Science Fiction

A critical guide

Science Fiction

A critical guide

Edited by
Patrick Parrinder

Longman
London and New York

Longman Group Limited London

*Associated companies, branches and representatives
throughout the world*

*Published in the United States of America
by Longman Inc., New York*

© Patrick Parrinder, Mark R. Hillegas, Marc Angenot, John
Huntington, Raymond Williams, T. A. Shippey, Tom Woodman, Scott
Sanders, J. A. Sutherland, Christopher Priest, Franz Rottensteiner
1979

First published 1979

British Library Catologuing in Publication Data

Science fiction.
  1. Science fiction – History and criticism
  I. Parrinder, Patrick
  809.3'876   PN3448.S45   78–40686

ISBN 0–582–48928–8
ISBN 0–582–48929–6 Pbk

Printed in Great Britain by
Richard Clay (The Chaucer Press) Ltd, Bungay, Suffolk

Contents

Editor's introduction

What do we mean by Science Fiction? What does it do, and why do so many people read it? What are its characteristic values, attitudes and procedures? Is it a creative force in our society, or merely a pathological symptom? How much of it is worth the attention of the ordinary 'non-scientific' or 'non-addicted' reader?

That these questions are frequently asked is a consequence of Science Fiction's current status as a highly popular and fashionable art-form. They are not easy to answer because SF is a confused concept and a confused field, varying from formula-repetition and institutionalized self-congratulation on the one hand to the most profound imaginative achievements on the other. This *Critical Guide* attempts a composite portrait of science fiction as a form of creative literature: not, that is, as a disembodied current of notions and ideas (e.g. about technological progress), nor as a 'sub-literature' which may only one day hope to aspire to literary status.

Though science fiction is now generally recognized as a literary form with its own history and traditions, its conventions and its major writers, critical pronouncements about it are still notoriously unreliable. Within the field overpraise is legion, reflecting the opportunism of publishers and the defensive clubbiness of editors, writers and fans. A paperback series edited by two well-known authors describes itself as 'the essential library of Science Fiction classics'. 'With one single story, X was instantly recognized as the world's best living science-fiction writer': writer Y, who put this in a paperback introduction to X's stories, has himself 'created an epic of nearly classic proportions' according to a publisher's blurb. Much of this is forgivable and easily discounted by those who know the field: SF writers are generous, exuberant fellows, the message goes, not much given to stabbing one another in the back. Critics who have tried to write of SF with more detachment have often fallen into an excessive primness of tone, as Kingsley Amis does at the conclusion to his pioneering and much-criticized survey *New Maps of Hell* (1961). 'At least a dozen current practitioners seem to me to have attained the status of the sound minor writer whose example brings into existence the figure of real standing', was how Amis summed up the genre. Science fiction *already* possesses its 'figures of real standing' (though, of course, it could do with a few more of them). But in the current critical climate it is still not easy for the layman to discover who they are.

With that in mind, the editor of a *Critical Guide* must reflect ruefully on Matthew Arnold's call for an authoritative 'hand to guide' the young poet through the confusion of contemporary literary values (Preface to *Poems*, 1853). It is my belief that to erect a definitive canon and lay down a series of final value-judgements is neither possible nor desirable in a field as dynamic and various as science fiction. What must be done, instead, is to work *towards* a consensus, which must always remain potential rather than actualized, and to demonstrate as far as one can the results of applying critical thought to the matter in hand. There is enough variety in present-day SF (not to mention present-day criticism) to make it highly unlikely that individual critics' attempts, however mutually compatible they may be, will fully coincide. A critical approach should aim, first of all, to state some widely acceptable truths and dispel some blatant falsehoods, and secondly, to show the grounds of its judgements and the consequences of its chosen methods. It is hoped that the *Critical Guide* does that.

The scope of this book may need some further explanation. In science-fiction criticism and scholarship the 'primitive accumulation' of facts is still being done, or has only very recently been done – as the flood of books and articles in the last four or five years testifies. The *Guide* does not aim at an exhaustive coverage of the literary field of SF, despite the largely chronological arrangement of its contents. The contributors are concerned less with surveying the bare facts of the genre than with interpreting their *significance*. With the exception of the essays on Verne and Wells, they have attempted to establish the common properties of science-fiction writing, whether in the treatment of a theme or in SF of a given period or nationality. Such common properties are stressed, by and large, at the expense of the continuity of the life-works of individual writers. Thus the *Critical Guide* does not set out to compete with the encyclopaedias and reference books of science fiction, on the one hand, nor with the growing volume of individual-author essays and monographs on the other. It tries to portray science fiction as a coherent system, not as a collection of facts or a random sequence of individual voices.

SF considered as a system – a small and recently colonized planet, let us say – itself belongs within much larger systems: the solar system of literary fictions, the galaxy of modern culture, the universe of human life as a whole. What are the peculiar features of the chosen planet, and how does it relate to the larger systems? These are the perennial problems of SF criticism, and it is not to be expected that the *Guide*'s contributors should be in complete agreement about them. Marc Angenot defines Jules Verne's science fiction as 'fiction about science in its global, historical effect, not in its scattering in specific discoveries'. Raymond Williams stresses SF's links with utopian writing and suggests that it is potentially a 'reworking, in imagination, of *all* forms and conditions'. Christopher Priest seems to repudiate this sort of critical pattern-building when he writes that the only completely reliable definition is that 'anything *labelled* as science fiction *is* science fiction' – an assertion which will not prevent some readers from suspecting that parts of the SF planet have been infiltrated by alien stock, or, at the very least, have served as a landing-ground for stray meteorites.

The SF planet is held in orbit in the literary system by a balance of gravitational forces. Franz Rottensteiner identifies one of the forces at work when he declares that 'any writer who would write *only* science fiction can only be a minor writer' (would Dr Rottensteiner argue a similar case, one wonders, about Jane Austen?) Scott Sanders and Patrick Parrinder discuss the nature of characterization in SF – the supposed deficiencies of which have been repeatedly used, even by SF authors themselves, to deny the genre any 'real' literary status. J. A. Sutherland makes the point that the form of a science-fiction novel – like most other kinds of modern writing – is hardly ever the result of totally unfettered individual choice. Readers, publishers and the censorship laws all play their part in determining what has appeared, and will in future appear, under the SF label. And T. A. Shippey, in the course of his defence of the SF magazines, asks 'whether the compulsive element in SF is at all reducible by the conventions of literary criticism'. To claim that SF has established itself as a literary form would be a mechanical exercise if it did not entail some challenge to, and some modification of, those conventions.

The same is true, of course, of the conventions of science-fiction history and hagiography as well. More attention is paid in this book to British and European SF, and less, perhaps, to the American magazines – especially in their early years – than the reader may have grown accustomed to. It is my personal conviction that the recent flood of coffee-table books featuring the chromatic covers of *Amazing*, *Astounding*, *Weird Tales*, and so on owes as much to a 'nostalgia boom' embracing 1930's musicals, 1930's fashions and ageing Hollywood film-stars as it does to serious literary criticism. The pulps undoubtedly had a major influence on modern science fiction, as T. A. Shippey's essay makes clear, but they were no better (and no worse) than the original science-fiction stories that they were able to print.

To say this may be to raise the ghost of an all-too-familiar argument between 'fans' and 'academics' in SF circles. Since this book is largely written by academics it is perhaps not surprising that some of the contributors favour writers who have (in the non-academic words of Christopher Priest) an 'uneasy relationship with the genre'. But what good writer *ever* had an easy relationship with a genre, except in those moments when he could feel he had mastered it and made it his own? It is only by following through the tensions that the pre-existence of a literary form sets up – between the new work and the old, and between the writer's desires and abilities and the reader's expectations – that an author can hope to achieve the 'aesthetic shock' which transcends the petty jealousies (fans versus academics, Old Guard versus New Wave, America versus the 'Best of the Rest') that SF, like all forms of cultural acitvity, breeds, When it does so, science fiction is no longer a hobby, a minority taste or a field to be dug over by the cultural archaeologist. It is a part of essential imaginative experience.

Note on the text

For ease of reading, notes and references to the ensuing text have been kept to an absolute minimum. Each essay is concluded by a bibliography of secondary material, and this should be consulted wherever a reference is in doubt. Novels cited are normally accompanied by the date of first publication, and, as most SF is now read in paperback form, chapter rather than page references are given for quoted passages.

Acknowledgements

I should like to thank my fellow-contributors, and especially Raymond Williams who first gave me the idea of producing a book of this kind. Without the patient encouragement of Stephen Davies, formerly of A. D. Peters & Co., this project would never have come to fruition. Darko Suvin, editor of *Science-Fiction Studies* and a living embodiment of the practical utopianism inherent in the notion of international scholarship, has been an unfailing source of advice, inspiration and well-timed rebuke. Neither he nor anyone else is, of course, responsible for my own errors and omissions. Finally, I would particularly thank my wife Ewa, initially so bemused by my passion for SF, who ended up by taking my mother-in-law to *Star Wars*.

Patrick Parrinder
June 1978

Acknowledgement is made to *Science-Fiction Studies* in which the essay entitled 'The disappearance of character' by Scott Sanders originally appeared under the title 'Invisible Men and Women'.

Part I
Early landmarks:
from the beginnings to 1900

The literary background to science fiction

Mark R. Hillegas

I

Any discussion of science fiction before Verne and Wells must necessarily begin with some agreement about the term itself. There have, over the years, been many attempts at a definition, but in my judgement the broadest, most accurate, and most comprehensive remains that of Kingsley Amis in *New Maps of Hell* (1961). At the heart of his definition is the concept that science fiction is a kind of narrative derived from 'some innovation in science or technology, or pseudo-science or pseudo-technology'. Contrasted with science fiction is fantasy, which pays no lip-service to fact but involves instead the supernatural or at least the obviously impossible. Science fiction according to this definition is not possible until the world-view shifts from a supernatural explanation of phenomena to a rational explanation based on known or hypothesized laws of the universe. The two forms are not always pure – fantasy can have science-fiction elements and science-fiction fantasy elements. Also to be emphasized is the fact that writers of science fiction have often drawn on literary traditions of fantasy.

response to the first scientific revolution, chiefly the new astronomy. Three voyages to other worlds, out of many, deserve particular attention: Kepler's *Somnium* (1634), Bishop Godwin's *The Man in the Moone* (1638), and Cyrano de Bergerac's *Voyages to the Moon and Sun* (1656). The classic, comprehensive treatment of early 'cosmic voyages' is Marjorie Nicolson's *Voyages to the Moon* (1948), to which, like all subsequent writers on the subject, I am greatly indebted.

Before turning to the first attempts in the seventeenth century at anything like science fiction, a few earlier works need to be discussed as a contrast with the new kind of imagination that begins with the first scientific revolution. Two works of Lucian, the second-century Syrian who wrote satires in Greek, illustrate the contrast. The first is his *True History*, which interestingly was initially published in English translation in 1634, the year Kepler's *Somnium* appeared in Latin. Mostly it is satiric fantasy, with a great deal of what today would be called obscenity. The *True History* involves a journey to the moon, but it is entirely an accident – Lucian's ship is picked up by a typhoon, whirled around at high speed, and lifted 1,800,000 feet into the sky. From there on he just sails to the moon: 'On the eighth day we sighted what looked like a big island hanging in mid-air, white and round and brilliantly illuminated, so we steered towards it, dropped anchor and disembarked.' Presto, the mariners are on the moon. It is a delightful book, and includes a meeting with the Greek heroes, a conversation with Homer (who had not been blind after all), and a giant whale whose stomach is inhabited. Besides an Island of the Blest, there is also an Island of the Damned, where the worst punishment is reserved for those who had written Untrue Histories. 'As my conscience was absolutely clear in that respect', writes Lucian, 'I was able to watch the poor fellow's sufferings without any serious fears for my future.'

The second, shorter work of Lucian's – its first paragraph is used by Wells as an epigraph to *The First Men in the Moon* (1901) – is the *Icaromenippus*. This time the traveller goes to the moon by design, having rigged for himself the wing of a vulture and that of an eagle. Besides Lucian, one might perhaps mention as in a sense predecessors of science fiction, various medieval visions of the heavens, the fantastic journeys of Rabelais's Pantagruel, or Astofo's visit to the moon in Ariosto's *Orlando Furioso*.

Another work – not science fiction – which inaugurates a tradition and also stands as part of the background to a good deal of science fiction is More's *Utopia* (1516). A diversely interpreted work, *Utopia* makes little sense unless one sees it as a kind of fiction, as C. S. Lewis pointed out in his *English Literature in the Sixteenth Century Excluding Drama*. It is, he wrote, 'a holiday work, a spontaneous overflow of intellectual high spirits, a revel of debate, paradox and (above all) of invention', a work looking forward to *Gulliver's Travels* but standing a long distance from Plato's *Republic*. In Book II, More's traveller, Raphael Hythloday, describes a democratic yet paternalistic agrarian society set on a crescent-shaped island, impregnable to foreign attack. In this communal state, people move at regular intervals between cities and farms, and food is stored in great warehouses, so that no Utopian need suffer starvation. Diversity of religious belief is permitted; gold and silver are despised and used for chamber pots and the chains of prisoners; and all people wear the same coarse clothing. But some of its features, such as slavery for the punishment for crime (including adultery) and restrictions on travel, would be repugnant to us today. Details from *Utopia* turn up in works as different as Wells's *The First Men in the Moon* and B. F. Skinner's *Walden Two* (1948). Utopian (and the mirror image, dystopian) elements are, of course, an important strand in much science fiction, particularly in the twentieth century.[1]

Kepler's *Somnium* is the first major example of anything like science fiction, and it is not science fiction in any way approaching pure form. In a dream the hero of the story, Duracotus, is transported to the moon by demons. But even in this supernatural journey there is some attention to scientific detail, notably the effects of gravitation and rarefied air in space. With the description of the moon and its inhabitants, we get what Kepler the scientist considered possibilities, though they seem utterly fantastic to us. (The conception of the moon appears to have had some influence on Wells's *First Men in the Moon*, and at one point Wells mentions Kepler.)

Kepler's moon is very briefly described, and then not too clearly. There are two halves to the moon: the Subvolva, which I take to be the hemisphere facing the earth, and the Privolva, the side we never see. For all the moon, 'Whatever is born on the land attains a monstrous size. Growth is very rapid. Everything has a short life, since it develops an immense body.' The Privolvans are apparently nomadic – some walk on very long legs (which may suggest the *sorns* of C. S. Lewis's *Out of the Silent Planet*, 1938) – some have wings to fly, others use boats, and all can apparently survive long periods under water. The Subvolvan hemisphere is more settled, equivalent to our 'cantons, towns, and gardens'.

Several details, as I have noted, suggest *The First Men in the Moon*. One sounds like the dawn of a lunar day witnessed by Cavor and Bedford;

If anything is exposed during the day, it becomes hard on top and scorched; when evening comes, its husk drops off. Things born in the ground — they are sparse on the ridges of the mountains — generally end their lives on the same day, with new generations springing up daily.

The caves in which some of the inhabitants hide from the sun during the lunar day are another detail that dimly foreshadows *The First Men in the Moon*. All in all, though, I have a feeling that Wells's indebtedness to Kepler is fairly slight.

Much more coherent and very charming is the next significant moon voyage, Bishop Francis Godwin's *The Man in the Moone*, published four years later. It is the story of a shipwrecked Spaniard, Domingo Gonsales, who discovers birds, called 'gansas', which he trains to carry him into the air. They are rather strange birds: 'one foote with Clawes, talons, and pounces, like an *Eagle*, and the other whole like a Swan or water fowle'. Escaping from savages on an island, the hero ascends into the sky: 'It was my good fortune that they tooke all one way, although not just the way I aymed at.' The birds, to his surprise, migrate to the moon. One of the most effective sections of the journey is the sight of the earth hanging in space:

Then I should perceive a great shining brightness to occupy the roome, during the like time (which was undoubtedly none other than the great Atlantick Ocean). After that succeeded a spot almost of an Ovall form, even just such as we see America to have in our Mapps. Then another vast cleernesse, representing the West Ocean; and lastly a medley of spots, like the Countries of the East Indies. So that it seemed unto me like no other than a huge Mathematical Globe, leasurely turned before me, wherein successively all the Countries of our earthly world within the compasse of 24 howers were represented to my sight.

What he sees leads Domingo to defend the Copernican theory.

Journeying for about twelve days (and without hunger, a common experience of many early space travellers), he finds himself hurtling towards the moon: 'Then, I perceived also, that it was covered for the most part with a huge and mighty Sea.' His description of the moon as he makes his approach seems to be fairly close to what observers in the seventeenth century had thought they had seen through their primitive telescopes.

When Domingo lands, he naturally discovers that the moon is inhabited. His description, though brief, portrays a simple utopian world. There is no waste of anything 'necessary for the use of man'; food of all sorts grows without labour; clothing, housing are provided virtually without labour, and that 'as it were playing'. All the women are extraordinarily beautiful, and no man desires any other than the one he has known. Naturally, there is no crime; the people, 'young and old, doe hate all manner of vice'. Occasionally, imperfect children are born, but they are shipped off to America.

The next major journeys to other worlds are Cyrano de Bergerac's *Voyages to the Moon and Sun*. The voyages, of which the first is the most interesting, are only marginally science fiction – chiefly they are satiric fantasies and delightful as such. Cyrano's first attempt to reach the moon is by a rather novel means. He fastens about him a number of bottles of dew, and, naturally, since dew rises, so does he. High above the clouds, he discovers he is not heading towards the moon, so he breaks some of the bottles of dew and lands instead in Canada. There he constructs another machine, activated by a spring; and, on his first attempt at launching from a rock, lands with a crash, bruising himself badly. Back in his room, he greases himself all over with beef marrow and returns to his machine, to which soldiers have attached fire-crackers. He jumps into his machine to break off the fire-crackers, but it is too late, and he finds himself shooting into the air. Eventually the firecrackers give out, but Cyrano keeps on going, since the moon in waning quarter sucks up the marrow of animals, and that is what he is covered with. Touch-down is in the Earthly Paradise, where Cyrano falls on the Tree of Knowledge. Briefly he joins the select company there of Adam, Eve, Enoch, Elijah, and Saint John the Evangelist. All goes well until he gets into an argument with Elijah, eats of the Tree of Knowledge, and finds himself suddenly in a land of beast men who walk on all fours. And so it goes. There is very little science in the voyage, except Cyrano's advocacy of the Copernican theory and speculation about a plurality of worlds. There are, however, some interesting inventions among the inhabitants of the moon, including movable houses and talking books.

For his Journey to the Sun, Cyrano constructs a more elaborate device, a 6-foot-tall box topped by a glass icosahedron. It is not exactly clear how the device is propelled; apparently it drives air out the top and sucks air in at the bottom. Meanwhile, though, it works, and Cyrano goes on a very long journey to the sun, giving him a chance to expound the Copernican theory. He lands first on one of the sunspots, which are actually little worlds circling the sun – a very good place to leave him.

A work that has had considerable influence on science fiction is, of course, Swift's *Gulliver's Travels* (1726), though except for the Voyage to Laputa, it is not itself science fiction. Instead it is a brilliantly satiric and ironic extension of travel literature, and something of the tone of the work lives on in many subsequent science-fiction stories and novels. Few, I think, would dispute that the most influential incident in the book is poor, bluff, not-too-bright Gulliver's inadvertent revelation of the depravity and cruelty of Western civilization in his interview with the King of Brobdingnag. After all that Gulliver has to tell about 'conspiracies, rebellions, murders, massacres, revolutions, banishments', the king offers his famous judgement: 'I cannot but conclude the bulk of your natives to be the most pernicious race of little odious vermin that nature ever suffered to crawl upon the surface of the earth.' One of the most important places where the incident reappears is in Wells's *The First Men in the Moon* in Cavor's interview with the Grand Lunar – except for his physics, Cavor is about as bright as Gulliver. It also appears again four decades after Wells in Lewis's *Out of the Silent Planet*, in the interview with the Oyarsa of Malacandra.

The only real science fiction in *Gulliver's Travels* is the Voyage to Laputa in Book III. Set adrift because of treachery, Gulliver lands on the island of Balnibarbi, only to discover 'a vast opaque body between me and the sun, moving towards the island'. This is the Flying Island of Laputa, and Marjorie Nicolson has argued that Swift's use of it is a moon voyage in reverse. Laputa, whose underside is adamantine, is powered by a giant magnet. With the Laputans, who are impractical mathematicians lost in abstract thought, Swift is making fun of knowledge which brings no practical human benefit.

Much more important as science fiction is Voltaire's *Micromégas* (1752), which was influenced by *Gulliver's Travels* (Voltaire admired Swift greatly and knew him during his four-year exile in England). The hero, an inhabitant of Sirius who is 120,000 feet tall, travels to our solar system with the aid of his 'marvellous knowledge of the laws of gravitation and of all the forces of attraction'. Making use now of a sunbeam, now of a comet, he finally lands on Saturn, where he picks a companion, a mere pygmy 6,000 feet tall. Together they travel the solar system, stopping at Jupiter and Mars and finally arriving at earth on 5 July 1737. They walk the planet in thirty-six hours: 'So here they are back where they started, after seeing that pool, almost imperceptible to them, that is called the Mediterranean, and that other pond,

which, under the name of the Great Ocean, surrounds the molehill.' At
first they find no sign of life, but then with the aid of a 'little microscope' – a diamond 150 feet in diameter – they finally detect a whale:
'The Saturnian, now convinced that our world was inhabited, very
soon made the assumption that it was inhabited only by whales.' But
further search reveals a ship on a scientific expedition, and one of its
members, with a quadrant, measures the height of the Saturnian
accurate to within a foot. Then he measures the Sirian, planting a 'big
tree in a place which Dr. Swift would name, but which I shall take good
care not to call by name because of my great respect for the ladies'.

The ensuing conversation with the mites of earth begins with a
marvellous speech by Micromégas:

*O intelligent atoms in whom the eternal Being has taken pleasure in
manifesting his skill and power, you must doubtless taste very pure joys
on your globe; for having so little matter, and, seeming to be all spirit,
you must spend your lives in love and in thought; that is the true life of
spirits. I have nowhere seen true happiness, but without doubt it is here.*

But the philosophers shake their heads and tell him it is not true.
Rather, except for a few not too well regarded men, humanity is an
'assemblage of madmen, wicked men, and unhappy men'. Micromégas
then wonders what the philosophers, who are apparently among the
select company of the wise, do with their time: 'We dissect flies . . . we
measure lines, we assemble numbers; we argue about two or three
points that we understand, and we argue about two or three thousand
that we don't understand.' At this point the visitors leave the mites
with a 'fine book of philosophy, written very small for their use'.
Opening it, the mites discover the pages are blank.

In concluding this section, I should note that there are, of course,
exceptions to the fact that most examples of science fiction in the
seventeenth and eighteenth centuries are journeys to other worlds in
space. With its research institute, the House of Salomon, and its
predictions of such scientific wonders as submarines and aircraft,
Bacon's *New Atlantis* (1627) is in part science fiction; but it is also part
of the utopian tradition and, unfortunately, a fragment.

II

Another new variety of science fiction is the voyage to a world underground, which makes its first important appearance in the eighteenth
century. It takes two forms: one is a journey into great caverns inside
the earth and the other a journey into a hollow earth. A small section of
Robert Paltock's *Peter Wilkins* (1750) is the first significant journey to
a cavern world (Jules Verne's *Journey to the Centre of the Earth* is, of
course, a later and much more important development of this form).
Shipwrecked near the South Pole, Wilkins's boat is sucked into a
cavern. The boat falls with incredible violence over a precipice, is

whirled round and round, then drifts down a river to a great lake surrounded by a wood. Indebted to *Robinson Crusoe*, Paltock has his hero set up camp in a grotto at the edge of the lake, taking supplies from his boat. The underground world is inhabited by flying men and women, and Wilkins marries Youwarkee, by whom he has numerous children. And that's about all there is to it. Paltock's book was familar to writers of the Romantic period, who often admired it; but except for the speculation about life within the great cavern, it cannot be considered science fiction.

The first important voyage to a hollow earth is Baron Holberg's *Journey of Niels Klim to the World Underground* (1741), a work which has been translated into at least thirteen languages and has gone through at least sixty editions. Although the work was initially translated into English in 1742, it is much better known to Europeans than it is to English-speaking people.

In 1664, after having passed his examinations at the University of Copenhagen, Niels returns to his native Norway and decides to clear up some points of natural philosophy by studying the nature of the earth. Lowered into a cave, he finds himself hurtling into the abyss when his rope breaks. At first he travels in complete darkness, but in time he comes out into the hollow earth, complete with its own sun, planet, and firmament. His initial thought is that he has arrived in the mansions of the Blessed, but he rejects the idea,

since I viewed myself armed with a harpoon, and dragging a mighty length of rope after me, knowing full well that a man just going to Paradise has no occasion for a rope or a harpoon, and that the celestial inhabitants could not possibly be pleased with a dress which looked as if I intended, after the example of the Titans, to take Heaven by violence.

Mature consideration leads him to believe 'that the conjectures of those men are right who held the Earth to be hollow, and that within the shell or outward crust there is another lesser globe, and another firmament adorned with lesser sun, stars, and planets.' Gradually his rate of descent slows and he becomes a satellite of the planet, Nazar, which he circles for three days:

For as without intermission I was whirled about the planet that was next to me, I could distinguish day from night; and observing the subterranean sun to rise and set, and retire gradually out of sight, I could easily perceive when it was night, though it was not altogether as it is with us. For at sunset the whole face of the firmament appeared of a bright purple, not unlike the countenance of our moon sometimes.

I find this a fascinating image, but I'm afraid it represents all that is science fiction in the book.

Niels lands on the planet Nazar when an attacking griffin he harpoons drags him down. The inhabitants of the various states of Nazar are all rational, talking trees, of whom the first he meets are the

Potuans. He starts off in trouble because, fleeing from a bull, he leaps into a tree, who turns out to be wife of a principal magistrate. After many adventures among the natives of Nazar, he gets exiled to the firmament, taken there by birds, called Cupacs, in the manner of Domingo Gonsales's trip to the moon. In the firmament he rises to be the Emperor of the Fifth Monarchy, but overreaching himself he has to flee, fortunately into the same hole by which he had arrived in the world underground. And so he arrives back on the surface of the earth. The book contains a great deal of satire, and in its details echoes works all the way back to Plato and Homer. Swift's influence seems to be pervasive, but *Gulliver's Travels* is a work of genius, while *Niels Klim* is merely competent.

After *Niels Klim* there are no important underground voyages until Jules Verne's *Journey to the Centre of the Earth* (1864). There is, however, a rather bizarre though minor utopian novel, the anonymous *Symzonia* (1820), which is important for its influence on Poe. It is based on the speculations of Captain John Cleves Symmes about a hollow earth open at both poles. Symmes first set forth his theory in a circular published in St Louis in 1818. Determined that the world should know of it as speedily as possible, he sent a copy of the pamphlet 'to every learned institution, and to every considerable town and village, as well as every distinguished individual of which he could gain any intelligence, throughout the United States, and to several learned societies in Europe'. The theory, instead of receiving the respectful attention he must have hoped for, became the subject of jest and ridicule in American newspapers, and men of science refused even to consider it. Undaunted, Symmes kept up the fight for more than ten years with letters to newspapers, pamphlets, and lecture appearances. His theory even got as far as the Congress of the United States, where a Bill was introduced in both House and Senate to finance a polar expedition to test its validity. The Bill didn't pass, but twenty-five senators voted for it.

'In the year 1817', writes the unknown Captain Seaborn in *Symzonia*, 'I projected a voyage of discovery in the hope of finding a passage to a new and untried world.' Seaborn sails south from New York, and after passing the ring of ice in latitude 70° to 80°, his ship moves toward the pole and an increasingly warmer climate. Imperceptibly the ship passes over the verge into the great opening which leads to the interior world. The heat becomes excessive, and the bewildered sailors nearly mutiny; but, quieting their fears, Seaborn is able to push on into the interior, where he discovers a utopian civilization technologically advanced beyond the outside world.

When Seaborn and the 'internals' overcome the language barrier, he is able to learn about their civilization and tell about his own. He learns that the selfish, greedy, and morally impure have been banished to a land near the northern polar opening. The exiles have lost their whiteness and become dark and misshapen, and Seaborn begins to suspect that his people may be the descendants of the exiles. Seaborn is careful to hide the faults of his people, but the ruler eventually uncovers them, and like Swift's King of Brobdingnag, he passes a severe judgement that shocks the worthy Captain: 'I was petrified with confusion and shame, on hearing my race thus described as pestiferous beings, spreading moral disease and contamination.' Seaborn and crew are ordered to sail out of the internal world, never to return again.

Apparently Poe knew about Symmes's theory and was interested in it, although he never really developed the idea of a hollow earth. 'The Unparalleled Adventures of One Hans Pfaall' (1835), the 'MS. Found in a Bottle' (1833), and *The Narrative of Arthur Gordon Pym* (1838) indicate that Poe had knowledge not only of Symmes's ideas but also of *Symzonia*. When Hans Pfaall passes over the North Pole, he sees the polar depression. The writer of the document in 'MS. Found in a Bottle' is evidently describing a descent into the earth through the south polar opening. The mysterious ghost ship on which he is an unwilling passenger moves steadily southward: 'Perhaps this current leads us to the southern pole itself.' Finally the ship penetrates the ice barrier and falls into the abyss: 'Oh, horror upon horror! the ice opens suddenly to the right, and to the left, and we are whirling dizzily in immense concentric circles, round and round the borders of a gigantic amphitheatre, the summit of whose walls is lost in darkness.' In *Arthur Gordon Pym* Poe makes greater use of Symmes's theory and of the imaginary voyage, *Symzonia*. Like Captain Seaborn's *Explorer*, the *Jane Grey*, the ship on which Pym finds himself after harrowing experiences of mutiny and shipwreck, passes through the southern ice hoop into a warmer region. When Pym escapes from the island of the dark savages after the massacre of the crew of the *Jane Grey*, his canoe heads into a current moving southward. The temperature, as demanded by Symmes's theory and portrayed in *Symzonia*, increases constantly until it becomes excessive. At the end of the narrative, the canoe carrying Pym is drawn into the vast chasm of falling waters at the South Pole:

And now we rushed into the embrace of the cataract, where a chasm threw itself open to receive us. But there arose in our pathway a shrouded human figure, very far larger in its proportions than any dweller among men. And the hue of the skin of the figure was of the perfect whiteness of snow.

The white figure suggests the utopians of *Symzonia* while the dark savages living on the islands outside the abyss suggest the descendants of moral misfits banished from the interior word. And, of course, Verne's late work, *The Sphinx of Ice* (1897), picks up where Poe left off.

III

The nineteenth century sees the development of a number of new science-fiction themes or devices. One of these has its first important expression in Mary Shelley's *Frankenstein* (1818), an immature work which nevertheless has been enormously influential. The theme is, of course, the creation of human life by supposedly scientific means – in this case, Victor Frankenstein's eight-foot monster. The story is romanticism at its worst, as is evident in the concluding paragraphs when the monster, having killed his creator, sets off across the polar ice fields:

I shall die, and what I now feel be no longer felt. Soon these burning miseries will be extinct. I shall ascend my funeral pile triumphantly, and exalt in the agony of the torturing flames. The light of that conflagration will fade away; my ashes will be swept into the sea by the winds. My spirit will sleep in peace; or if it think, it will not surely think thus. Farewell.

The novel, in presenting the dilemma of the monster in relation to Frankenstein, is a variation on Satan's response to God and at the same time a re-working of the Prometheus theme. It is also science fiction, since it is by his researches into the principles of life that Frankenstein is able to fabricate his monster from the dead bodies of human beings. This to me seems surely to be one of the sources for Wells's *The Island of Doctor Moreau* (1896). It has also been suggested that *Frankenstein* had some influence on his *The Invisible Man* (1897).

Another new form of science fiction appears early in the nineteenth century, the voyage to another world by optical means. During August and September 1835, a series of articles in the New York *Sun* employed scientific verisimilitude to perpetrate one of the most famous newspaper hoaxes of all times, Richard Adams Locke's 'Great Astronomical Discoveries Lately Made by Sir John Herschel at the Cape of Good Hope'. Better known today as the *Moon Hoax*, the story told how life had supposedly been seen on the moon by Herschel through a new type of telescope that brought the moon to within an apparent distance of 40 feet. The great public interest in the story and the widespread acceptance of its truth have too often been described to require repetition here. It is sufficient to note that the only thing in modern experience comparable to the *Moon Hoax* was Orson Welles's 1938 dramatization of H. G. Wells's *The War of the Worlds*.

In his portrayal of our satellite and its inhabitants, Locke made no effort to achieve the realism which characterized his account of Herschel's great telescope. The description of the moon is completely fantastic; and, as Professor Nicolson notes, it suggests the spectacular settings employed in several popular plays which were indebted to the stories of Godwin and Cyrano for their presentation of another inhabited world. Vast lunar forests, level green plains, beaches of brilliant white and ringed with green marble, blue amethysts ninety feet high, hills topped with orange and yellow crystals form the stage on which Locke's animals and flying men perform. There are one-horn goats, cranes with outrageously long legs and bills, biped beavers that use fire, miniature zebras and bison, and a strange amphibious animal, spherical in shape, that rolls along the beaches. Most romantic of all the creatures on the moon are the flying men, who have 'wings composed of a thin membrane, without hair, lying snugly upon their backs, from the top of the shoulders to the calves of the legs'. These remarkable creatures are, as Poe remarked, a 'literal copy' of the glums and gawries, the flying men and women described in Robert Paltock's *The Life and Adventures of Peter Wilkins*.

Locke's peculiar mixture of verisimilitude and fantasy seems to have been imitated in Fitz-James O'Brien's 'Diamond Lens' (1859). In this story the narrator constructs a super-microscope which reveals a world in a drop of water inhabited by a beautiful girl. The kind of pseudo-scientific terminology employed to explain the Cape Town telescope appears in the description of the microscope while the names of famous microscopists are conjured up as are Sir John and Sir William Herschel in the *Moon Hoax*. The world in the atom is like Locke's world in the moon, completely fantastic and full of rich colours and strange shapes:

Far away into the illimitable distance stretched long avenues of the gaseous forest, dimly transparent, and painted with prismatic hues of unimaginable brilliancy. The pendent branches waved along the fluid glades until every vista seemed to break through the half-lucent ranks of many-colored drooping silken pennons. What seemed to be either fruits or flowers, pied with a thousand hues, lustrous and ever varying, bubbled from the crowns of this fairy bridge.

Although Animula, the beautiful girl in the atom, is a perfectly formed human being and hence unlike Locke's subhuman bat men, there are other strange creatures reminiscent of the *Moon Hoax*, including an apparently intelligent tree which the narrator sees handing fruit to the lovely Animula.

But Poe and Hawthorne develop several new themes in stories of higher quality and sophistication, if not of greater interest. It is convenient to discuss Hawthorne first.

'Dr Heidegger's Experiment' (1837) barely qualifies as science fiction and can be quickly dismissed. Water from the Fountain of Youth changes four old people into youths again, or does it? Hawthorne plays his familiar game of ambiguity:

Yet, by a strange deception, owing to the duskiness of the chamber, and the antique dresses which they still wore, the tall mirror is said to have reflected the figures of three old, gray, withered grandsires, ridiculously contending for the skinny ugliness of a shrivelled grandam.

More clearly science fiction, though anti-science science fiction, is 'Rappaccini's Daughter' (1837). Like *Frankenstein*, it is right out of the Romantic period. In this familiar story, Rappaccini, the 'tall, emaciated, yellow, and sickly-looking' scientist, raises his daughter, Beatrice, to be immune to the deadly scents of poisonous plants, but, alas, poisonous to other human beings. Caring infinitely more for science than mankind, '[Rappaccini] would sacrifice human life, his own among the rest, or whatever else was dearest to him, for the sake of adding so much as a grain of mustard seed to the great heap of accumulated knowledge'. Beatrice, the only admirable character in the story, dies at his feet at the end of the story.

In 'The Birthmark' (1843) Hawthorne seems to equate science with magic and makes it out to be an evil tampering with nature – Aylmer destroys his beautiful wife by trying to remove a birthmark and thereby make her perfect. The story sounds even more like *Frankenstein* in its philosophy:

In those days when the comparatively recent discovery of electricity and other kindred mysteries of Nature seemed to open paths into the regions of miracle, it was not unusual for the love of science to rival the love of woman in its depth and absorbing energy.

Hawthorne's moral is that Nature permits us to 'mend, and, like a jealous patentee, on no account to make'. This is, of course, a familiar sentiment among many Romantics.

I would like to conclude this essay with a few stories of Edgar Allan Poe, surely the most important writer of science fiction in the nineteenth century before Verne and Wells. I shall first deal with two which are fairly effective and, like some we have just discussed, represent the treatment of other themes than the voyage to another world.

The first is 'The Facts in the Case of M. Valdemar' (1845). It deals with a man hypnotized at the point of death, only to be awakened seven months later. As the narrator makes his 'mesmeric passes', M. Valdemar is drawn from his trance, with the following results:

. . . [Valdemar's] whole frame at once — within the space of a single minute, or less, shrunk — crumbled — absolutely rotted away beneath my hands. Upon the bed, before that whole company, there lay a nearly liquid mass of loathsome — of detestable putrescence.

The story is clearly science fiction: it is, after all, built on what is at least a pseudo-scientific hypothesis.

The second story is 'Von Kempelen and His Discovery' (1849). Less macabre but also less effective, it develops an ancient idea, the transmutation of lead into gold, but gives it a certain scientific plausibility. Several references are made to the 'Diary of Sir Humphry Davy', and it is hinted that the great English chemist was attempting the same transformation. We are also shown the laboratory, a room ten by eight filled with chemical apparatus:

. . . a very small furnace, with a glowing fire in it, and on the fire a kind of duplicate crucible — two crucibles connected by a tube. One of these crucibles was nearly full of lead, which was close to the brim. The other crucible had some liquid in it, which, as the officers entered, seemed to be furiously dissipating in vapor.

The end product of the process is gold, gold 'without the slightest appreciable alloy', a fact which is discovered when the contents of a trunk, hidden under a bed, are analysed.

But in spite of the development of several new science-fiction themes in the early nineteenth century, the most common form remains the journey to another world in space.[2] Its most important manifestation is in Poe's flawed story, 'The Unparalleled Adventures of One Hans Pfaall' (1835). Before discussing it, brief mention should be made of his 'Mellonta Tauta' (1849), a satire in the form of an account of a balloon journey in the year 2848. Its science-fiction elements include dirigible balloons carrying 200 people, aircraft propelled by magnetically operated propellers, floating telegraph wires, and 300-mile-an-hour trains running on tracks 50 feet wide.

The new realism in the journey to another world made its first significant appearance in Poe's 'Hans Pfaall'. Poe, who understood the change which the journey to another world was undergoing, discussed the new realism in his Notes and found the old, familiar moon voyages wanting because they lacked 'plausibility'. Although he boasted of his own scientific accuracy, Poe did not write a first-rate story. One part of 'Hans Pfaall' is a parody of the seventeenth- and eighteenth-century lunar voyage, the other a realistic story of space travel; and the two are not successfully blended together. At first he planned an entirely serious story along the lines of complete verisimilitude and took the idea to his friend Kennedy, who advised against it. 'I fell back', he wrote later, 'upon a style half plausible, half bantering.' The story as finally published in the *Southern Literary Messenger* (June 1835) consisted of the realistic narrative of the journey from the earth to the moon and the fantastic enveloping plot.

More than anyone before, Poe lavished attention on the preparations for the trip and the actual journey to the moon, and details follow details in rapid sequence. To explain the use of the balloon for the journey through space, Poe carefully marshals evidence to prove that a very thin atmosphere may exist in space, and to complete the process of winning credibility, he attempts to picture a balloon of amazing buoyancy. No effort is spared to furnish a plausible-sounding description of this, the last as well as the only important lighter-than-air spaceship. It is made of cambric muslim, treated with three coats of varnish caoutchouc and filled with 40,000 cubic feet of a remarkable new gas '37.4 times lighter than hydrogen'. Suspended beneath is a wicker passenger car covered by 'a very strong, perfectly air-tight, but flexible gum-elastic bag'. To maintain a breathable atmosphere inside the sealed car, Hans Pfaall has 'one of M. Grimm's improvements upon the apparatus for the condensation of atmospheric air' and a 'small valve at the bottom of the car' to eject foul air. A supply of water and 'compact provisions like pemmican' complete the arrangements, while Hans also collects animal passengers, in this case a cat and two pigeons. Because he plans to make scientific observations during the trip, he assembles various instruments: 'a telescope, a barometer, a thermometer, an electrometer, a magnetic needle, and a seconds watch'.

The journey itself is characterized by a similar effort to achieve technical verisimilitude. As Hans Pfaall rises in the air, he observes the earth and sky, and watches his instruments more attentively than had any previous space traveller. The barometer indicates the altitude, and the rate of fall of feathers thrown from the car the density of the air. At seventeen miles elevation the atmosphere becomes so thin that Hans, gasping for breath and bleeding at the nose, ears, and eyes, adjusts the air-tight bag around his car, and during the rest of the trip he wakes himself periodically with an ingenious water clock in order to operate his air-replenishing machine. Throughout the whole experience he carefully records observations in his notebook.

In the narrative of the voyage to the moon, all the stereotyped conventions are employed, and certain incidents seem to have been copied from previous stories. The earth is a great globe hanging in space; the reversal of the ship at the point of equal attraction between the earth and the moon and then the growing bulk of the moon, are all included. But Poe does make one original contribution to the journey to another world. Far out in the depths of space a flaming meteor comes booming past the balloon, a convention which becomes standard in nineteenth-century stories of interplanetary travel.

Poe omitted the description of the moon when he gave up the idea of writing an entirely realistic story and decided instead to add the facetious enveloping plot. However, internal evidence seems to indicate that his original intention was to portray the moon of contemporary astronomy. Far out in space, Hans notes the 'entire absence of ocean or sea, and indeed of any lake or river, or body of water whatever' on our satellite, and he sees 'vast level regions of a character decidedly alluvial' and also 'innumerable volcanic mountains conical in shape'. Later Hans mentions the moon's 'wonderful alterations of heat and cold; of unmitigated and burning sunshine for one fortnight, and more than polar frigidity for the next'. It might seem that Poe was following Kepler's conception of the moon. Poe, however, explained in a later article that inspiration for 'Hans Pfaall' had come from the description of the moon in Sir John Herschel's *Treatise on Astronomy*, the American edition of which had been published a few months before 'Hans Pfaall'. Poe read Herschel's book with great care as soon as it appeared and found himself 'very much interested in what is there said respecting the possibility of future lunar investigations', but Kennedy's unfortunate advice put an end to his plan of embodying in a story the description of the moon contained in the *Treatise on Astronomy*.

In order to write the enveloping plot, which tells how the manuscript account of Hans's trip is delivered by a ridiculous Selenite who arrives in a balloon made of dirty newspapers, Poe was forced to alter his conception of the moon-world from which the Selenite had come. Though not described at any length, this moon-world is fantastic in the tradition of those discovered by voyagers like Domingo Gonsales and Cyrano de Bergerac. After nineteen days in transit, Hans, clutching the framework of his balloon, crashes into the 'very heart of a fantastical-looking city, and into the very heart of a vast crowd of ugly little people'. The Selenites, about 2 feet 2 inches tall, are absurdly rotund, have enormous red noses, and are without ears. Their description, while obviously related to the seventeenth-century tradition of the cosmic voyage, also seems to echo the ideas of the nineteenth-century selenographer Schröter about the little people who inhabit the moon.

It is interesting to note that, in *From the Earth to the Moon* (1865), Verne, in concluding a survey of previous journeys to the moon in literature, ends with mention of 'Hans Pfaall': 'But, to bring this rapid sketch to a close, I will only add that a certain Hans Pfaall, of Rotterdam, launching himself in a balloon filled with a gas thirty-seven times lighter than hydrogen, reached the moon after a passage of nineteen hours.'

Finally a postscript. Voyages to the planets became more common in the period after Verne's trip to the moon (which will be discussed later in this volume). One kind, though very minor, was to a world less advanced in evolution, usually either Jupiter or Mars. The other kind, the journey to an advanced Mars, was inspired by Schiaparelli's detection of the so-called canals in 1877. The public responded enthusiastically to the implication that intelligent life had produced artificial waterways on Mars, and writers began to capitalize on this enthusiasm at least as early as Percy Greg's *Across the Zodiac* (1880). But it is not until Wells's *The War of the Worlds* (1898) that the story of the advanced Martians achieves substantial development.

Notes

1. See Raymond Williams's essay in this volume (p. 52–66).
2. See my survey of the many minor nineteenth-century journeys to other worlds in 'Victorian "Extraterrestrials" ', *The Worlds of Victorian Fiction*, ed. Jerome H. Buckley (Harvard U.P., 1975). Another minor form of science fiction in the period is the future war story, which is discussed in I. F. Clarke, *Voices Prophesying War* (Oxford U.P., 1966).

Bibliography

Primary texts

Anon. *Symzonia, A Voyage of Discovery by Captain Adam Seaborn*. Gainesville: Scholars' Facsimiles and Reprints, 1965.

Cyrano de Bergerac, Savinien. *Voyages to the Moon and Sun.* Trans. Richard Aldington. New York: The Orion Press, 1962.

Godwin, Francis. *The Man in the Moone.* Hereford: The Hereford Times Ltd, 1959.

Hawthorne, Nathaniel. *The Complete Novels and Selected Tales of Nathaniel Hawthorne.* Ed. Norman Holmes Pearson. New York: Modern Library, 1937.

Holberg, Ludwig. *The Journey of Niels Klim to the World Underground.* Ed. James I. McNelis, Jr. Lincoln: University of Nebraska Press, 1960.

Kepler, Johann. *Kepler's 'Somnium'.* Trans. Edward Rosen. Madison: The University of Wisconsin Press, 1967.

Locke, Richard Adams. *The Moon Hoax.* New York: William Gowans, 1859.

Lucian. *True History and Lucius or the Ass.* Trans. Paul Turner. Bloomington: Indiana U.P., 1958.

O'Brien, Fitz-James. *The Diamond Lens and Other Stories.* New York: William Edwin Rudge, 1932.

Paltock, Robert. *The Life and Adventures of Peter Wilkins.* Ed. Christopher Bentley. London: Oxford U.P., 1973.

Poe, Edgar Allan. *The Narrative of Arthur Gordon Pym.* Intro. Sidney Kaplan. New York: Hill and Wang, 1960.

Poe, Edgar Allan. *The Short Fiction of Edgar Allan Poe.* Ed. Stuart and Susan Levine. Indianapolis: Bobbs-Merrill, 1976.

Shelley, Mary. *Frankenstein.* Ed. M. K. Joseph. London: Oxford U.P., 1969.

Voltaire [François Marie Arouet]. *Voltaire's Candide, Zadig and Selected Stories.* Trans. Donald M. Frame. Bloomington: Indiana U.P., 1961.

Secondary sources

Bailey, J. O. *Pilgrims Through Space and Time.* Westport: Greenwood Press, 1972.

Franklin, H. Bruce. *Future Perfect: American Science Fiction of the Nineteenth Century.* New York: Oxford U.P., 1966.

Nicolson, Marjorie Hope. *Voyages to the Moon.* New York: Macmillan, 1948.

Philmus, Robert M. *Into the Unknown: The Evolution of Science Fiction from Francis Godwin to H. G. Wells.* Berkeley: University of California Press, 1970.

Jules Verne:
the last happy utopianist

Marc Angenot

Life and work

Jules Verne was born in Nantes in 1828. His father, a well-to-do
provincial bourgeois, wanted his son to follow the respectable career of
a lawyer or financier. Jules was sent to Paris to study law. Endowed
with an independent and adventurous character, he did not show much
enthusiasm for his first profession, that of a stockbroker. He wanted to
write and actually tried without great success to become a playwright.
It was rather late in his life and, apparently, by pure chance that Verne
discovered the literary formula that was to bring him success, wealth,
and some sort of international fame.

In 1862, encouraged by his friend and publisher Hetzel (who some
years later would launch the *Magasin d'Education et de Récréation*, the
most successful magazine for young people at the time), Jules Verne
wrote his first scientific adventure novel, *Five Weeks in a Balloon*
(1863), to be followed shortly by *Journey to the Centre of the Earth*
(1864), *From the Earth to the Moon* (1865), and many others. Their
success was immediate, as evidenced by an ever-increasing demand
from a public never entirely limited to teenagers. A host of imitators
soon followed, among them André Laurie, le Faure and Graffigny,
Nagrien, Calvet, Berthet, and Danrit.

Without trying to disparage his genius, it should be noted that,
although he has so often been called the 'Father of Science Fiction',
Verne was not among the first to write 'scientific romances'. From the
French Revolution to 1862 in France, there had been dozens of
narratives which, in retrospect, have to be called science fiction. C.
Defontenay's *Star* (*Psi Cassiopoea*) (1854), recently published in
English, gives evidence of the hitherto unrecognized value and audacity of these works. Nevertheless, before Verne, SF never established
a tradition. It was a production without cultural continuity, deprived of
any institutional legitimacy.

In sociological terms, the contrast between Verne's commercial
success and the failure of his predecessors may be explained by supposing that SF had for years sought in vain for an institutional 'landing
point' and an ideological model. It is as if powerful resistances had
impeded the success of genres with an intense speculative boldness or
with strong elements of social satire, so that the fiction of scientific

conjecture was finally forced into a more timid framework, namely the promotion of a literature for teenagers, progressivist and 'virile'.

And in fact – though a few early enthusiasts recognized him immediately as an important author – Verne was generally considered nothing more than a respectable writer for young people. It is only in the last twenty years that such critics as Michel Butor, Marcel Moré, Roland Barthes, Michel Serres, Michel Foucault, Pierre Macherey, Jean Chesneaux, and Simone Vierne have discovered in Verne a writer whose coherence, subtlety, and complexity of vision place him among the greatest. These recent works in French (see Bibliography) place Jules Verne at the centre of the methodological debates on literary criticism, since each is representative of a particular approach; thus, Verne has been brought within the horizons of psychoanalysis, archetypal criticism, formalism, Marxism, structuralism, and other types of sociocritical analysis.

Verne wrote eighty novels or so and, although he reached the peak of his career in the 1870s, there are only a few of his later works that are decidedly uninteresting. In this essay, I shall attempt to circumscribe a specific world-view that in my opinion underlies all his books: not only the actual 'scientific romances' – which would leave us with a balance of travelogues, fantasy tales, and adventure stories that are usually labelled as 'less interesting' by critics of SF – but his opus as a whole.

Circulation as theme

Let us begin with something obvious on the surface of the text: all the narratives of Jules Verne, or almost all, are narratives of circulation and even – as Michel Serres has pointed out – of circular circulation. All his practically minded characters are bodies in motion; but one can also see that this mobility does not apply to the actors alone. Other things circulate also: desires, information, money, machines, celestial bodies. Everything circulates – *mobilis in mobili*: what can be more suitable than to use Captain Nemo's own motto as the *leitmotif* of the entire opus?

It has often been noted that Verne's most significant characters are people with fixations: Lidenbrock in *Journey to the Centre of the Earth*, Hatteras in *English at the North Pole* (1866), Phileas Fogg in *Around the World in Eighty Days* (1873) and, to the point of being ridiculous, Jos Merritt in *Mistress Branican* (1891) who goes all the way to Australia in search of a hat won by Queen Victoria. Yet, paradoxically, all these fixations are ambulatory fixations.

What of the 'supreme point' towards which the characters tend, as Michel Butor has noted? No doubt it exists, but it is always a question, not of remaining there, but of *attaining* it. In fact, by virtue of its being a fixed point, it cannot be occupied: the geographic pole is an erupting volcano, while the centre of the earth is never reached by Professor

Lidenbrock and his nephew. The 'American' qualities of the characters – energy, tenacity, steadiness, insensitivity – are qualities of an object bound to a periplus or circumnavigatory voyage, the trajectory of which ought to be accelerated, but cannot be bent inwards. 'This gentleman asked for nothing. He did not travel, he described a circumference', says Verne very accurately of Phileas Fogg.

In *Captain Antifer* (1894), the hunt for treasure, determined by geographic coordinates, results in the tracing of a 'circle of circles', but the treasure (the fixed point, meaning or value) has been swallowed up by the sea. Equally, Verne's frequent cryptogram is a machine which causes meaning to circulate: it has a key but no referent; circulation comes to a halt with the last message. The entire *œuvre* is a 'cycle of cyclical voyages', says Michel Serres, who returns to Hegel, but could just as easily refer to Marx's concept of the commodity circuit (commodity → money → commodity). To add a Freudian element, the theme of 'triangulation' can be interpreted as analogous to the Oedipus triangle, in a work where the Oedipus myth is present through a number of avatars.

Before attempting an interpretation, it is important to take into account the polysemy, the circulation of meaning throughout the intertextual system.

At a cosmological level, for example, Verne's celestial mechanics correspond to his circular voyages. The celestial bodies also turn in relation to a fixed point: thus the aphelion of Gallia in *Off on a Comet!* (1877) does not pass beyond the solar system, and the comet returns to skim the earth's atmosphere after its revolution. And since mythological interpretations have a good time with Jules Verne, it remains to be noted that Verne uses only the *ambulatory* myths which are, in effect, transposed, and very systematically, in his work: Ulysses being the model for *Mathias Sandorf* (1885); Orpheus, the ancestor of Franz de Telek in *Castle of the Carpathians* (1892); Icarus, the ancestor of Robur in *Clipper of the Clouds* (1886); Oedipus being reversed in *Michael Strogoff* (1876); ARiadNE being the archetype of ARNE Saknussemm, the thread in the labyrinth where Lidenbrock and Axel make their way. . . . These myths, of which Verne retains the general configuration, are superficial features; to look here for the essence of the work, as the archetypal critics do, would be a mistake. It is the 'theme' of circulation (for lack of a more appropriate expression) which gives unity to the work, and which permits the bringing together of the scientific romances and the 'simple' travel narratives such as *Michael Strogoff, Eight Hundred Leagues on the Amazon* (1881), and *Cesar Cascabel* (1890).

Verne reactivates in his work *all* the fictional models of the voyage. *Around the World in Eighty Days* revives the picaresque model of flight and pursuit stories: Figgs behind Fogg, policeman and thief. Fogg is accused of having invented his extravagant bet to cover a bank robbery. Fogg is the movable body and Figgs's is fixed, an obstacle to circulation, attempting to head back the circulating gold to the 'fixed capital' of the Bank of England, the victim of the theft. This confusion of Phileas Fogg with a *gold thief* is worth emphasizing. In the economic image that I shall describe, gold is an imaginary equivalent for capitalization, i.e. sedentariness, as opposed to the circulation of commodities in the axiomatic paradox of the capitalist system.

Keraban the Inflexible (1883), a narrative of simple circulation, gives us a clue. Keraban wants to go from Constantinople to Scutari, but the protectionist government of the Young Turks has just imposed a toll on the Bosporus. The reactionary Keraban becomes, in spite of himself, a hero of economic liberalism: he cannot put up with this blocking element, a tax imposed on commodities and people. Since he is prevented from circulating as he pleases, he decides to circulate in an accelerated fashion: he will travel around the Black Sea to avoid submitting to this protectionist nuisance! The novel comes down to this and nothing else, but it reads in expressly economic terms. Let us keep in mind the equation: 'blockage implies acceleration'.

There are other epics of *release* and *circulation*. *L'Invasion de la Mer* (1905) predicts that the Sahara Desert, travelled by wretched and culturally stagnant people, will become an ocean, open to commercial ventures, if a canal can be dug between the Gulf of Gabes and the Tunisian Schotts. *The Underground City* (1877) is likewise the story of a struggle between the engineer, Starr, who wants to reopen the Aberfoyle coal mine, and Silfax, the Hermit of the mine and the superstitious guardian of stagnation and autistic obscurity. In *Off on a Comet!* Gibraltar, symbol of imperialist protectionism and blockading, is sucked away by the comet Gallia, so that its obtuse garrison begins to circulate within the solar system. The same goes for the 'polar' novels, narratives of the struggle against entropy and 'zero degree': 'I do not believe in uninhabitable areas', Captain Hatteras had said. . . .

It has often been noted that all Verne's imaginary machines are machines meant to circulate more rapidly: the Steam House, the Albatross, the *Nautilus*, the Épouvante, the Columbiad rocket, Propellor Island; and even (minus the machinery) the giant raft of la Jangada, and the gypsy wagon of Cesar Cascabel. One is reminded of the love for railways shared by Verne and his juvenile readers. Verne even invented lines which did not exist (and still do not), such as the Transcaspian, and the Transasiatic. *Claudius Bombarnac* (1892) is a railroad romance from the first page to the last.

At the end of the nineteenth century, electricity was no longer a dream; the dynamo dates from 1861, the electric railway from 1879, the elevator from 1880. But electricity is, in itself, natural energy, and, in its effects, a source *par excellence* of mobility, the negation of space by speed: the telegraph, acclaimed by Verne, presages a McLuhanesque shrinking of the world to the dimensions of an 'electronic village'. It should be noted that electricity is an accelerating agent, not a transforming one in Verne: there are *accelerated circularities*, not qualitatively irreversible mutations: the acceleration does not reach attrition speed, the circle never becomes asymptote.

These circulating machines finally permit a dialectical transcendence of values attached to sedentariness: the vehicles are homely and comfortable, deterritorialized territories. Hence, the paradoxes of the Steam House, the Floating City, and the Propellor Island. What is meant by this means of travelling which carries its shelter along with it? By the hero who is both a sedentary bourgeois and a stateless person, like Captain Nemo in the rococo stateroom of the *Nautilus*, with its opulent pictures and tapestries, its marble statues and its magnificent organ?

Circulation for circulation's sake

Let us ask ourselves the most obvious question: why does one circulate? And what can be gained at the end of the periplus which very often is the point of departure? Among Verne's recent critics, Simone Vierne replies that the Voyage is always an 'initiation', in the quasi-religious sense of the world. But the idea of initiation is, to a large extent, an artificial critical device which has been superimposed on Verne's texts. M.-H. Huet declares: 'the exploration, the voyage would be incomplete if the hero did not return to communicate his discovery'. This is the official ideology which rationally justifies the voyage. But Nemo and Robur never return. Hatteras and Telek do return, to the 'civilized' world, but go mad. . . .

Let us go back to our question, 'why circulate?' in the light of the 'cryptogram voyages', such as *Journey to the Centre of the Earth*, *Captain Grant's Children* (1867), *Captain Antifer* and *Eight Hundred Leagues on the Amazon*. The cryptogram is a text without a signified: it is a mutable signifier, the mobility of which involves that of the decipherers. With the exception of *Captain Grant's Children*, the referent of the cryptogram is never really found at the end of the voyage (the centre of the earth is not reached, the islet Julia is engulfed). Captain Grant – the father – is found on his island, but the voyage around the world was an investment without return, and Paganel's 'treasures' of ingenuity were in vain. All the cryptograms, then, give rise to circulation (of meaning and characters).

The 'Icarian' novels, such as those featuring Nemo and Robur, are flights forward: Icarus is a Prometheus without a beneficiary for his gift. In *The Will of an Eccentric* (1889), J. W. Hipperbone leaves his fortune to the winner of a strange contest: the United States becomes a chart for the game of snakes-and-ladders, each State representing a square of the game. But to have travelled across the USA is the only thing the competitors will have to show for their efforts; J. W. Hipperbone not being dead, the inheritance escapes them. The paradigm for all this is to be found in the pre-capitalist fable of Jean de la Fontaine, 'The Ploughman and the Children'. A ploughman, 'sensing his approaching death', summons his children and directs them to plough the fields he leaves them, since 'a treasure is hidden within'. The children plough, the plough digs its furrows, and they find nothing (no value, no capital, no fetish), but they know henceforth, seeing the earth improved and productive, that 'work is treasure'. In Verne also, circulation is the true wealth and capitalization is accursed.

Phieeas Fogg makes his trip around the world; the expenses and benefits of the bet cancel each other out; his voyage was a case of circulation (monetary) without the surplus-value of *investment*. But Fogg obtains something which could be called a 'surplus-value of circulation', one day gained in travelling eastward. He also obtains another unsought-after value – fortune, gift, not investment – 'What was the yield of this voyage? Nothing, we would say.' . . . 'Nothing were it not for a wife.' And Verne, tongue in cheek, concludes: 'Would one not make a trip around the world for less than this?' In addition, the bet, a frequent motif in Verne, is the Romantic image of a time transaction, a 'future'; Fogg is a 'speculator' in both the intellectual's and the stockbroker's sense of the word.

Why does one circulate? One circulates in order to circulate, and one gains no profit from it, except a 'capital' of knowledge (but science is an immanent accelerator). Circulation is an end in itself; the only thing to do is to speed it up, and the highest moral quality is haste, which is always valued.

All the narratives are bound to this principle of acceleration: Lidenbrock and his companions are thrown forth by the Stromboli, while Phileas Fogg moves more and more rapidly in spite of the obstacles. A ludicrous variant of this is to be found in *Dr Ox's Experiment* (1874). The experiment consists of exposing a placid Flemish village to the effects of pure oxygen. Over a period of several hours, the normally phlegmatic behaviour of these people becomes more and more frantic, but finally everything goes back to normal. That's all: the narrative has no other interest than to stage this incongruous acceleration.

The paradox is that this accelerated circulation takes place in a closed circuit, in a limited universe, a world without transcendence, where science is identified with an integrated and accrued acceleration. I will try to interpret this essential feature in economic and political terms (but on other levels also), by opposing two isotopias, the terms of which are correlated:

Sedentariness	*vs*	Circulation
stagnation, entropy		acceleration
centripetal absorption		centrifugal expansion
territory		deterritorialization
blockages, territorial obstacles		fluidification
feudalism, closed societies		imperialism, deculturation
permanent or fixed capital		circulation of commodities

Sedentariness	*vs*	Circulation
monosemy _____		circulation of meaning, cryptogram
Jehovah figure _____		positivism and immanence
father figure _____		orphan figure
protectionism, State apparatus _____		liberalism, anarchism
superstition _____		free examination and science
marriage _____		celibacy
etc _____		

I shall attempt to demonstrate the immanent intelligibility of these contrasts, certain of which seem incongruous. Let me add a possible interpretative paradigm:

Robinsonade, as the paradigm of primitive capitalism, the physiocratic epic of landed property.	*vs*	Vernian narrative, as the paradigm of 'Keynesian' consumption society, acceleration without exterior limit (or crisis).

(Hence the need for examining Verne's *robinsonades* or desert-island narratives, such as *The Mysterious Island* (1874).)[1]

From the eighteenth century to the end of the nineteenth, we progress from the ideological figure of the Island to that of the accelerated Voyage, from the appropriation of nature to the economy of consumption. Movement is measured in time and energy; progress is a drive having neither limit nor backlash. As Lewis Mumford writes in *Technics and Civilization*, 'Progress was motion toward infinity, motion without completion or end, motion for motion's sake. One could not have too much progress, it could not come too rapidly, it could not spread too widely and it could not destroy the "unprogressive" elements in society too swiftly and ruthlessly.'

In this hypothesis, capitalism, as an ideological form, is perceived as the paradoxical coexistence of sedentary capital and circulating abundance (technical progress, consumption). The necessity for increased circulation leads to the valorization of science as a solvent of social contradictions, an immanent anticipative apparatus, a Utopia without rupture or setback, constantly producing divergences and integration. In a society which is torn apart by its transformation, Vernian fiction produces an imaginative synthesis of the contradictions of sedentariness and circulation.

Circulation in economic terms

Let us begin with the most commonplace quotations of Marx, not to look here for the 'source' of Vernian ideological phantasms, but rather for an intertextual vector which passes through Verne's text:

All capital values are engaged in the continuous circulation. . . . The movement of the commodity is therefore a circuit.

Money is a perpetuum mobile.

The circulation of money as capital possesses its end in itself, because it is only by this continuously renewed motion that value continues to make itself valuable.

(Karl Marx, Capital, *I, i, Ch. 3, sect. 1, a, b*)

Circulation is a 'process without end', $M \rightarrow C \rightarrow M$, a circle; after undergoing changes of form, the same value returns to that of the universal equivalent. Circulation seems to *create* value in the shortened circuit $M \rightarrow M'$ (as exemplified by the bet in *Around the World in Eighty Days*). Verne privileges circulation as a social axiom; it is here that one is tempted to compare his idea of circulation with Keynes's antistagnationism: 'lack of consumption as the chief cause of depression'.

This circulation is tied to a generalized accountability – energy is measurable. Phileas Fogg is a neurotic of accountable time. Verne disregards the fact that circulation is tied to a sedentary pole, *Capital*. Everything is seen as accelerated fluidity; all unproductive accumulation (of meaning, knowledge, riches) is condemned in the story itself. For instance, his condemnation of permanent capital is illustrated in the character of Isaac Hakkabut, a merchant and usurer, in *Off on a Comet!* Carried away through the solar system, Hakkabut thinks only of centralizing the economic exchanges on Gallia in order to increase his small hoard of money. What the parable shows is that capital, once made 'unsedentary', no longer has any value. First because the comet itself is made of gold – which never more merited the name of a 'dirt cheap metal'! Second, because in orbit around Saturn, gold no longer weighs what it weighed on earth. The novel is a metaphorical critique of capitalist 'fetishism'.

There is no encoding which resists mobility, which is to say that capitalism destroys itself, not through crises, but in the very process of its reproduction. Private property is not a major element in modern society, it is an archaism, a contradiction. All of Verne's imaginative art puts this mobility and its liberating effects on stage. Science opposes fixed Capital: they are the positive and negative aspects of modernity. On this level, we already see Verne's ideological paradox: a utopia without rupture for a capitalism without capital. Verne portrays expense, not accumulation; circulation, not surplus value.

If capitalism tends to become, in economic terms, undifferentiated circulation, it is also undifferentiated circulation in its *lateral* effects. Here Verne sometimes expresses most directly the presuppositions which we ascribe to his world-view. The political effect of industrial capitalism is an effect of deterritorializing and anonymizing. In suppressing by force the archaic axioms dependent on territorial investments, it creates a universe of stateless persons and orphans, in which everybody can be called a *Nemo*.

The capitalist market, and the apparatus of political expansion that it relies on, pitilessly eliminates particularisms, local traditions, old cultures which interfere with its expansion, and subverts the closed social nuclei – families, tribes – to mix up everything in the insignificance of exchange. Imperialist mobilization involves alienation, but equally the liberation from traditional bonds: the peasant uprooted from the soil becomes a proletarian, and the Hindu prince brutally expelled from his feudal world becomes Captain Nemo (Latin: nobody), the anonymous avenger, builder of a submarine, the *Nautilus*, which circulates more rapidly than the fleets of the imperialist powers pursuing him. Nemo does not try to reconstitute what 'inevitable progress' has crushed. He haunts a non-territory which no one will appropriate, the Ocean, with its inexhaustible abundance. He is the figure of the Wandering Jew, the Romantic image of the man without a territory.

Let us consider the ideological elements which Nemo's case transposes:

1. His motto *mobilis in mobili* is at once ambiguously Romantic theme ('Homme libre, toujours, tu chériras la mer!') and the epitome of circulation and technological modernity.
2. The *Nautilus*, a machine which produces no surplus value, makes for the coexistence of deterritorialization and territorial nostalgia; it is a closed whole, a museum and an encyclopaedia.
3. For Nemo to become an anarchist rebel who seeks to avenge himself on the imperialist powers, imperialism had to tear him from his static and condemned feudal world and to strip him of his identity as the former Prince Dakkan, a leader of the Sepoys in the Indian Mutiny of 1857. (Nemo's past is not revealed in *Twenty Thousand Leagues under the Sea*, but is established retrospectively in *The Mysterious Island*.) Nemo is both a new Prometheus and a Frankenstein's monster; he is at once the Creature dehumanized by progress, and the Creator who makes use of progress in accelerating it. His mobility is a fate which he transforms into a Romantic choice, and this is why the Saint-Simonian hero Cyrus Smith (Cyrus Harding in the English translation) must both admire and condemn him: 'Your error lay in supposing that the past could be resuscitated and in contending against inevitable progress' (*The Mysterious Island*, III, Ch. 16). It should be noted that 'inevitable progress' includes the genocide of the Sepoys and that Verne is perfectly conscious of this.
4. Nemo intervenes politically by financing the Cretans' liberation

movement against the English imperialists, but he draws the money from the unproductive treasure of the Spanish galleons sunk in the Bay of Vigo. In other words, here again he places in circulation 'sedentary' capital.

5. His voyage, zigzagging without a goal, a case of conspicuous consumption in undersea lands, is deterritorialized circulation, thus reproducing the capitalist axiom.

6. Imperialism, by stripping Nemo of his name, his property, and his flag made of him a 'free' man, a negative liberty that he changes into a positive one. Is Nemo a father figure, as Marcel Moré would have it? An odd father whose name is no-one! He is an orphan rather, like many Vernian heroes, born of a 'family without a name', in the violent midwifery of Capital made History. This outcast is not in reaction against, but rather ahead of history – he struggles against 'inevitable progress', but it must be said that in doing so, he passes beyond it. In the last chapters of *Twenty Thousand Leagues under the Sea*, when a British frigate blocks him up in an estuary, he can avenge himself, because he has, in the circumstances, the ultimate value of circulation against blockage.

7. This is also clearly stated in *The Mysterious Island*. Verne is forced to admire the power of imperialism to place things in circulation, at the very time when he tries to vindicate the right. Of the crushing of the Sepoys he says: 'Right, once again, had succumbed in the face of might. But civilization never recedes and it seems that it borrows all its rights from necessity.'² This is an ambiguous and frightening phrase to which no one has paid sufficient attention.

Blocking figures

In this epic of acceleration, what are the elements which represent the blockage of flow, the obstruction of energy, the stasis? First of all, there is frequently a critique of the State (the State, not the nation: nationalism is a liberating stage, but its clotting in a repressive apparatus inhibits it; the 'libertarian' Verne condemns the police forces while the free-trader Verne condemns the customs duties). From a Saint-Simonian point of view, the withering away of the State is tied to the free development of the industrial system.

We have seen the example of Keraban the Inflexible who cannot accept the toll on the Bosporus. If Verne is anglophobic, it is when he speaks of Gibraltar, Malacca, Aden, and all the hegemonic protectionism for which he nourishes a stubborn hatred. Verne even wrote a short story which is apparently supportive of the South in the American Civil War, but its title explains this paradox: 'The Blockade Runners' (1865). In *North Against South* (1887) and other novels, he is, on the contrary, for the Northerners, because philanthropic anti-slavery is consonant with the theme of deterritorialization.

Is he a racist, hostile to archaic or primitive peoples? That depends. No, if they free themselves from feudal stagnation. Yes, if, like the Tunisian nomads, they want to preserve for themselves a desert where nothing circulates: Verne invents a tidal wave which sweeps them away, but this natural catastrophe assists the cause of Progress and Exchange by creating the 'Saharan Sea' (*L'Invasion de la Mer*)!

Verne has a high regard for profit, trade and riches, but gold is doomed: a Romantic theme, if one wishes, but also an echo of a Saint-Simonian loathing, since what is spurned is unproductive accumulation. The ideological ethic which valorizes accelerated circulation, condemns the reduction of economic flow to an immobile centre. Marx in *Capital* saw that the two phenomena are correlated:

As soon as the circulation of commodities develops, the necessity and the desire to conserve the product of the first metamorphosis also develops.

But it is the 'fetishists of metal money', fascinated by the 'material glow of precious metals', who are condemned by Verne.

In other words, gold is valorized if it is put into circulation. Thus the Spanish treasures recovered by Nemo supply the revolt of the Cretans. In *Off on a Comet!*, in which Isaac Hakkabut is, as has been seen, the figure of unproductive capital, it is ironic that Verne thought it fit that the comet be made of gold telluride: 'It was indeed the mineral reign in its horrible aridity. . . .'

In *The Golden Volcano* (1906) and *The Survivors of the 'Jonathan'* (1909), Verne remembers the Australian and Californian gold rushes of the 1850s. Kaw Djer, the libertarian leader, throws back into the sea the first gold nugget that he finds. But he cannot prevent this discovery from bringing the disintegration of the colony. The colonists of Hoste Island become gold-washers, and the abandonment of productive labour ruins the economy of the island. 'The eternal desire to possess' is equally at the heart of *The Vanished Diamond* (1884), in which alchemical delusion is transposed into the theme of the chemical manufacture of diamonds.

If it is absurd to ask whether Verne was a closet anarchist, one may venture to see what in libertarian thought could be inscribed in his fictional system: and that is the absurdity of private property:

Everyone would say, as though it were the most natural thing in the world: this is mine! And no one was aware of this intense comedy, this pretention of a being so fragile to monopolize for himself and for himself alone some fraction of the universe.   (The Survivors of the 'Jonathan')

Here again it is unproductive property which is condemned, such as that of Silfax in *The Underground City*, guardian of an unknown gold vein in an abandoned mine. As soon as Starr starts working the mine again, the tone changes and the praise of industrial capital modestly conceals the exploitation of the workers.

Science as accelerator

Science, for Verne, is at the same time exterior to social vicissitudes, innocent of society's contradictions and completely understood in its effects. In the place of need and labour it is the transcendental subject of history, whose inscription in the social body is called *progress.* Exterior to social relations but the agent of their transformations, it is the *alibi*, in the etymological sense, of the dominant class. It cannot be enslaved. It does not, then, have an institutional dimension: there are isolated scientists, but there is no technostructure; the rocket to the moon is launched by a private society supported by gifts. With isolated scientists as heroes, the passage from knowledge to praxis is made in the same person.

But science is not described for its own sake, and never does the narrative focus on isolated gadgets. The referent of Vernian discourse is the *effect* of science, as the successive projection of discrete inventions on the social body. This effect is essentially a quantifiable acceleration. Science is thus at once the guardian of the social *status quo,* and the means of its immanent transcendence.

Verne is far from manifesting the futurological fantasy of Rosny the Elder or Albert Robida, as his ideological project lies elsewhere: to show the social and historical effect of the introduction of new techniques into a state of society – his own. (Although Verne has for a long time been seen as the 'prophet of the twentieth century', it has been discovered that there is scarcely an 'invention' in his work which did not already exist in blueprint form.) His works are a portrayal of the influence of science in history. It is a one-way effect: science accelerates general circulation, but it is not influenced by the conflicts or the interests which were pre-existent. This lack of realism is proportional to Verne's optimism. Science cannot progress, however, without freedom (free criticism, free diffusion): it demands an unbounded and fluid society which it, in turn, contributes to produce; a dialectical harmony to which Verne holds.

Identifying Progress and Growth – an idea which our century has learned to distrust – Verne sees science taking the place of the immediate means of manual industry. 'They *knew*', he says of the colonists of Lincoln Island, comparing their progress to the failure of other, more primitive colonists. Progress is a continual process, unequivocal; its contradictions are only archaic resistances, reminders of a former order which will erode. It is fully positive. Does Verne write *science fiction*? Yes, as fiction about science in its global, historical effect, not in its scattering in specific discoveries.

In *The Golden Meteor* (1908), Verne confronts science and capitalism. An eccentric scientist, by means of a small apparatus manufactured in two or three days, brings the fall of a golden meteor; the result is diplomatic panic, universal bankruptcy, and military crisis. Science can wipe out the capitalist system which cannot do it any harm in return. Verne, however, hesitated in seeing it through, and at the end of the novel nothing has happened. There are some transfers of fortune and the Republic of Greenland where the meteor had fallen (only to be engulfed by the sea) remains as poor as it was before. Something can be retained nonetheless: the impotence of the capitalist system when a simple scientific initiative strikes at its heart.

Verne's ideological image of unlimited acceleration unfolds in a closed universe. There is no externality: in terms of fiction, no mutant, no alien, no humanoids, no social catastrophe, no epistemological break, no interplanetary expansion. It is a world without externality, a geocentric circulation which remains totalizable: the cartographic dream fills up a limited space: 'The earth is the primitive and savage unity of desire and production.' All Vernian islands are the synecdoche of this primitive unity which echoes that of the first capitalist fiction, *Robinson Crusoe* (1719) by Daniel Defoe.

There is no anticipation in Verne, because the future is *in* the present. As Michel Serres writes, 'We are of a world where everything happens: one has almost the right to say: where everything has happened.' In this closed universe, Verne postulates the unlimited development, absolute growth without crises that will go on until the natural resources become exhausted. Some have wanted to see in his idea of the end of the world by 'natural exhaustion' a sign of pessimism, but, to me, it indicates an extreme optimism!

Narrative presuppositions and ideology

I have presented the theme of 'accelerated circulation' – a theme which postulates a *generalized economy* (circulation of commodities, people, ideas, desires) – as the invariable feature that confers a dynamic unity on Verne's work.

After having traditionally treated Verne as an inspired entertainer, literary critics have sought recently to throw light on his political ideology. Was he a good watch-dog of the bourgeois order, or rather a closet socialist, a libertarian, or a nationalist in the 1848 tradition? Perhaps it is useful to outline some significant vectors.

1. Saint-Simonianism

The social doctrine of Saint-Simon is often considered quite improperly as being socialist (i.e. as a class ideology of the proletariat). Saint-Simon expressed the social aspirations of the petty-bourgeois industrial vanguard, yearning for a 'government of the producers' when 'engineers would be kings'. The division of labour is seen as functional: a common and effective exploitation of Nature will eradicate exploitation of man by man.

2. '1848' nationalism

Verne praises the struggle of oppressed ethnic groups and nations, but he also tends to justify a 'civilizing' imperialism. Here there are potential contradictions in his work. Class struggle is not ignored but is usually associated with ethnic struggles: Quebecers, Irishmen, Greeks, Balts, Slavs, etc.

3. Libertarian socialism

Jules Verne, a well-to-do provincial bourgeois, but also a friend and admirer of the anarchist doctrinaire Elisée Reclus, had in principle a certain reticent admiration for anarchism. At least in theory, anarchy stands for individual freedom as science stands for the freedom of mankind. Anarchy was probably in his opinion a 'noble chimera'. Bourgeois liberalism and anarchism are not totally incompatible in the spirit of 'accelerated circulation'. Free trade is a factor in the decay of the absolutist state.

4. 'Authoritarian' socialism

Here, Verne's reticence is more profound. The bourgeois parliamentary system is satirized in *Propellor Island* (1895); imperialist chauvinism is denounced in *The Golden Meteor*. *The Survivors of the 'Jonathan'* conceals a deeper critique of socialist theories. If Verne talks about 'les Lassalle, les Karl Marx, Les Guesde', it is to say that 'none of them take into account contingencies of life'. The 'dictatorship essential for the working of a collectivist society' is what his hero rejects. Verne sees in socialism only the blocking of circulation, economic exploitation being shifted to political hyper-repression. The parable is very clear: immigrants, displaced persons, are shipwrecked on the coast of southern Magellania, the last part of the world that in 1900 was not claimed by any political power. Yet, as soon as they are settling in this inhospitable area, they re-create powers, policies, prisons, and some sort of collective property that does not eliminate hatred and competition. The ideological conclusions are obvious. Collectivism cannot exist in scarcity: it cannot but entail tyranny. Science remains, for Verne, the only factor of social liberation.

Conclusions

Verne is not a doctrinaire but rather a man of fiction and fantasy. His tales display a certain ideological fuzziness along a major vector: that is, the circulation and acceleration of flux in a closed universe.

Verne is paradoxically a utopianist without an alternative society; he is the last SF writer who believes in industrialist euphoria, even if some pessimism overshadows his last books. H. G. Wells or Rosny the Elder are of another generation, prey to a cataclysmic world-view counterbalanced by a quest for mutations and radical changes. At the cost of some oversimplifications, Verne is able to harmonize most of the social ideas of his time.

Rather than a precursor of the twentieth century, he is the last 'happy' SF writer. Hence his everlasting seduction. Nostalgically, the reader sees this world-view which is neither critical, nor tragic, nor clouded with resentment, and is free from the paranoia that invades conjectural fiction after him. Verne is a great writer, whose profundity and aesthetic richness were discovered only recently. Far from anticipating the twentieth century, he only marks the end of certain illusions.

Notes

1. Pierre Macherey tries to see in *The Mysterious Island* a regression to early capitalist ideology. One should rather talk of a critical transcendence of this ideology. Marx himself clearly delineated such a project. Verne, had he read *Das Kapital*, would only have had to follow this scheme (I, i, sect. 3): 'Let us now picture to ourselves a Community of free individuals, carrying on their work with the means of production in common, in which the labour power of all the different individuals is consciously applied as the combined labour-power of the community. All the characteristics of Robinson's labour are here repeated, but with this difference, that they are social, instead of individual. . . . The total product of our community is a social product. . . . The social relations of the individual producers, with regard both to their labour and to its products, are in this case perfectly simple and intelligible, and that with regard not only to production but also to distribution.'
   Here is the ideological 'source' of *The Mysterious Island,* substituting for individual property the overall product of united workers. This 'Robinsonade' is anti-Robinson; the reign of scarcity is supplemented by technical knowledge. The 'colonists' begin at a prehistorical stage (one match, one watch-glass) and, in four years, recapture the technical development of the 1870s. The novel is a reflection on scientific 'surplus value' replacing landed surplus value.
2. My translation. In the (abridged) British version one only reads: 'Civilization never recedes. The law of necessity ever forces it onwards.' This is typical of the state of Vernian translations.

Bibliography

Les Voyages extraordinaires

The dates given in the text of this essay refer to the first publication of the French original in book form. The titles, however, are those of the English translations, where translations exist. In the following cases, the English title differs noticeably from that of the French original: *English at the North Pole* (*Voyages et aventures du Capitaine Hatteras*), *Off on a Comet!* (*Hector Servadac*), *Clipper of the Clouds* (*Robur le Conquérant*), *Eight Hundred Leagues on the Amazon* (*La Jangada*), *The Underground City* (*Les Indes noires*), *The Golden Meteor* (*La Chasse au météore*).
The only reliable reprints of Verne in any language today are the *Œuvres de Jules Verne*, Lausanne (Rencontre) 1966-71, and the twenty titles or so published by Hachette in their 'Livre de Poche' series. The latter reproduce the original texts and illustrations. All other texts on the market are bowdlerized.

Secondary material

Allott, Kenneth. *Jules Verne*. London: Cresset Press, 1940.

Allotte de la Fuye, Madame, *Jules Verne*. London: Staples Press, 1954.

Barthes, Roland. 'Par où commencer?', in *Le Degré zéro de l'écriture, Suivi de Nouveaux essais critiques*. Paris: Seuil, 1972.

Barthes, Roland. 'The *Nautilus* and the Drunken Boat', *Mythologies*. Trans. Annette Lavers. London: Paladin, 1973, pp. 65-7.

Bellemin-Noel, Jean. 'Analectures de Jules Verne', *Critique*, Nos. 279-80 (1970).

Butor, Michel. 'The Golden Age in Jules Verne', in *Inventory*. Ed. Richard Howard. London: Jonathan Cape, 1970, pp. 114-45.

Chesneaux, Jean. *The Political and Social Ideas of Jules Verne*. London: Thames and Hudson, 1972.

Evans, Idrisyn Oliver. *Jules Verne and his Work*. London: Arco, 1965; New York: Twayne Publishers, 1966.

Huet, Marie-Hélène. *L'Histoire des 'Voyages extraordinaires', essai sur l'œuvre de Jules Verne*. Paris: Minard, 1973.

Jules-Verne, Jean. *Jules Verne: A Biography*. New York: Taplinger, 1976.

Macherey, Pierre. 'Jules Verne ou le récit en défaut', in *Pour une théorie de la production littéraire*. Paris: Maspero, 1966.

Moré, Marcel. *Le très curieux Jules Verne*. Paris: Gallimard, 1960.

Moré, Marcel. *Nouvelles explorations de Jules Verne*. Paris: Gallimard, 1963.

Serres, Michel. *Jouvences sur Jules Verne*. Paris: Editions de Minuit, 1974.

Suvin, Darko, 'Communication in Quantified Space: The Utopian Liberalism of Jules Verne's Science Fiction', *Clio*, **4**, No. 1 (1974), 51-71.

Touttain, Pierre-André, ed. 'Jules Verne', *Cahiers de l'Herne*, No. 27 (1974).

Vierne, Simone. *Jules Verne et le roman initiatique*. Paris: Editions du Sirac, 1974.

The science fiction of H. G. Wells

John Huntington

I

Wells's early works are remarkable for the way they do justice to conflict. In these stories and novels Wells does not set out to defend a specific point of view or assume a position of advocacy; instead, he constructs contradictions and then explores their structures and possibilities. His imaginative strategy is to establish acute conflict, the sharper and the more irresolvable the better, and then to find ways of overcoming the opposition without denying the validity of either side. The process involves either finding areas of identity that transcend the antithesis (*The War of the Worlds*), or, more usually, inventing symbols, images, and characters that bridge the gap between opposites. These early works thereby develop, not answers, but intricately balanced patterns which, by helping us focus clearly on the contradictions within civilization, force us to ponder, though hardly resolve, central moral issues of our world. Science fiction, or Scientific Romance as Wells himself termed it, is useful for such imaginative play because it offers a wider range of situations and images than does conventional realistic literature, and it permits new and eccentric orderings of old images.

The core of work that most interests us today was all published before 1900. It consists of four novels (*The Time Machine*, 1895; *The Island of Doctor Moreau*, 1896; *The Invisible Man*, 1897; and *The War of the Worlds*, 1898) and three collections of stories (*The Stolen Bacillus and Other Incidents*, 1895; *The Plattner Story and Others*, 1897; and *Tales of Space and Time*, 1899). This body of work forms a coherent unit which, despite the variety of ingenious plots and situations, is the product of a consistent imaginative method. There are, to be sure, important and influential pieces of science fiction that lie outside this central core (such as the great allegory of the limitations of human imagination, 'The Country of the Blind,' 1904), but they are for the most part works of a more didactic purpose and products of a new and different mode of imagination which, as has been frequently observed, enters Wells's fiction around 1900. After that date Wells frequently attempts to resolve the kind of conflict which he sustains in his early work, and often such resolutions take place at the expense of the truth one of the two sides expresses. Increasingly, he sees his art as committed to depicting a single truth, and the crises he invents are warnings of the consequences of not seeing or not acting according to his vision of sanity. Such works have their own excitement and generate their own kind of enlightenment; they are the works that Zamyatin focused on when he praised Wells as a genuine heretic; but in their concern for solutions, for being 'useful', they differ significantly from the stories and novels of the early years which offer no solutions, but delight in questions and paradoxes.

II

The key to Wells's early work is his use of irony, not to mock, nor to express moral outrage, but to explore civilization's form and potential. At its purest this irony is not even a linguistic device; it is situational and consists of simple, radical physical juxtaposition and contradiction. A number of the early tales have extraordinarily simple plots and no explicit moral ideas, but focus entirely on the strange conflict of two incongruous worlds. 'The Remarkable Case of Davidson's Eyes', for example, seems to have no other aim than to work out the ways two discrepant worlds fit and do not fit. Davidson, an acquaintance of the narrator, is working with electromagnets when lightning strikes particularly close by and suddenly he sees, instead of a laboratory in London late on a stormy afternoon, a semi-arid South Sea island early in the morning. But his body still resides in London, and for a while he has a difficult time getting around since he sees a world quite unlike the physical world he actually inhabits. The story spends some time working out oppositions – it is day there when it is night here; when he goes downstairs Davidson thinks he is going underground and gets claustrophobia; likewise, when he goes upstairs he thinks he is suspended in mid-air and gets vertigo. Nothing of narrative interest is happening in London, yet it is certainly no hell of boredom; and the island with its flock of filthy penguins is terribly drab, hardly a paradise. The story ends with evidence to suggest that Davidson was actually seeing a real island; there is neither a thematic nor a psychological explanation for the strange event. It is enough to sketch the exotic aspect of one world and the quotidian aspect of the other to set up a powerful and disturbing opposition, and it is simply that opposition, that superimposition of one world on another, that interests the author and his reader. Such radical juxtaposition of two incongruous opposites, what I shall call a 'two-world system', represents Wells's most basic imaginative structure.

Throughout the early tales we find instances of the two-world system enjoyed for itself. 'The Crystal Egg', though it hints at plots tangential to the central structure of physical contrast (Mr Cave's unhappy home life and the mysterious customers who want to buy the crystal egg lead one to seek some value in the Martian world viewed in the egg) is at its core exactly like 'Davidson's Eyes'. The crystal egg is the device, like the mysterious twist to Davidson's sight, that links London and a strange landscape. 'The Plattner Story', in which Gottfried Plattner disappears into a parallel world and then later reappears, ornaments the two world structure by raising the issue of fraud (is Plattner perpetrating a hoax?), by making the other world that of the dead rather than just some other 'space', and by hinting at a complicated plot at the end (we watch a dying husband being tended by his greedy wife). But as in the other tales of this type, nothing develops from these suggestions, and ultimately they are secondary to the dichotomy between the two worlds and the odd intimacy between them. In 'Under the Knife' the narrator, after worrying through the last days before an operation, escapes from his body under the influence of the anaesthetic and thinks he sees himself die. Wells's main imaginative effort goes towards describing the approach to immortality: the narrator finds himself free from matter and therefore not subject to the motion of the Earth or even of the Universe, and the time between impressions becomes increasingly vast for him. At the end Wells forces us to see the exercise in contrast itself as the story's point by having the narrator regain consciousness, thereby leaving the experience of immortality unexplained. The possibilities of complicated plot develop into nothing; imagining the opposition is itself pleasurable and sufficient.

At the edge of the two-world system, as an almost inevitable consequence, is the balanced opposition between the true and the false. Just as stories using the two-world system establish a situation encapsuling a contradiction, the stories of fraud develop a double perspective by which we see that the same event can be read two different ways. One of Wells's shortest and most elegant stories, 'The Triumphs of a Taxidermist', renders the whole form and its pleasurable irony perfectly. An old, drunken taxidermist tells a reporter, Bellows (the name hides that of the author), about the 'secrets' of his profession. The greatest triumph of taxidermy has been, not merely to stuff well a damaged pelt, not merely to make a whole specimen out of a few shreds of the original, but to create species:

'I have created birds', he said in a low voice. 'New birds. Improvements. Like no birds that was ever seen before'.

He resumed his attitude during an impressive silence.

'Enrich the universe; rath-er. Some of the birds I made were new kinds of humming birds, and very beautiful little things, but some of them were simply rum. The rummest, I think, was the Anomalopteryx Jejuna. *Jejunus-a-um – empty — so called because there was really nothing in it; a thoroughly empty bird — except for stuffing. Old Javvers has the thing now, and I suppose he is almost as proud of it as I am. It is a masterpiece, Bellows. It has all the silly clumsiness of your pelican, all the solemn want of dignity of your parrot, all the gaunt ungainliness of a flamingo, with all the extravagant chromatic conflict of a mandarin duck. Such a bird. I made it out of the skeletons of a stork and a toucan*

*and a job lot of feathers. Taxidermy of that kind is just pure joy, Bellows,
to a real artist in the art.'*

The Taxidermist, like the writer of scientific romances, generates an
alternative fictional world which infiltrates the real one and which
thereby generates the 'pure joy' of the friction of ironic juxtaposition.

The essentially abstract structure of the two-world system allows
Wells to treat such concrete historical issues as imperialism and racism,
but the structure enforces balance rather than judgement, though
judgement is not necessarily excluded. Frequently, secondary oppositions follow from the imperialist one: the British–alien opposition
becomes an opposition between technology and primitive craft, or
between science and superstition. The ultimate division, which sub-
sumes the imperialist situation itself, is that between Civilization (usually explicitly British) and Nature. We can see the potential for such a
division in the pure two-world structure of 'Davidson's Eyes' where
the author could have begun to explore the implications of the South
Sea island's pastoral and its relation to urban civilization. And though
Wells often ornaments his tales with verbal ironies that contain some
harsh judgements of the imperialist enterprise, in their largest and
deepest structures such tales support neither side but stabilize and
balance the opposition.

Such symmetry can be quite elaborate, as in the story of 'The Flying
Man'. The central opposition here is that between the British Army
and the savage Chin. Initially, this cultural opposition is given simple
geographic expression: the English camp is downstream; the Chin
village is upstream in a wilderness without roads. As the English
approach the Chin they lose any superiority that might have unbalanced the opposition: the Lieutenant hero loses his rifle; the troop
loses its mule; and as they approach the interior they find the going 'as
slippery as ice'. By the middle of the story the inequality of British
power and native vulnerability has been rectified, and the opposition
has become a stand-off: the English, trying to retreat, are trapped on a
high ledge which is completely safe but lacks water and offers no way
out. Beneath the ledge runs the river, escape and life, but it is patrolled
by the Chin. Thus, what at first looked to be a somewhat unbalanced
opposition between technological civilization and primitive savagery
gradually balances and becomes a graphic opposition between a high,
dry, safe trap and a low, moist, dangerous escape.

At this point Wells goes beyond the oppositions that we have been
looking at; the story turns into science fiction: by inventing a new mode
of travel, an unheard-of kind of movement, the Lieutenant bridges the
static opposition. He improvises a parachute and leaps out of
the English world into that of the Chin. As he descends he sees that the
Chin have decapitated a Sepoy who earlier had leapt off the cliff in
despair, and the Lieutenant in landing replays the savage gesture:
'Then my boot was in the mouth of one [of the Chin], and in a moment

he and I were in a heap with the canvas fluttering down on the top of us. I fancy I dashed out his brains with my foot.' Under the fluttering canvas the union of Englishman and native is complete, so complete that when he arrives at the English camp the Lieutenant's comrades, mistaking him for a native, fire on hom. The Lieutenant's daring and ingenious act, while it leaves intact the central opposition, allows traffic between the two sides. And it also transcends both sides. The Lieutenant relinquishes civilization (the act of leaping is strongly associated with suicide in the story) and enters nature: he becomes a bird (he is called later the 'gay Lieutenant bird') and also commits an act of savage violence. He finally becomes a myth. But Wells tucks the end of the story back into the original opposition by having the Lieutenant refuse to accompany the rescue squad, choosing to sit safely at the English camp drinking whisky and soda. The story sides with neither the English nor the Chin; it creates a physical opposition, a visual irony, and then discovers a mode a bridging the abyss, not to unify, but to open the possibilities of thought.

III

The machine which travels in time instead of space sets up a pure two-world system. In *The Time Machine*, however, Wells goes beyond 'The Flying Man' in the number and complexity of the antitheses and in the ingenuity of the links. The novella confronts the great, consoling myths of progress and of social harmony of the late Victorian period (and of our own) with myths of degeneration, entropic decline, and of absolute class division. But the conflict, while it entails a severe rebuke to the complacency and injustice of the present, remains balanced, and the possibilities of both optimism and pessimism remain open. After the Time Traveller has disappeared into time at the end of the novella, the narrator remarks that the Time Traveller 'thought but cheerlessly of the Advancement of Mankind, and saw in the growing pile of civilization only a foolish heaping that must inevitably fall back upon and destroy its makers in the end'. But that pessimism is balanced by the narrator himself, who is more sanguine about the future: 'I, for my own part', he has said a moment earlier, 'cannot think that these latter days of weak experiment, fragmentary theory, and mutual discord are indeed man's culminating time.' This juxtaposition of opposite attitudes is but the last of a sequence of open antitheses that define the tale. *The Time Machine* is not simply a prognosis of what will occur in the distant future, nor simply a judgement of the present, but a series of balances and of symbolic bridges between opposites which lead us to meditate on the nature of humanity and on the virtues and drawbacks of technological civilization itself.

The Time Traveller finds that in the future the human race has split into opposed species: the Eloi, who have descended from the owning classes, and the Morlocks, who have descended from the working classes. Quite apart from the issue of who controls whom and the problems of general decline the two species represent, this division gives expression to a deep confusion in what we admire in human civilization. The Morlocks – who, though certainly frightening, have been severely misrepresented in the movie of *The Time Machine* and can be seen as considerably less monstrous than is usually assumed – are masters of machinery. Their world is terribly diminished, and their understanding, what little we know about it, feeble, but nevertheless they do control their world, and they are capable of such basic social techniques as working in a group, and of such basic survival mechanisms as laying a trap for the Time Traveller. Though caricatures, they operate a civilization based on an overwhelming technology. On the other hand, the Eloi express the leisure and aesthetic pleasure that are supposed to be the benefits of technological civilization: they are beautiful; they enjoy flowers; they dance and sing. Thus, in spite of the transformation into diminished versions of present humanity, the opposition of the two renders a basic puzzle about what we value in modern civilization itself. The opposition is rendered painful and ironic but is not resolved when the Time Traveller realizes that the laborious Morlocks are the predators and that the seemingly aristocratic but mindless and feeble Eloi are their prey.

Upon his return to the present the Time Traveller explicitly associates himself with both aspects of civilization: he shows the strange flower that Weena, the Eloi woman who accompanied him, gave him, a badge of his link with the Eloi and their gentle, affectionate, and trivial aestheticism, and he aggressively demands some meat and complains about his eight days as a vegetarian, thereby associating himself with the carnivorous and dominating Morlocks. Like the flying Lieutenant, he can acknowledge the opposition and bridge it.

As in 'The Flying Man' the division of civilization finds vivid spatial expression. The Eloi belong above the surface in the light; the Morlocks belong below in darkness. Yet this Manichean war of opposites is not absolute and is mediated at a number of levels. The Time Traveller himself bridges this predatory antithesis by the technology of matches which allow him to bring light to the lower darkness. The match serves both as a source of aesthetic pleasure, thereby linking the Time Traveller with the Eloi, and as a tool and weapon of a sort more fittingly associated with the Morlock aspect of civilization. He wastes matches entertaining the childish Eloi, but he also frightens off Morlocks with them. The division between up and down, light and dark, is further bridged by the Palace of Green Porcelain, an aesthetic construction that houses a museum of technology and whose most curious feature is its ability to translate the Time Traveller underground without his being aware of any descent. A mysterious editor enters at this point to underline this special quality by observing in a footnote that the museum may have been built into a hill (Ch. XI). Thus, though lateral, it manages to participate in both the upper and the lower worlds.

But architecture and technology, though they may bridge the opposites, are valueless without the ingenuity of human intellect. While in the Palace of Green Porcelain the Time Traveller recovers fire, but also, importantly, he improvises a club from the lever of a machine. This act of creating a tool by misusing one is a favourite of Wells and appears frequently in the early work. One remembers that the Lieutenant in 'The Flying Man' makes a parachute from a tent; the young man in 'In the Avu Observatory' smashes a bottle to make a weapon against the monstrous bat: Prendick in *The Island of Doctor Moreau* makes a lethal club from the arm of a chair; the narrator in *The War of the Worlds* turns a meat cleaver into a blunt club; Denton in 'A Story of the Days to Come' uses a lamp as a bludgeon. Such improvization usually involves a healthy regression from an incapacitating sophistication back to a more primitive ingenuity. It is the ability to make a tool, however simple, that is the sign of the human mind at its highest, not the mere ability to use tools already made. Thus the act of making a club, more than the knowledge of matches, sets the Time Traveller above the inhabitants of the future, for it reveals his ability to do more than serve machines the way the Morlocks do, but to improvise and invent.

However, tools are not seen simply as unqualified benefits. Fire, the instrument on one level of mediation between the Eloi and the Morlocks, has its severe limitations, even dangers. After the Time Traveller leaves the Palace of Green Porcelain, he sets a fire to ward off Morlocks as he moves through the forest at night. Later he has to set a second fire, by which he and Weena go to sleep. The second fire goes out, and the Morlocks almost overcome the Time Traveller, but the first fire has turned into a forest fire which threatens both the Morlocks, as intended, and the Time Traveller himself. On one hand the fire fails to perform; on the other it overperforms. This undependability of tools is most graphically expressed by matches. As the major symbol of technological merit, matches represent a hope of unlocking the unhappy opposition of Eloi and Morlock, as we have seen, and yet matches are also undependable toys that lead us to misplaced self-confidence: elementary as they seem, they nevertheless represent a stage of technological sophistication a fraction too intricate to be entirely trustworthy. As he leaves the year 802701, the Time Traveller, confidently mounted on his time machine, tries to strike a match to drive off the Morlocks and discovers that he has conserved safety matches that will strike only on the box, which he has lost. Again, however, he proves his mastery by improvising an elementary weapon, a club from a lever of the time machine itself. The 'message' of all this, it should be observed, is neither for nor against technology as such. The novella is more interested in setting up ironic balances and oppositions, and the author's primary imaginative energy is directed towards creating a pattern that is symmetrical and linked.

The Time Machine is neither strictly prophetic nor is it merely a

revealing nightmare of the author; it is a very special narrative configuration that contains within its structure the dynamic awareness of the
promising and disastrous potentialities of the present. Wells here
engages central contradictions of his civilization, not to propagandize
for one side or the other, but to permit them to conflict. Such an ironic
pattern sets the novella apart from the gothic aspects of some and the
utopian aspects of others of Wells's models. One has only to read the
fantasies of writers whom Wells admired, Grant Allen or William
Morris, for example, to see how elegantly organized and open, in the
sense of tolerating contradiction, *The Time Machine* is. To allow us to
think clearly, Wells here gives us a pattern that in its symmetries both
emphasizes contradiction and values connections.

IV

A recurrent opposition in Wells's work is that between the human and
the alien. At one pole one finds the complete failure to communicate
between humans and such creatures as regimented and armed ants in
'The Empire of the Ants'. The comic Captain Gerilleau can only shrug
his shoulders and exclaim, 'What can a man do against ants? Dey
come, dey go.' His one military act is to fire off the Big Gun, a
pompous, empty gesture he later regrets when he contemplates having
to explain the waste of ammunition. Similarly, in 'The Sea Raiders',
organized, intelligent, flesh-eating octopi visit the English coast
briefly, wreak some few atrocities, and retire with the narrator's vague
intimations of future hostilities. Like the simplest two-world systems,
these stories enjoy incongruous juxtaposition, and frequently they
balance in the sense that Wells's sympathy seems suspended between
the incompetent humans and the efficient aliens who have the sanction
of being underdogs. However, in Wells's longer works the opposition
between human and alien becomes more complicated and the possible
bonds and links between the two sides become a source of extensive
investigation.

The human–alien opposition is central to *The Time Machine*. The
Time Traveller finds the humanity of 802701 remote, and while the
humanoid appearance of the Eloi leads him to treat them as human,
even though he is aware how inhuman they are, the sloth-like appearance of the Morlocks leads him to make what may be a no less artificial
disjunction and treat them as separate and alien, even after he suspects
the truth of their descent. The Time Traveller's relation with Weena
catches the first of these problematic identity-separations: the more
intimate the bond is between the Time Traveller and Weena, the more
disturbing it is. While he instinctively treats her as a human child, he
repeatedly forces himself to acknowledge how remote her behaviour is
from that of a human. In the last lines of the tale the narrator piously
observes that 'even when mind and strength had gone, gratitude and
mutual tenderness still lived in the heart of man'. We may take this as

true, but given the real facts of Eloi mindlessness, this may be a sentimental illusion. The novella leaves it entirely ambiguous what bond of affection is possible across the species difference. The uneasiness critics have expressed about the depiction of the relationship with Weena is, therefore, exactly right. On the other hand, the Morlocks, who are equally close to (and distant from) today's humanity, do not appear human at all. Like Gulliver who at first can see no human aspect in the Yahoos, the Time Traveller dismisses the Morlocks as ape-like ghosts for half the tale. If Weena represents a false identity that the Time Traveller has to keep reminding himself of, the Morlocks establish a false division that the progress of the tale makes the Time Traveller begin to overcome. When the forest fire reaches him the Time Traveller experiences a moment of symbolic fellowship with the Morlocks: he ceases to batter them and shares with them a common refuge from the fire. But, if Weena's alienness is muted by her human appearance, the Morlock identity never gets much beyond horror.

In all of Wells's early novels the human–alien opposition generates a process of constant reinterpretation and re-examination of the bases of similarity and of difference. *The War of the Worlds* is a clear case of such restructuring of the initial opposition. While the cruelty and the repulsive appearance of the Martians are sources of antipathy and terror early in the novel, their very amorality becomes a source of identity with humanity when it is pointed out by the narrator that the Martians are merely doing to humans what humans have done to other species and races. Perhaps the Martians are not aliens at all but simply super-humans, a possibility that Wells underlines by playfully reminding us how close they come to his own vision of future humanity in his early essay, 'The Man of the Year Million'.

The irony of this connection is exquisitely rendered by the Artilleryman who accepts the evolutionary implications of the Martian invasion and who plans for a long-term combat culminating in a melodramatic reversal:

Just imagine this: Four or five of their Fighting Machines suddenly starting off— Heat-Rays right and left, and not a Martian in 'em. Not a Martian in 'em, but men — men who have learned the way how. It may be in my time, even — those men. Fancy having one of them lovely things, with its Heat-Ray wide and free! Fancy having it in control! What would it matter if you smashed to smithereens at the end of the run, after a bust like that? I reckon the Martians'll open their beautiful eyes! Can't you see them, man? Can't you see them hurrying, hurrying — puffing and blowing and hooting to their other mechanical affairs? Something out of gear in every case. And swish, bang, rattle, swish! Just as they are fumbling over it, swish *comes the Heat-Ray, and, behold! man has come back to his own.* (Book II, Ch. 7)

The triumph of 'man' in the Artilleryman's vision is not for humanity to enforce civilizing activity in place of Martian ruthlessness, but simply for humanity to become Martian. The irony is made all the more powerful by the naive exhilaration of the passage.

Towards the end of *The War of the Worlds* a more humane link between the Martians and us is proposed by the narrator who, disillusioned by the models for human behaviour set forth in the pathetic Curate, who treats God as his 'insurance agent', and the ruthless and ineffective Artilleryman, finds a powerful consolation in the Martian hootings:

Abruptly, as I crossed the bridge, the sound of 'Ulla, ulla, ulla', ceased. It was, as it were, cut off. The silence came like a thunder-clap.

The dusky houses about me stood faint, and tall and dim; the trees towards the park were growing black. All about me the Red Weed clambered among the ruins, writhing to get above me in the dim. Night, the Mother of Fear and Mystery, was coming upon me. But while that voice sounded, the solitude, the desolation, had been endurable; by virtue of it London had still seemed alive, and the sense of life about me had upheld me. Then suddenly a change, the passing of something — I knew not what — and then a stillness that could be felt. Nothing but this gaunt quiet. (Book II, Ch. 8)

'The passing of something': what we had expected to be the end of humankind has turned out to be the end of the Martians. Wells's consummate stroke in the novel is not simply to have truly evolutionary forces defeat the Martians, but to transpose the tragedy of the human race that the whole novel has been working towards to a tragedy of the Martians. Such a transformation is possible only if we acknowledge, as the narrator does, the bond of intelligence in the midst of evolutionary chaos. The enemy at the end of the novel is not the Martians, but the wild dogs and the black birds, symbols of nature's vast machinery of death against which all intelligent life, human and Martian, organizes itself.

Though the bond of intellect is recognized powerfully at the end of *The War of the Worlds*, the novel also acknowledges the problem of domination inherent in the split between higher and lower stages of evolution. *The Island of Doctor Moreau*, though earlier than *The War of the Worlds*, examines this dilemma more subtly and with a finer eye to the obligations that may extend across species difference. The novel develops a symmetrical system in which the principle of opposition works at almost all levels. On the one hand the line between human and non-human is defined with acute precision by both humans and beast-men in the terms of the 'law' that Moreau's creations chant:

'Not to go on all-Fours; *that* is the Law. Are we not Men?
Not to suck up Drink; *that* is the Law. Are we not Men?
Not to eat Flesh nor Fish; *that* is the Law. Are we not Men?
Not to claw Bark of Trees; *that* is the Law. Are we not Men?
Not to chase other Men; *that* is the Law. Are we not Men?' (Ch. 12)

The tension here arises from our strong sense that only a non-human would need such a law to be human. And yet many of the very characteristics that here define man – posture, food, language, treatment of other men, etc. – are violated by real men at some time in the novel. We see Prendick himself on all fours. We see Montgomery drinking brandy the way beasts drink blood; Montgomery himself teaches the beast-man, M'ling, how to cook a rabbit. At the beginning of the novel we see men in a life-boat planning on cannibalism, and it is only because they are clumsy that cannibalism does not occur. The Captain of the *Ipecacuanha*, the ship that rescues Prendick at the beginning of the novel and which has destroyed itself by the end, is clearly bestial: he drinks heavily and reduces language to the simple term of command, 'Shut up'. Just as the beast-men once they taste blood revert, the Captain and Montgomery both become drunks. Prendick even drinks something that 'tasted like blood' (Ch. 2) early in the novel, and near the end Montgomery gives brandy to M'ling with the injunction, 'drink and be men' (Ch. 19), the obvious implication being that what defines man is the ability to degenerate. Thus, throughout the novel the activity of distinguishing between man and beast is mirrored by the activity of bridging that carefully established boundary.

Besotted Montgomery, who as he becomes more degenerate as a human exhibits greater humanity towards the beast-men, points to the strong bond that extends between men and beasts. When they are stranded with the beast-men attacking them, he bitterly remarks to Prendick, 'We can't massacre the lot, – can we? I suppose that's what *your* humanity would suggest?' (Ch. 19). This sarcastic remark draws our attention to Prendick's tendency to use the difference between human and beast to justify acts less than humane: he refrains from murder, but later when Montgomery is dead and he is alone and threatened, Prendick 'had half a mind to make a massacre of them' (Ch. 21). We recall the Time Traveller smashing Morlock skulls with joy, and again we sense how it is the act of restraint more than anything else that defines the human act as against the bestial for Wells. A similar moment occurs in *The War of the Worlds* when the narrator in order to prevent the Curate from revealing their hiding place to the Martians hits him with a meat cleaver, but at the very last moment, in what he calls a 'last touch of humanity' (Book II, Ch. 4), turns the instrument and uses the butt rather than the cutting edge.

The Invisible Man, which since its characters are all Englishmen and women might seem to lie outside this general concern with the human and the non-human and the paths between them, actually fits exactly. As an albino, Griffin has always been slightly alien, but his obsessive genius and his brutal carelessness about other humans set him increasingly apart until, as the invisible man, he becomes an alien in the sense we are used to in the other novels. The war between species that is the issue of *The Time Machine* and *The War of the Worlds* occurs in *The*

Invisible Man only at the end when Griffin begins his reign of terror and Kemp suddenly realizes that it is 'Griffin *contra mundum*' (Ch. 27).

Griffin's role of scientist places him in the company of the Time Traveller and Dr Moreau. Wells works through a chain of transformations by which the scientist, who originally offered the hope of bridging a future conflict by means of present-day technology in the service of conventional humane moral concerns, becomes in Moreau a figure of terribly ambiguous power who in the act of bridging generates monstrosities that threaten both sides of the opposition, and then in Griffin becomes himself the alien, the opposite. The benign relation of the Time Traveller to the Eloi, the adult among children, becomes sinister in the later works. Moreau is a cruel and demanding patriarch; Griffin becomes a tyrannical maniac. The chain describes a natural set of permutations of power. One should note, however, that if Griffin offers the darkest picture of the scientist, Wells's quest for balance does not allow him simply to render Griffin horrible. Griffin generates a special version of the questions of mastery and cooperation that civilization raises, for to enjoy the power of invisibility he must go naked and thus expose himself to weather, cold, and such common hazards of civilization as broken glass. On the other hand, dressed in his disguise, his range of expression and interaction is so limited that he becomes powerless. Like the Time Traveller's match, Griffin's invisibility is a terribly ambiguous tool.

V

The nature and problems of such power as Griffin's never ceased to fascinate Wells, but as time goes on the complexity of his vision of them diminishes. In *The First Men in the Moon* (1901) he divides the power between Cavor, the absent-minded and therefore at times quite dangerous scientific genius, and Bedford, the quick-witted and unscrupulous con-man. One reason the Selenites silence Cavor at the end of the novel is to prevent him from sending to earth the secret that would allow the Bedfords on earth to invade and exploit the moon. But if separating Cavor from Bedford seems to simplify thought about the problem, the civilization on the moon, which deforms individuals to adapt them for specific jobs, offers a strangely ambiguous critique of such separation. The Selenite 'hive' is in part a satiric horror, but one senses that its efficiency has a fascination for Wells that weakens the sense of abomination, and a part of him responds by seeing an inefficient individualism as the ultimate horror. Cavor reports:

Recently I came upon a number of young Selenites, confined in jars from which only the fore-limbs protruded, who were being compressed to become machine-minders of a special sort. The extended 'hand' in this highly developed system of technical education is stimulated by irritants and nourished by injection, while the rest of the body is starved. Phi-oo, unless I misunderstood him, explained that in the earlier stages these queer little creatures are apt to display signs of suffering in their various cramped situations, but they easily become indurated to their lot; and he took me on to where a number of flexible-limbed messengers were being drawn out and broken in. It is quite unreasonable, I know, but these glimpses of the educational methods of these beings have affected me disagreeably. I hope, however, that may pass off, and I may be able to see more of this aspect of their wonderful social order. That wretched-looking hand sticking out of its jar seemed to appeal for lost possibilities; it haunts me still, although, of course, it is really in the end a far more humane proceeding than our earthly method of leaving children to grow into human beings, and then making machines of them. (Ch. 23)

This justly celebrated passage with its dialectical ironies fits into the main tradition of Swiftian satire, but like Pierre Menard's *Quixote*, it must be read in a twentieth-century way. Though Wells never went so far as to argue for education on the Selenite model, the ideal of a 'wonderful social order' in which all men grew to their places and took pleasure in doing their bit to make the social machine work smoothly and efficiently appealed to him, and more and more he concentrated on envisioning such an order.

The First Men in the Moon retains some of the complexity of vision that has characterized the early work, but in an important story, 'The Land Ironclads', published in 1903, we see a distinct simplification of the issues of mastery and order. This Vernian tale of technological competence begins in military stalemate and then describes how one side achieves stunning victory by introducing the military tank. The story is impatient with balance. The oppositions – country–town, man–machine, heroic athlete–engineer – do not express serious puzzles. Wells sees one side as simply stupidly traditional while the other is intelligent and imaginative. Technological efficiency becomes self-justifying and blinds him to moral complexity. The hypocrisy of the engineers' position, which seems to be Wells's own, is, I hope, self-evident:

For the enemy these young engineers were defeating they felt a certain qualified pity and a quite unqualified contempt. . . . 'If they must make war', these young men thought, 'why in thunder don't they do it like sensible men?' They resented the assumption that their own side was too stupid to do anything more than play their enemy's game, that they were going to play this costly folly according to the rules of unimaginative men. They resented being forced to the trouble of making man-killing machinery; resented the alternative of having to massacre these people or endure their truculent yappings; resented the whole unfathomable imbecility of war.

Meanwhile, with something of the mechanical precision of a good clerk posting a ledger, the riflemen moved their knobs and pressed their buttons. . . .

This is, if you will, Martian reasoning: the invaders blame the defenders for making war and consider that technological superiority equals moral superiority. But whereas in *The War of the Worlds* Wells explored the complexities of the moral problem by conscious irony, here the irony is unconscious and as far as one can tell unintended. We see here the style of the new Wells, the prophet of the efficient future state.

Years later, in 1940, Wells would bear testimony to the centrality of 'The Land Ironclads' in his vision of himself by objecting at length to Major-General Swinton's claiming credit for inventing the military tank when, so Wells insisted, he himself was responsible for it. The point is that by 1903 Wells has come to see himself, not as the artist creating complex structures by which to explore human possibilities, but as the prophet of an efficient future that has little tolerance for the subtleties and discriminations so carefully developed in the earlier work. Around the turn of the century Wells decided that it was not enough to build balanced imaginative forms, no matter how educational such exercises might be, but that he must put his energies into changing the world. In part this new view of the writer's function comes from a need to get beyond a system of thought which, however elegant, is clear and complete in its basic structure and which tends to repeat itself even as the details of the surface change. In part it comes from an imperative intrinsic in the need for balance itself: artistic equilibrium is itself one-sided and requires its opposite, the disequilibrium of committed advocacy that leads to action and change. Wells wants to get beyond an art that, while doing justice to complexity, leaves the world in the same sorry state it found it.

The problem Wells is feeling is clear in 'A Story of the Days to Come' (1899). The story is paired with 'A Story of the Stone Age'; they are adventures which take place at the same place at different times, so together they constitute a two-world system much like *The Time Machine*. But 'A Story of the Days to Come' is surprisingly clumsy, given the skill we have seen. Like *The Time Machine*, the story builds a tension between an intense anticipation of a better future and an angry pessimism about the dragging sameness of human behaviour and of civilization's constraints. But in 'A Story of the Days to Come' the contradictory attitudes are unintegrated; while balance is maintained, the reader nevertheless senses Wells's impatience with the complexities it entails. At the middle of the long story occurs a passage that captures well the new tone. The passage starts off enthusiastic about the promise of change, but then, almost without being aware of the shift, it complains about the lack of change:

Prominent if not paramount among world-changing inventions in the history of man is that series of contrivances in locomotion that began with the railway and ended for a century or more with the motor and the patent road. That these contrivances, together with the device of limited liability joint stock companies and the supersession of agricultural labourers by skilled men with ingenious machinery, would necessarily concentrate mankind in cities of unparalleled magnitude and work an entire revolution in human life, became, after the event, a thing so obvious that it is a matter of astonishment it was not more clearly anticipated. Yet that any steps should be taken to anticipate the miseries such a revolution might entail does not appear even to have been suggested; and the idea that the moral prohibitions and sanctions, the privileges and concessions, the conception of property and responsibility, of comfort and beauty, that had rendered the mainly agricultural states of the past prosperous and happy, would fail in the rising torrent of novel opportunities and novel stimulations, never seems to have entered the nineteenth-century mind. That a citizen, kindly and fair in his ordinary life, could as a shareholder become almost murderously greedy; that commercial methods that were reasonable and honourable on the old-fashioned countryside, should on an enlarged scale be deadly and overwhelming; that ancient charity was modern pauperisation, and ancient employment modern sweating; that, in fact, a revision and enlargement of the duties and rights of man had become urgently necessary, were things it could not entertain, nourished as it was on an archaic system of education and profoundly retrospective and legal in all its habits of thought. (Ch. III)

This is a wonderful indictment, but of the present, not of the future, and there lies the problem. The tone at the end here is outrage at human stupidity. The sense of the deep contradictions in human desires for civilization is gone; instead Wells seems to say that the way to a true civilization is open and only a fool will refuse or botch it.

The same dilemma can be felt in *When the Sleeper Wakes* (1899); in place of the ingenious analysis we see in the early works, Wells here relies on melodramatic clichés about love and revolution in order to escape the closed system his logic generates. Later novels, such as *In the Days of the Comet* (1906) and *The World Set Free* (1914), resolve the problems of alienation and oppression by changing humanity. These novels may be said to participate in a remote way in the two-world system, but the balance is gone; the old world is simply dismissed as primitive and insane, and the new world, created by miracle, is celebrated as emancipated and sane. The promise is exhilarating but unconvincing

However, Wells is never incapable of irony. Though the engineer who invents and runs the new machine or society becomes an ideal for him, he is able to use irony to give contour and shading to the projector's stark enthusiasms. For instance, *A Modern Utopia* (1905), one of Wells's most concrete projections, does not lose sight of the difficulties of human interaction. The narrator never is able to give up the habits of mind which give him pleasure in the present world, and he and his friend find that, once the present does not exist, they do not enjoy each other's company. Not everything is predictable, and Wells, even when he is most proud of his ability to predict, does not quite forget that. But in general the later work is arrogantly complacent when compared to the works we have been looking at. Wells's early work is profoundly disturbing, not because it is pessimistic, nor because it is optimistic, but because it abjures the solace of simple solutions and attains balance, not by sacrificing detail and honesty, but by probing situations deeply, by maintaining sceptical openness, and by developing symmetrical structures that by mirroring illuminate. To render such complexity so simply is the gift of genius.

Bibliography

The standard edition of Wells remains the *Atlantic Edition* (1924-7) of which 600 copies were for sale in England and 1,050 in the USA. Most of the short stories have been collected in the *Complete Short Stories* (London: Ernest Benn, 1927), which remains in print, and Dover has published two good selections: *Best Science Fiction Stories of H. G. Wells* and *28 Science Fiction Stories*. The novels have been reprinted many times; there are bowdlerized editions, but the Dover, Berkley, and Dutton editions follow the Atlantic texts. *The Time Machine* presents a special problem since the serialized version of 1895 contains an episode that Wells dropped in all later book editions. The version that appears in *Three Prophetic Novels of H. G. Wells*, ed. E. F. Bleiler (New York: Dover, 1960) contains the expanded text, and I have taken my chapter references from it. *A Modern Utopia* has been reissued with an introduction by Mark Hillegas (Lincoln, Nebraska: University of Nebraska Press, 1967) and Robert Philmus and David Y. Hughes have recently edited an important collection of Wells's early, previously uncollected and unreprinted work, *Early Writings in Science and Science Fiction by H. G. Wells* (Berkeley and Los Angeles: University of California Press, 1975).

The major biography of Wells is Norman and Jeanne Mackenzie's *The Time Traveller* (London: Weidenfeld & Nicolson, 1973).

Criticism of Wells by his contemporaries has been usefully collected in *H. G. Wells: The Critical Heritage*, ed. Patrick Parrinder (London: Routledge and Kegan Paul, 1972). During Wells's lifetime most of his critics focused on his sociological and technological ideas and tended to dismiss the early core of science fiction as entertaining but not serious. As late as 1960 Kingsley Amis would continue this tradition in his *New Maps of Hell* (London: Gollancz, 1961). Nevertheless, the following works published during Wells's lifetime are important for our understanding of the man's total accomplishment; Van Wyck Brooks, *The World of H. G. Wells* (New York: 1915, repr. New York: Scholarly Reprints, 1970); J. D. Beresford, *H. G. Wells* (New York: 1915, repr. New York: Haskell House, 1973); Yevgeny Zamyatin, 'H. G. Wells', in *A Soviet Heretic: Essays by Yevgeny Zamyatin*, ed. and trans. Mirra Ginsburg (Chicago and London: University of Chicago Press, 1970) (a different translation of this essay appears in the Parrinder collection); Christopher Caudwell, 'H. G. Wells: A Study in Utopianism', in his *Studies in a Dying Culture* (New York: Dodd, Mead and Co., 1938); and George Orwell, 'Wells, Hitler, and the World State', in *Collected Essays, Journalism and Letters of George Orwell*, vol. 2 (London: Secker & Warburg, 1968).

In the last twenty years the importance of the early science fiction has been more generally recognized. Anthony West's essay on his father, 'H. G. Wells', in *Principles and Persuasions* ed. Anthony West (London: Eyre Methuen, 1958) is central. The major books are Bernard Bergonzi, *The Early H. G. Wells* (Manchester: Manchester U.P., 1961); J. Kagarlitski, *The Life and Thought of H. G. Wells*, trans. Moura Budberg (London: Sidgwick & Jackson, 1966); Mark Hillegas, *The Future as Nightmare: H. G. Wells and the Anti-Utopians* (New York: Oxford U.P., 1967); Patrick Parrinder, *H. G. Wells* (New York: Capricorn Books, 1977); and Robert M. Philmus, *Into the Unknown: Science Fiction from Francis Godwin to H. G. Wells* (Berkeley and Los Angeles:

University of California Press, 1970). Important essays on Wells's science fiction are collected in the volume on Wells, in *The Twentieth Century Views* series, edited by Bernard Bergonzi (Englewood Cliffs, New Jersey: Prentice-Hall, 1976) and in *H. G. Wells and Modern Science Fiction*, ed. Darko Suvin and Robert Philmus (Lewisburg: Bucknell U.P., 1977).

Part II

Two formative traditions

Utopia and science fiction

Raymond Williams

I

There are many close and evident connections between science fiction and utopian fiction, yet neither, in deeper examination, is a simple mode, and the relations between them are exceptionally complex. Thus, if we analyse the fictions that have been grouped as utopian we can quickly distinguish four types:

1. *the paradise*, in which a happier kind of life is described as simply existing elsewhere;
2. *the externally altered world*, in which a new kind of life has been made possible by an unlooked-for natural event;
3. *the willed transformation*, in which a new kind of life has been achieved by human effort;
4. *the technological transformation*, in which a new kind of life has been made possible by a technical discovery.

It will of course be clear that these types often overlap. Indeed the overlap and often the confusion between (3) and (4) are exceptionally significant. One kind of clarification is possible by considering the negative of each type: that negative which is now commonly expressed as 'dystopia'. We then get:

1. *the hell*, in which a more wretched kind of life is described as existing elsewhere;
2. *the externally altered world*, in which a new but less happy kind of life has been brought about by an unlooked-for uncontrollable natural event;
3. *the willed transformation*, in which a new but less happy kind of life has been brought about by social degeneration, by the emergence or re-emergence of harmful kinds of social order, or by the unforeseen yet disastrous consequences of an effort at social improvement;
4. *the technological transformation*, in which the conditions of life have been worsened by technical development.

Since there can be no *a priori* definition of the utopian mode, we cannot at first exclude any of these dystopian functions, though it is clear that they are strongest in (3) and (4), perceptible in (2) and barely evident in (1), where the negative response to Utopia would normally have given way to a relatively autonomous fatalism or pessimism. These indications bear with some accuracy on the positive definitions, suggesting that the element of transformation, rather than the more general element of otherness, may be crucial.

We can then consider these types in relation to science fiction, an even more difficult general category. What we are looking for are the differential ways in which 'science', in its variable definitions, can be an element in each of the types. We find:

1. *The paradise and the hell* can be discovered, reached, by new forms of travel dependent on scientific and technological (space-travel) or quasi-scientific (time-travel) development. But this is an instrumental function; the mode of travel does not commonly affect the place discovered. The type of fiction is little affected, whether the discovery is made by a space voyage or a sea voyage. The place, rather than the journey, is dominant.

2. *The externally altered world* can be related, construed, foretold in a context of increased scientific understanding of natural events. This also may be an instrumental function only; a new name for an old deluge. But the element of increased scientific understanding may become significant or even dominant in the fiction, for example in the emphasis of natural laws in human history, which can decisively (often catastrophically) alter normal human perspectives.

3. *The willed transformation* can be conceived as inspired by the scientific spirit, either in its most general terms as secularity and rationality, or in a combination of these with applied science which makes possible and sustains the transformation. Alternatively, the same impulses can be negatively valued: the 'modern scientific' ant-heap or tyranny. Either mode leaves open the question of the social agency of the scientific spirit and the applied science, though it is the inclusion of some social agency, explicit or implicit (such as the overthrow of one class by another), that distinguishes this type from type (4). We must note also that there are important examples of type (3) in which the scientific spirit and applied science are subordinate to or simply associated with a dominant emphasis on social and political (including revolutionary) transformation; or in which they are neutral with respect to the social and political transformation, which proceeds in its own terms; or, which is of crucial diagnostic significance, where the applied science, though less often the scientific spirit, is positively controlled, modified or in effect suppressed, in a willed return to a 'simpler', 'more natural' way of life. In this last mode there are some pretty combinations of very advanced 'non-material' science and a 'primitive' economy.

4. *The technological transformation* has a direct relation to applied

science. It is the new technology which, for good or ill, has made the new life. As more generally in technological determinism, this has little or no social agency, though it is commonly described as having certain 'inevitable' social consequences.

We can now more clearly describe some significant relations between utopian fiction and science fiction, as a preliminary to a discussion of some modern utopian and dystopian writing. It is tempting to extend both categories until they are loosely identical, and it is true that the presentation of *otherness* appears to link them, as modes of desire or of warning in which a crucial emphasis is attained by the element of discontinuity from ordinary 'realism'. But this element of discontinuity is itself fundamentally variable. Indeed what has most to be looked at, in properly utopian or dystopian fiction, is that form of continuity, of implied connection, which the form is intended to embody. Thus, looking again at the four types, we can make some crucial distinctions which appear to define utopian and dystopian writing (some of these bear also on the separate question of the distinction of science fiction from older and now residual modes which are simply organizationally grouped with it):

1. *The paradise and the hell* are only rarely utopian or dystopian. They are ordinarily the projections of a magical or a religious consciousness, inherently universal and timeless, thus commonly beyond the conditions of any imaginable ordinary human and worldly life. Thus the Earthly Paradise and the Blessed Islands are neither utopian nor science-fictional. The pre-lapsarian Garden of Eden is latently utopian, in some Christian tendencies; it can be attained by redemption. The medieval *Land of Cokaygne* is latently utopian; it can be, and was, imagined as a possible human and worldly condition. The paradisal and hellish planets and cultures of science fiction are at times simple magic and fantasy: deliberate, often sensational presentations of *alien* forms. In other cases they are latently utopian or dystopian, in the measure of degrees of connection with, extrapolation from, known or imaginable human and social elements.

2. *The externally altered world* is typically a form which either falls short of or goes beyond the utopian or dystopian mode. Whether the event is magically or scientifically interpreted does not normally affect this. The common emphasis is on human limitation or indeed human powerlessness: the event saves or destroys us, and we are its objects. In Wells's *In the Days of the Comet* (1906) the result *resembles* a utopian transformation, but the displacement of agency is significant. Most other examples, of a science-fiction kind, are implicitly or latently dystopian: the natural world deploys forces beyond human control, thus setting limits to or annulling all human achievement.

3. *The willed transformation* is the characteristic utopian or dystopian mode, in the strict sense.

4. *The technological transformation* is the utopian or dystopian mode narrowed from agency to instrumentality; indeed it only becomes utopian or dystopian, in strict senses, when it is used as an image of *consequence* to function, socially, as conscious desire or conscious warning.

II

No contrast has been more influential, in modern political thought, than Engels's distinction between 'utopian' and 'scientific' socialism. If it is now more critically regarded, this is not only because the scientific character of the 'laws of historical development' is cautiously questioned or sceptically rejected; to the point, indeed, where the notion of such a science can be described as utopian. It is also because the importance of utopian thought is itself being revalued, so that some now see it as the crucial vector of desire, without which, in one version, even the laws are imperfect; in another version are mechanical, needing desire to give them direction and substance. This reaction is understandable, but it makes the utopian impulse more simple, more singular, than, in the history of utopias, it is. Indeed the variability of the utopian situation, the utopian impulse and the utopian result is crucial to the understanding of utopian fiction.

This can be seen from one of the classical contrasts, between More's *Utopia* (1516) and Bacon's *New Atlantis* (1627). It is usual to say that these show, respectively, a humanist and a scientific Utopia:

that excellent perfection in all good fashions, humanitye and civile gentilness (More);

the end of our foundation is the knowledge of causes and secret motions of things and the enlarging of the bounds of human empire, to the effecting of all things possible (Bacon).

It can be agreed that the two fictions exemplify the difference between a willed general transformation and a technological transformation; that More projects a commonwealth, in which men live and feel differently, while Bacon projects a highly specialized, unequal but affluent and efficient social order. But a full contrast has other levels. Thus, they stand near the opposite poles of the Utopia of free consumption and the Utopia of free production. More's island is a cooperative subsistence economy; Bacon's a specialized industrial economy. These can be seen as permanent alternative images, and the swing towards one or another, in socialist ideology as in progressive utopianism, is historically very significant. (One might indeed write a history of modern socialist thought in terms of the swing between a Morean cooperative simplicity and a Baconian mastery of nature, except that the most revealing trend has been their unconscious fusion.) Yet what we can now perceive as permanent alternative images was rooted, in each case, in a precise social and class situation.

More's humanism is deeply qualified: his indignation is directed as much against importunate and prodigal craftsmen and labourers as against the exploiting and engrossing landlords – his social identification is with the small owners, his laws regulate and protect but also compel labour. It is qualified also because it is static: a wise and entrenched regulation by the elders. It is then socially the projection of a declining class, generalized to a relatively humane but permanent *balance*. Bacon's scientism is similarly qualified: the scientific revolution of experiment and discovery becomes research and development in an instrumental social perspective. Enlarging the bounds of human empire is not only the mastery of nature; it is also, as a social projection, an aggressive, autocratic, imperialist enterprise; the projection of a rising class.

We cannot abstract desire. It is always desire for something specific, in specifically impelling circumstances. Consider three utopian fictions of the late nineteenth century: Bulwer-Lytton's *The Coming Race* (1871); Edward Bellamy's *Looking Backward* (1888); William Morris's *News from Nowhere* (1890).

The Coming Race is at one level an obvious example of the mode of technological transformation. What makes the Vril-ya, who live under our earth, civilized is their possession of Vril, that all-purpose energy source which lies beyond electricity and magnetism. Outlying underground peoples who do not possess Vril are barbarians; indeed the technology *is* the civilization, and the improvement of manners and of social relations is firmly based on it alone. The changes thus brought about are the transformation of work into play, the dissolution of the State and in effect the outlawing of competitive and aggressive social relations. Yet it is not, for all the obvious traces of influence, either a socialist or an anarchist Utopia. It is a projection of the idealized social attitudes of an aristocracy, now generalized and distanced from the realities of rent and production by the technological determinism of Vril. In its complementary liberation of sexual and family relations (in fact qualified, though apparently emphasized, by the simple reversal of the relative size and roles of women and men) it can be sharply contrasted with the rigidities of these relations within More's humanism. But this is of a piece with the aristocratic projection. It is (as in some later fantasies, with similarly privileged assumptions) a separation of personal and sexual relations from those problems of care, protection, maintenance and security which Vril has superseded. Affluence delivers liberation. By contrast the greed, the aggression, the dominativeness, the coarseness, the vulgarity of the surface world – the world, significantly, both of capitalism and of democracy – are easily placed. They are what are to be expected in a world without Vril and therefore Vril-ya. Indeed there are moments when Vril can almost be compared with Culture, in Matthew Arnold's virtually contemporary *Culture and Anarchy* (1869). Arnold's spiritual aristocracy, his spiritual force beyond all actual classes, has, though, been magically achieved, without the prolonged effort that Arnold described, by the properties of Vril. It is in each case desire, but desire for what? A civilizing transformation, beyond the terms of a restless, struggling society of classes.

What has also to be said, though, about *The Coming Race* is that the desire is tinged with awe and indeed with fear. The title introduces that evolutionary dimension which from this period on is newly available in utopian fiction. When the Vril-ya come to the surface they will simply replace men, as in effect a higher and more powerful species. And it is not only in his unVril humanity that the hero fears this. Towards the end he sounds the note that we shall hear so clearly later in Huxley's *Brave New World*: that something valuable and even decisive – initiative and creativity are the hovering words – has been lost in the displacement of human industry to Vril. This was a question that was to haunt the technological Utopia. Meanwhile, back in nineteenth-century society, an entrepreneur took his own short-cut. Inspired by Lytton he made a fortune from a beef extract called Bovril.

Bellamy's *Looking Backward* is unquestionably a Utopia, in the central sense of a transformed social life of the future, but it is in a significant way a work without desire; its impulse is different, an overriding rationalism, a determining total organization, which finds its proper institutional counterpart in the State-monopoly capitalism which is seen as the inevitable 'next stage in the industrial and social development of humanity' (the order of adjectives there is decisive). That this forecast, rather than vision, was widely taken as socialism is indicative of a major tendency in Bellamy's period, which can be related to Fabianism, but has also now to be related to a major current in orthodox Marxism: socialism as the next higher stage of economic organization, a proposition which is taken as overriding, except in the most general terms, questions of substantially different social relations and human motives. Morris's critique of Bellamy repeated almost exactly what is called the Romantic but is more properly the radical critique of utilitarian social models: that 'the underlying vice . . . is that the author cannot conceive . . . anything else than the *machinery* of society': the central point made, in this tradition, from Carlyle's *Signs of the Times* onward. Morris's fuller response was his *News from Nowhere*, but before we look at this we should include a crucial point about the history of utopian writing, recently put forward by M.-H. Abensour.

Abensour establishes a crucial periodization in the utopian mode, according to which there is, after 1850, a change from the *systematic* building of alternative organizational models to a more open and *heuristic* discourse of alternative values. E. P. Thompson has interpreted this latter mode as the 'education of desire'. It is an important emphasis, since it allows us to see more clearly, by contrast, how examples of the mode of 'willed social transformation' can be shifted, in their essence, to the mode of 'technological transformation', where the technology need not be only a marvellous new energy source, or some industrial resource of that kind, but can be also a new set of laws, new abstract property relations, indeed precisely new *social machinery*. But then, when we have said this, and recognized the contrasting value of the more heuristic mode, in which the substance of new values and relations is projected, with comparatively little attention to institutions, we have to relate the change to the historical situation within which it occurred. For the shift from one mode to another can be negative as well as positive. To imagine a whole alternative society is not mere model-building, any more than the projection of new feelings and relationships is necessarily a transforming response. The whole alternative society rests, paradoxically, on two quite different social situations: either that of social confidence, the mood of a rising class, which knows, down to detail, that it can replace the existing order; or that of social despair, the mood of a declining class, or fraction of a class, which has to create a new heaven because its earth is a hell. The basis of the more open but also the vaguer mode is different from either. It is a society in which change is happening, but primarily under the direction and in the terms of the dominant social order itself. This is always a fertile moment for what is, in effect, an anarchism: positive in its fierce rejection of domination, repression and manipulation; negative in its willed neglect of structures, of continuity and of material constraints. The systematic mode is a response to tyranny or disintegration; the heuristic mode, by contrast, seems to be primarily a response to a constrained reformism.

It is then not a question of asking which is better or stronger. The heuristic Utopia offers a strength of vision against the grain; the systematic Utopia a strength of conviction that the world really can be different. The heuristic Utopia, at the same time, has the weakness that it can settle into isolated and in the end sentimental 'desire', a mode of living with alienation, while the systematic Utopia has the weakness that, in its insistent organization, it seems to offer little room for any recognizable life. These strengths and weaknesses vary, of course, in individual examples of each mode, but they vary most decisively, not only in the periods in which they are written but in the periods in which they are read. The mixed character of each mode then has much to do with the character of the twentieth-century dystopias which have succeeded them. For the central contemporary question about the utopian modes is why there is a progression, within their structures, to the specific reversals of a Zamyatin, a Huxley, an Orwell; of a generation of writers of science fiction.

It is in this perspective that we have now to read *News from Nowhere*. It is commonly diagnosed and criticized as a generous but sentimental heuristic transformation. And this is substantially right, of the parts that are made ordinarily to stick in the mind: the medievalism of visual detail, and the beautiful people in the summer along the river, are inextricable from the convincing openness and friendliness and relaxed cooperation. But these are residual elements in the form: the Utopians, the Houyhnhnms, the Vril-ya would have found Morris's people cousins at least, though the dimensions of universal mutuality have made an identifying difference. But what is emergent in Morris's work, and what seems to me increasingly the strongest part of *News from Nowhere*, is the crucial insertion of the *transition* to Utopia, which is not discovered, come across or projected – not even, except at the simplest conventional level, dreamed – but fought for. Between writer or reader and this new condition is chaos, civil war, painful and slow reconstruction. The sweet little world at the end of all this is at once a result and a promise; an offered assurance of 'days of peace and rest', after the battle has been won.

Morris was strong enough, even his world is at times strong enough, to face this process, this necessary order of events. But when Utopia is not merely the alternative world, throwing its light on the darkness of the intolerable present, but lies at the far end of generations of struggle and of fierce and destructive conflict, its perspective, necessarily, is altered. The post-religious imagining of a harmonious community, the enlightened rational projection of an order of peace and plenty, have been replaced, or at least qualified, by the light at the end of the tunnel, the sweet promise which sustains effort and principle and hope through the long years of revolutionary preparation and organization. This is a genuine turning-point. Where the path to Utopia was moral redemption or rational declaration – that light on a higher order which illuminates an always present possibility – the mode itself was radically different from the modern mode of conflict and resolution.

Morris's chapters 'How the Change Came' and 'The Beginning of the New Life' are strong and convincing. 'Thus at last and by slow degrees we got pleasure into our work': this is not the perspective of reformism, which in spirit, in its evasion of fundamental conflicts and sticking points, is much nearer to the older utopian mode; it is the perspective of revolution – not only the armed struggle but the long and uneven development of new social relations and human feelings. That they have been developed, that the long and difficult enterprise has succeeded, is crucial; it is the transition from dream to vision. But it is then reasonable to ask whether the achieved new condition is not at least as much rest after struggle – the relaxed and quiet evening after a long, hard day – as any kind of released new energy and life. The air of late Victorian holiday is made to override the complexities, the divergences, the everyday materialities of any working society. When the time-dreamer finds himself fading, as he looks in on the feast at the old church, the emotions are very complex: the comforting recall of a medieval precedent – 'the church-ales of the Middle Ages'; the wrench of regret that he cannot belong to this new life; and then also, perhaps, for all the convinced assent to the sight of the burdens having been lifted, the impulse – and is it only unregenerate? – of an active, engaged, deeply vigorous mind to register the impression, though it is put into a voice from the future, 'that our happiness even would weary you'. It is the fused and confused moment of the longing for communism, the longing for rest and the commitment to urgent, complex, vigorous activity.

III

When Utopia is no longer an island or a newly discovered place, but our familiar country transformed by specific historical change, the mode of imagined transformation has fundamentally changed. But the historical agency was not only, as in Morris, revolution. It was also, as in Wells, some kind of modernizing, rationalizing force: the vanguard of Samurai, of scientists, of engineers, of technical innovators. Early rationalist Utopias had only, in the manner of Owen, to be declared to be adopted; reason had that inevitability. Wells, refusing popular revolution, belonged to his time in seeing agency as necessary, and there is a convincing match between the kind of agency he selected – a type of social engineering plus a rapidly developing technology – and the point of arrival: a clean, orderly, efficient and planned (controlled) society. It is easy to see this now as an affluent state capitalism or monopoly socialism; indeed many of the images have been literally built. But we can also, holding Morris and Wells together in our minds, see a fundamental tension within the socialist movement itself; indeed in practice within revolutionary socialism. For there are other vanguards than those of Wells, and the Stalinist version of the bureaucratic Party, engineering a future which is primarily defined as technology and production, not only has its connections to Wells but has to be radically distinguished from the revolutionary socialism of Morris and of Marx, in which new social and human relations, transcending the deep divisions of industrial capitalist specialization, of town and country, of rulers and ruled, administrators and administered, are from the beginning the central and primary objective. It is within this complex of tendencies – of efficient and affluent capitalism set against an earlier capitalist poverty and disorder; of socialism against capitalism in either phase; and of the deep divisions, within socialism itself, between the reformist free-riders with capitalism, the centralizing social engineers, and the revolutionary democrats – that we have to consider the mode of dystopia, which is both written and read within this extreme theoretical and practical complexity.

Thus Aldous Huxley's *Brave New World* (1932) projects a black amalgam of Wellsian rationality and the names and phrases of revolutionary socialism, in a specific context of mobile and affluent corporate capitalism. This sounds and is confused, but the confusion is significant; it is the authentic confusion of two generations of science fiction itself, in its powerful dystopian mode. 'Community, Identity, Stability': this is the motto of the Brave New World State. It is interesting to track these ideals back into the utopian mode. Stability, undoubtedly, has a strong bearing; most of the types of Utopia have strongly emphasized it as an achieved perfection or a self-adjusting harmony. Huxley adds the specific agencies of repression, manipulation, pre-natal conditioning and drugged distraction. Western science fiction has been prolific in its elaboration of all these agencies: the models, after all, have been close to hand. Stability blurs to Identity: the manufac-ture of human types to fit the stabilized model; but this, crucially, was never an explicit utopian mode, though in some examples it is assumed or implied. Variability and autonomy, within the generally harmoni-ous condition, are indeed among its primary features. But now, under the pressures of consumer capitalism and of monopoly socialism, the mode has broken. As in the later stages of realist fiction, self-realization and self-fulfilment are not to be found in relationship or in society, but in breakaway, in escape; the path the Savage takes, like a thousand heroes of late-realist fiction, getting out from under the old place, the old people, the old family, or like a thousand science-fiction heroes, running to the wastes to escape the machine, the city, the system. But then the last and most questionable irony: the first word of the motto of this repressive, dominating, controlling system is Com-munity: the keyword, centrally, of the entire utopian mode. It is at this point that the damage is done or, to put it another way, is admitted. It is in the name of Community, the utopian impulse, and in the names of communism (Bernard Marx and Lenina) that the system is seen as realized, though the actual tendencies – from the degradation of labour through an ultimate division and specialization to the organized mobil-ity and muzak of planned consumption – rely for their recognition on a contemporary capitalist world. In his 1946 foreword Huxley continued his running together of historically contrary impulses but then, inter-estingly, returned to Utopia, offering a third way beyond the incubator society and the primitive reservation: a self-governing and balanced community, little different in spirit from Morris's future society except that it is limited to 'exiles and refugees', people escaping from a dominant system which they have no chance or hope of changing collectively. Utopia then lies at the far end of Dystopia, but only a few will enter it; the few who get out from under. It is the path travelled, in the same period, by bourgeois cultural theory: from the universal liberation, in bourgeois terms, through the phase in which the minority first educates and then regenerates the majority, to the last sour period in which what is now called 'minority culture' has to find its reserva-tion, its hiding-place, beyond both the system and the fight against the system. But then what is so strange is that this last phase, in some writing, returns to the utopian mode, throwing strange questions back to the whole prior tradition: questions which disturb the apparently simple grammar of desire – that desire for another place and another time which, instead of being idealized, can be seen as always and everywhere a displacement, but which can itself be transformed when a history is moving:

Not in Utopia – subterranean fields –
Or in some secret island, Heaven knows where!
But in the very world, which is the world
Of all of us – the place where in the end
We find our happiness, or not at all!

Wordsworth's emphasis, it is true, can go either way: into revolutionary effort, when the history is moving; into a resigned settlement when it goes wrong or gets stuck. The utopian mode has to be read, always, within that changing context, which itself determines whether its defining subjunctive tense is part of a grammar which includes a true indicative and a true future, or whether it has seized every paradigm and become exclusive, in assent and dissent alike.

For the same consideration puts hard questions to the now dominant mode of dystopia. George Orwell's 1984 is no more plausible than Morris's 2003, but its naturalized subjunctive is more profoundly exclusive, more dogmatically repressive of struggle and possibility, than anything within the utopian tradition. It is also, more sourly and more fiercely than in Huxley, a collusion, in that the State warned against, satirized – the repression of autonomy, the cancellation of variations and alternatives – is built into the fictional form which is nominally its opponent, converting all opposition into agencies of the repression, imposing, within its excluding totality, the inevitability and the hopelessness which it assumes as a result. No more but perhaps no less plausible than Morris's 2003, but then, in the more open form, there is also Morris's 1952, and the years following it: years in which the subjunctive is a true subjunctive, other than a displaced indicative, because its energy flows both ways, forward and back, and because in its issue, in the struggle, it can go either way.

IV

The projection of new heavens and new hells has been a commonplace of science fiction. Yet perhaps a majority of them, just because they are so often literally out of this world, are functions of fundamental alteration: not merely the intervention of altered circumstance, which in the type of the externally altered world is a minor mode of the utopian, but a basic recasting of the physical conditions of life and thence of its life-forms. And then in most stories this is a simple exoticism, generically tied to the supranatural or magical romance. There is a range from casual to calculated fantasy, which is at the opposite pole from the hypothesized 'science' of science fiction. Yet, perhaps inextricable from this genre, yet bearing different emphases, there is a mode which is truly the result of a dimension of modern science: in natural history, with its radical linkages between life-forms and life-space; in scientific anthropology, with its methodological assumption of distinct and alternative cultures. The interrelation between these is often significant. The materialist tendency of the former is often annulled by an idealist projection at the last, mental phase of the speculation; the beast or the vegetable, at the top of its mind, is a human variation. The differential tendency of the latter, by contrast, is often an overriding of material form and condition: an overriding related to idealist anthropology, in which alternatives are in effect wholly voluntary. Yet it is part of the power of science fiction that it is always potentially a mode of authentic shift: a crisis of exposure which produces a crisis of possibility; a reworking, in imagination, of *all* forms and conditions.

In this at once liberating and promiscuous mode, science fiction, as a whole, has moved beyond the utopian; in a majority of cases, it is true, because it has also fallen short of it. Most direct extrapolation of our own conditions and forms – social and political but also imminently material – has been in effect or in intention dystopian: atomic war, famine, overpopulation, electronic surveillance have written 1984 into millennia of possible dates. To live otherwise, commonly, is to be other and elsewhere; a desire displaced by alienation and in this sense cousin to phases of the utopian, but without the specific of a connected or potentially connecting transformation and then again without the ties of a known condition and form. So that while the utopian transformation is social and moral, the science-fiction transformation, in its dominant Western modes, is at once beyond and beneath: not social and moral but natural; in effect, as so widely in Western thought since the late nineteenth century, a mutation at the point of otherwise intolerable exposure and crisis; not so much, in the old sense, a new life as a new species, a new nature.

It is then interesting within this largely alternative mode to find a clear example of an evidently deliberate return to the utopian tradition, in Ursula K. Le Guin's *The Dispossessed* (1974). It is a return within some of the specific conditions of science fiction. The alternative society is on the moon of a far planet, and space-travel and electronic communication – to say nothing of the possibilities of the 'ansible', that device for instantaneous space-wide communication developed from the theory of simultaneity – permit interaction between the alternative and the original society, within a wider interaction of other galactic civilizations. At one level the space-ship and the ansible can do no more, technically, than the sea voyage, the cleft in the underground cavern and, crucially, the dream. But they permit, instrumentally, what is also necessary for another and more serious reason: the sustained comparison of the utopian and the non-utopian options. The form of the novel, with its alternating chapters on Anarres and Urras, is designed for this exploratory comparison. And the reason is the historical moment of this looking again at Utopia: the moment of renewed direct social and political hope, a renewed alternative social and political morality, in a context with one variable from the ordinary origins of the utopian mode, that within the world in which the hope is being interestedly if warily examined, there is not, or apparently not, the overwhelming incentive of war, poverty and disease. When Morris's dreamer goes back from twenty-first- to nineteenth-century London the questions are not only moral; they are directly physical, in the evidently avoidable burdens of poverty and squalor. But when Le Guin's Shevek goes from Anarres to Urras he finds, within the place provided for him, an abundance, an affluence, a vitality, which are sensually overwhelming in comparison with his own moral but arid world. It is true that when he steps out of his place and discovers the class underside of this dominant prosperity the comparison is qualified, but that need only mean that the exuberant affluence depends on that class relationship and that the alternative is still a shared and equal relative poverty. It is true also that the comparison is qualified, in the text as a whole, by what is in effect a note that our own civilization – that of Earth, which in its North-American sector Urras so closely and deliberately resembles – has been long destroyed: 'appetite' and 'violence' destroyed it; we did not 'adapt' in time; some survivors live under the ultimate controls of 'life in the ruins'. But this, strictly, is by the way. Urras, it appears, is not in such danger; Anarres remains the social and moral option, the human alternative to a society that is, in its extended dominant forms, successful. It is among its repressed and rejected that the impulse stirs, renewing itself, after a long interval, to follow the breakaway revolution, anarchist and socialist, which took the Odonians from Urras to a new life on Anarres. Shevek's journey is the way back and the way forward: a dissatisfaction with what has happened in the alternative society but then a strengthened renewal of the original impulse to build it. In two evident ways, then, *The Dispossessed* has the marks of its period: the wary questioning of the utopian impulse itself, even within its basic acceptance; the uneasy consciousness that the superficies of Utopia, affluence and abundance, can be achieved, at least for many, by Non-utopian and even anti-utopian means.

The shift is significant, after so long a dystopian interval. It belongs to a general renewal of a form of utopian thinking – not the education but the learning of desire – which has been significant among Western radicals since the crises and also since the defeats of the 1960s. Its structures are highly specific. It is a mode within which a privileged affluence is at once assumed and rejected: assumed and in its own ways enjoyed, yet known, from inside, as lying and corrupt; rejected, from in close, because of its successful corruption; rejected, further out, by learning and imagining the condition of the excluded *others*. There is then the move to drop out and join the excluded; the move to get away, to get out from under, to take the poorer material option for a clear moral advantage. For nothing is more significant, in Le Guin's contrasted worlds, than that Anarres, the Utopia, is bleak and arid; the prosperous vitality of the classical Utopia is in the existing society that is being rejected. This is a split of a major kind. It is not that Anarres is primitivist: 'they knew that their anarchism was the product of a very high civilization, of a complex diversified culture, of a stable economy and a highly industrialized technology'. In this sense, the modification of Morris is important; it is clearly a future and not a past, a socially higher rather than a socially simplified form. But it is significantly only available in what is in effect a waste land; the good land is in the grip of the Urran dominance. It is then the movement that Huxley imagined, in his 1946 foreword. It is not the transformation, it is the getaway.

It is a generous and open getaway, within the limited conditions of its waste-land destination. The people of Anarres live as well, in all human terms, as Morris's cooperators; mutuality is shown to be viable, in a way all the more so because there is no abundance to make it easy. The social and ethical norms are at the highest point of the utopian imagination. But then there is a wary questioning beyond them: not the corrosive cynicism of the dystopian mode, but a reaching beyond basic mutuality to new kinds of individual responsibility and, with them, choice, dissent and conflict. For this, again of its period, is an open Utopia: forced open, after the congealing of ideals, the degeneration of mutuality into conservatism; shifted, deliberately, from its achieved harmonious condition, the stasis in which the classical utopian mode culminates, to restless, open, risk-taking experiment. It is a significant and welcome adaptation, depriving Utopia of its classical end of struggle, its age of perpetual harmony and rest. This deprivation, like the waste land, may be seen as daunting; the cutting-in of elements of a dominant Dystopia. But whereas the waste land is voluntary deprivation, by the author – product of a defeatist assessment of the possibilities of transformation in good and fertile country – the openness is in fact a strengthening; indeed it is probably only to such a Utopia that those who have known affluence and known with it social injustice and moral corruption can be summoned. It is not the last journey. In particular it is not the journey which all those still subject to direct exploitation, to avoidable poverty and disease, will imagine themselves making: a transformed this-world, of course with all the imagined and undertaken and fought-for modes of transformation. But it is where, within a capitalist dominance, and within the crisis of power and affluence which is also the crisis of war and waste, the utopian impulse now warily, self-questioningly, and setting its own limits, renews itself.

Bibliography

Morton, A. L. *The English Utopia*. London: Lawrence & Wishart, 1952.
Abensour, M.-H. *Utopies et dialectique du socialisme*, forthcoming.
Suvin, Darko. 'The Alternate Islands', *Science-Fiction Studies*, **3**, Part 3 (1976), 239-48.
Thompson, E. P. *William Morris: Romantic to Revolutionary* (new edn). London: Merlin Press, 1977.

Goode, John. 'William Morris and the Dream of Revolution', in *Literature and Politics in the Nineteenth Century*. Ed. John Lucas. London: Methuen, 1971.

Parrinder, Patrick. *H. G. Wells*. New York: Capricorn Books, 1977.

Williams, Raymond. *Orwell*. London: Fontana, 1971.

Fekete, John. *The Critical Twilight*. London: Routledge & Kegan Paul, 1978.

Science fiction and the scientific world-view

Patrick Parrinder

I

The problems of writing about the relationship between science and science fiction are manifold. It is necessary not only to define one's terms but to dispel a widespread suspicion that the relationship is accidental rather than essential. Do the initials 'SF' have to stand for '*science* fiction'? Many have wished that they didn't. One could compile an anthology of dismissive or patronizing references to SF by practising scientists (though Arthur C. Clarke has suggested that they might mostly be second-rate scientists). A much livelier anthology would display SF writers, particularly recent ones, pouring scorn on the idea that their work has anything to do with institutionalized knowledge. 'Like most science-fiction writers', Kurt Vonnegut assures us (referring to his fictional hero, Kilgore Trout), 'Trout knew almost nothing about science, was bored stiff by technical details.' And Brian Aldiss once asserted that 'Most of science fiction is about as firmly based in science as eggs are filled with bacon.'

One could answer these statements by saying that they are demonstrably untrue; there are probably very few significant developments in modern physics, astronomy, cybernetics, biology and genetics – to go no further – which have not been reflected in science-fiction stories. One could also note that the denial of any connection between SF and science is a species of deliberate heresy. For many years SF writers in England and America formed a largely ingrown community, cut off from the mainstream of literary culture by their outspoken support for the values of scientists and technologists. By the 1960s there was an understandable desire to break out of the ghetto and to assert the continuity between SF and other forms of contemporary fiction. At the same time, there was a loss of confidence in the scientific world-view which had inspired so many writers of earlier decades. The period of ascendancy of the scientific outlook – an ideology justifying scientific research as intrinsic to the nature and purpose of human existence – began with the technological triumphs and the erosion of traditional religious beliefs caused by the Industrial Revolution. The growth of science fiction as a separate genre would be unthinkable without this ascendancy. Up to the present, SF has continued to be moulded and shaped by scientific thought, even in its moments of rebellion against it.

Hugo Gernsback introduced the first number of his magazine *Science Wonder Stories* (June 1929) with the declaration that 'it is the policy of *Science Wonder Stories* to publish only such stories that have their basis in scientific laws as we know them, or in the logical deduction of new laws from what we know'. At the same time, he announced that he was enlisting a panel of experts to pronounce on the scientific correctness of stories submitted to the magazine.[1] The necessity of getting the technical details right has always been a precept with some SF writers, as Jules Verne's famous put-down of Wells's *The First Men in the Moon* ('I make use of physics. He invents') illustrates. More important than detailed correctness, however, is the general imaginative debt which SF writers owe to scientific ideology. This ideology has often received its fullest expression in stories – such as those concerning time travel – which at some point flagrantly violate 'scientific fact'.

Mary Shelley's *Frankenstein* (1818) would undoubtedly have been thrown out by the *Science Wonder Stories* panel of scientific experts. Yet, as Mark R. Hillegas has already argued, this is one of the earliest SF novels because it takes us into the laboratory and shows the horrifying results of a scientist's researches into the principle of life. Victor Frankenstein creates life by collecting the materials of a human body from dissecting-rooms and slaughterhouses, and then galvanizing the creature with the 'vital spark' of electricity. The power of electricity is suggested by the thunderstorms which crackle through the novel, as well as by the blackened lips and shrivelled skin of the hideous creature itself. Science, in this Gothic melodrama, stands accused of perverting the awesome power of natural forces to ungodly ends. Frankenstein's researches do irreparable damage to himself and his family, and his last words are a warning against the ambition of distinguishing oneself in science and discoveries.

The isolated, demonic inventor remains a classic SF figure, but the development of the genre throughout the nineteenth century reflects the steady institutionalization of science, as uncoordinated 'discoveries' and 'inventions' gave way to the organized connection of education and research. Jules Verne's romances have a strong element of scientific education without tears. H. G. Wells was an ex-science student, his first book was *A Text-Book of Biology* (1893) and several of his early novels were reviewed in the scientific periodical *Nature* as well as in more conventional journals. Though he has a residual fondness for the Frankenstein figure, most of his heroes have had a scientific training and some, like Dr Moreau, are outlaws from the community of professional scientists. The widespread foundation of learned societies, professional journals, laboratories and degree courses during the Victorian period conferred on the 'scientist' (the word was coined by William Whewell in 1840) a growing degree of public esteem. What T. H. Huxley called the 'ethical spirit' of science, sceptical, experimental and rigorously impersonal, had a wide impact on social thought, literature and the arts. Science and technology held the key to 'progress' and thus represented bourgeois society's invest-ment in its own future. One expression of this climate is the technologi-cal utopianism of Bellamy and Bulwer-Lytton, as analysed in Raymond Williams's essay in this volume.

Two strands of late nineteenth-century science appeared to chal-lenge this prospect of the social perfectibility of man. These were the Darwinian theory of evolution, with its implication that the biological constitution of man was open to perpetual change and instability, and the Second Law of Thermodynamics which posited an irreversible process of entropy, or what became known as the 'running-down universe'. In the conclusion to *The Origin of Species* (1859), Darwin contrasted the fixed nature of planetary movements with the dyna-mism of biological evolution, which throws up 'endless forms most beautiful and most wonderful'. Natural selection, he writes, 'works solely by and for the good of each being', so that in man 'all corporeal and mental endowments will tend to progress towards perfection'. The noble optimism of these words conceals the fact that natural selection is based on competitive struggle and the 'elimination of the unfit' – in this case, of present-day man. Moreover, the perfection of the human race is being pursued on a planet that, in the long run, must inevitably cool to the point where it becomes uninhabitable. (The belief that the earth must eventually be abandoned is one of the imperatives underly-ing science fiction's characteristic vision of space travel.) These para-doxes at the heart of the scientific outlook are the province of the early fiction of H. G. Wells, beginning with *The Time Machine* (1895).

Scientific thought has most decisively influenced science fiction where it has itself contained a strong vein of futurological fantasy. The prospects of space travel and of evolution beyond man have played an important part in this. Space travel is an age-old dream of mankind, which appealed to the Victorian rationalist as representing the final goal of human progress. Thus Winwood Reade's *The Martyrdom of Man* (1872), a Positivist account of human history which remained in print for fifty years and was still selling in its tens of thousands in the 1920s, looks forward to a time when disease has been extirpated, immortality has been 'invented' and man has migrated into space. 'The earth will become a Holy Land', Reade predicts, 'which will be visited by pilgrims from all quarters of the universe.' Finally, men will master the forces of nature and will set out to build their own universes. What Reade is putting forward here is a 'religion of humanity' very obviously modelled on the Christian religion, with scientists eventually usurping the function of God. It is not surprising that a sober-minded observer such as Huxley, in his lecture 'On the Advisableness of Improving Natural Knowledge' (1860), should pooh-pooh the idea of science as a fairy godmother bringing 'omnipotent Aladdin's lamps' and 'tele-graphs to Saturn'. In the early twentieth century, however, the inven-tion of powered flight made space travel no longer seem an absurdity. Meanwhile, developments in biology led not only to the control of ageing and disease but to the prospect of a planned 'improvement' of the human race by means of genetic engineering. Yet it was not until the 1920s that there emerged a coherent body of thought bringing together all the elements of the future vision that we have come to call 'science-fictional'. It is in this body of popular scientific thought, and most notably in works by H. G. Wells, J. B. S. Haldane and J. D. Bernal, that we may find a significant link between the scientific outlook and modern SF.

The reasons why this futurological perspective or 'scientific world-view' took coherent shape when and where it did are highly complex, and only a few suggestions can be made here. Modern scientific optimism reached its peak in the 1920s as a reaction against the traditionalist thinking which was thought to have caused the First World War. Although an international movement, it received its most authoritative intellectual statement in Europe, and especially Britain, while in the United States it was most fully represented by Gernsback and his successors in the SF pulps. It has often been suggested that the scientific world-view was the ideology of a new social class of engineers and technicians, a sector of the petty-bourgeoisie who hoped to gain enormously in power and influence as the planned society that they foresaw came about. H. G. Wells saw himself as the prophet of an 'Open Conspiracy' of scientists, technicians and industrialists who would take over world government, while both Haldane and Bernal were advocates of the combination of collectivism and the high status of the specialist that they found in the Soviet Union. Nevertheless, the specifically British origins of these three thinkers might be detected in their tendency to envisage a future of cosmic expansion; at the height of the Empire, the conquest of space would seem to have had a special appeal even for the most anti-imperialistic of Englishmen.

In Britain and Europe the vision of a scientific, collectivist future was in sharp contrast to the established or (in the Soviet Union) the recently destroyed social structure. The United States, however, was thought of as an inherently dynamic society which already represented 'the future' (see, for instance, Wells's book *The Future in America*, which finds – in 1906 – that the major flaw of American society is its lack of any collectivist ideology). In America technological developments were more immediately put in the service of consumer-oriented capitalism than in Europe, where the first priority was often national defence. It may have been for these reasons that the most influential American proponents of the scientific outlook expressed a much narrower and more manipulative attitude than their European counterparts. Pragmatism, the philosophy of 'if it works, it's right' originating in the works of C. S. Peirce and William James, prepared the ground for the techniques of 'social engineering' advocated by F. W. Taylor in *The Principles of Scientific Management* (1911), and later by the behaviourist school of psychologists. The aim of social engineering is to increase efficiency by 'modernizing' all aspects of industrial production; its range thus extends from the time-and-motion study advocated by Taylor (and satirized in Zamyatin's *We*, 1921) to the social welfare programmes of the New Deal in the 1930s. The extension of 'scientific management' into the control of all human behaviour is envisaged in B. F. Skinner's utopian novel *Walden Two* (1948), which portrays a perfect community set up within the existing capitalist system. Skinner's behaviourism, which holds that human fulfilment can be attained as a result of psychological techniques to be applied, without any structural or political change, in the here and now, seems a typical – though extreme – product of the pragmatic American outlook.

More recently, a similarly hard-headed, materialistic attitude has been reflected in the establishment of 'futurology' as a so-called science in which likely technological developments are scrutinized in isolation from any wider social and political changes which might influence them. The tendency to universalize the acquisitiveness and individualism of the capitalist epoch is also widespread in American SF. At the same time, SF writers interested in the longer perspectives of science, such as space travel or biological and cultural evolution, had to turn to European thinkers; either to the proponents of the scientific world-view, or to the apologists of a modern, post-scientific irrationalism such as Oswald Spengler, whose Darwinian sense of the rise and fall of civilizations made *The Decline of the West* (1922) one of the main source-books for SF's future histories.

II

The first element in the scientific world-view of Wells, Haldane, Bernal and their successors is the entity 'man'; man considered not as a divinely created being or a paragon of reason, but as a competing biological species. Wells (unlike many other late-Victorian 'social Darwinists') was concerned with the fortunes of mankind as a whole, not with particular class or racial groups. Nevertheless, a degree of conceptual slippage is very widespread in scientific materialism; 'man' comes to stand for 'civilized man' and, in effect, for 'modern Western man', with modernity being equated with the capacity to pursue scientific research. Scientific pronouncements about 'man's survival' pretend to a universalism which is often false, since they tend to represent the interests of the social groups to which scientists belong. Typically, they look to action by world bodies such as the United Nations (or its predecessor the League of Nations) to bring about the changes which are desired. The 'League of Nations' idea of joint action by governments to ensure peace and prosperity reflects an idealism that arose naturally out of the carnage of the First World War, but it also suggests a desire to stave off the 'anarchy' of proletarian revolutions like that which had taken place in Russia. The common interest of 'mankind' is taken for granted by some (if not all) of the scientific thinkers of the 1920s and 1930s. Their articulation of the problems and prospects of 'man' – an articulation largely present in Wells, and yet considerably extended by his scientific followers, including some SF writers – may be loosely summarized as follows.

1. The immediate challenge to mankind is the self-destructiveness inherent in the present phase of social and technological evolution. The nightmare of technological warfare, as foreseen by Wells and other SF novelists, was unleashed in the First World War of 1914-18. Future wars, it is anticipated, will be world wars, destructive of civilization as a whole. War has become irrational because no one side stands any longer to gain by it. (Thus, scientists often incline towards a pacifist position on purely rational grounds, but such pacifism has little to say about localized wars, strike-breaking, colonial 'police actions' and other forms of violence which are not self-evidently irrational.) If major wars are to be avoided, the advanced societies must learn to control their own 'inner demons' and those of others. Such control is to be achieved by a framework of international legal and political coordination, by the use of social engineering (i.e. social reform directed from above) to remove the frustrations and inequalities which lead to demagogy and mass hysteria, and by the transfer of power to a scientific élite.

2. It is when it looks beyond the horizons of the immediate twentieth-century crisis that scientific thinking enters the 'eschatological' dimension which is the territory of much SF. Once the problems of war, poverty, frustration and ignorance have been overcome, what is to come next? From an evolutionary point of view, man is now free to apply the principles of social engineering at will to his own further development. Since there is no finality in the evolutionary process – except that of extinction – he cannot look to the stabilization or conservation of any features of his present civilization as a long-term goal. Man's aim, accordingly, must be to transcend his own present cultural, and eventually biological, identity. The vision of 'evolution beyond man' is usually presented by some grotesque marriage of biology and cybernetics; the inheritors of human civilization will be either organisms with vastly distended brains (as in Wells and Stapledon) or machines which have liberated themselves from their human constructors. The first steps toward further development will be taken as human beings learn to inhabit wholly artificial environments, to consume artificial foods and adopt artificial means of reproduction and the prolongation of life.

3. As consolation for this loss of natural life there is the last and greatest of the physical challenges that man faces: the conquest of space. Today, with the US and USSR space programmes well into their third decade, space exploration and research are usually

justified on pragmatic grounds, either as a satisfaction of basic impulses ('Because it's there') or as an exercise in *Realpolitik* ('Because the Russians might get there first'). Once the gospel of a small number of writers and thinkers mocked by the public at large, space research is now both an economic and military reality and one of the staple components of mass-entertainment fantasy.

While the practicability of star travel awaits the discovery of some mode of faster-than-light propulsion, travel within the solar system depends upon simple extensions of the transport technology which has produced the motor-car and the jet aeroplane. The mid-twentieth-century revolution in attitudes to space is vividly recorded in the files of periodicals like the *Journal of the British Interplanetary Society*, founded in 1934 by a small group of visionaries, which by the late 1940s had become a professional journal for rocket engineers, most of whom were employed on government-assisted research projects. Writing in the *Journal* for December 1946, Arthur C. Clarke (already a veteran contributor) recalled that in *Possible Worlds* (1927) J. B. S. Haldane had predicted space travel around the year 8 000 000. Now, Clarke suggested a little too optimistically, there was a possibility of a guided missile crashing onto the moon by 1950! For decades before this, however, scientific thinkers and SF writers had discussed the possibilities of colonizing neighbouring planets, the exploitation of mineral resources and the sale of real estate on them, and the likelihood of discovering alien life-forms. 'Space' had become a new frontier of the imagination, at once the last repository of the colonist's dream of a clean break and a new start, and the ultimate target of capitalism's drive towards perpetual expansion.

Beyond the practical advantages of opening up the solar system, space travel has always had a powerful quasi-religious attraction for certain minds. Winwood Reade's *The Martyrdom of Man* has already been cited as an example of this, and perhaps the most important writer to echo the strain of religious exaltation in which Reade writes of space is H. G. Wells. In his lecture 'The Discovery of the Future' (delivered at the Royal Institution and subsequently published in *Nature* for 6 February 1902) Wells looks forward to a time when 'beings who are now latent in our thoughts and hidden in our loins, shall stand upon this earth as one stands upon a footstool, and shall laugh and reach out their hands amidst the stars'. Like the universe-makers prophesied by Reade, these human children who take the heavens for their playground are substitutes for the traditional gods. But, since Wells wrote, they have also become the brain-children of an ever-increasing social group – the readers of science fiction.

In the long term there is a more sombre reason for embarking on space travel, which scientific thinkers have seldom failed to point out. The time will come (though maybe not for millions of years) when the earth will no longer be able to support human life. Whether as a result of the planet's natural cooling or of some purely man-made disaster, enforced migration will become the key to human survival. The certainty that man, having survived the most immediate dangers, must one day face the choice of leaving the earth or becoming extinct makes space travel appear as a form of positive evolutionary adaptation. Space, in effect, is of the essence of the scientific world-view, for it represents not only man's future playground but his destiny.

4. It is not likely that man is alone in the universe. If he were, he might soon be able to master it – thus finally proving the Darwinian reduction of *Homo sapiens* to a biological entity to be an irrelevance – but, in the long run, what could be more boring than to be a lone ranger on a frontier without Red Indians? While statistical probability seems to support the inference that there is or has been intelligent life elsewhere in the universe, there is no doubt that scientific thinkers have by and large *wanted* to believe this. In the 1890s popular astronomy championed the idea that intelligent beings must have constructed the newly discovered 'canals' on Mars. Now that we no longer expect to encounter a rival civilization anywhere in the solar system, speculation centres on the possibility of establishing a communications network across interstellar space. The astronomer Fred Hoyle has written that, while travel outside the solar system may be 'not merely difficult but impossible', the rate of information-exchange may be such that we could stumble across a 'galactic library' and a 'galactic telephone directory'. In this way we might even profit from the experience of other civilizations which have learned to avoid nuclear war! These speculations from Hoyle's *Of Men and Galaxies* (1965) do not differ in essence from those of SF writers who imagine extra-terrestrials arriving out of the blue and establishing a benevolent despotism to save mankind from its follies. Against this, Arthur C. Clarke suggested in *The Exploration of Space* (1951) that although the chances of intelligence existing elsewhere in the universe are very high, the probability of our encountering a civilization at a stage of development recognizably close to our own is infinitesimal. But even if contact with other civilizations turns out to be a purely fictional prospect, the doubt whether human intelligence is alone in the universe does much to mitigate the bleakness of scientific cosmology.

5. Modern scientific thought places man in a time and space so large as to annihilate the individual with a normal human life-span. This perspective has no obvious relevance to the problems of individual behaviour or of social justice and liberty, so that it would be quite rational to refuse to base one's ethical or political views on it. Nevertheless, the inherently anti-individualistic quality of the

evolutionary outlook has constituted one of its most powerful attractions. Scientific thinkers such as Wells, Haldane and Bernal reject the 'short-sighted' materialistic and pragmatic goals of modern democracy in favour of a more self-sacrificing concern for the welfare of the species as a whole. It may be that in rejecting individualism, more fundamentally than in its dreams of space travel, artificial environments and alien intelligence, the scientific world-view reflects some of the deeper and as yet unsatisfied yearnings of human culture.

The 'spiritual' goal of the evolutionary process, according to Wells and his successors, is the establishment of some sort of collective mind or intelligence incorporating the whole human race. Such a collective mind is a materialization of a metaphorical idea which already exists; phrases such as 'collective mind' and 'collective wisdom' have a long history, and Wells gave a book of his arguing for an integrated, world-wide information service the title *World Brain* (1938). Nevertheless, the realization of collective mind implies the attainment of an unprecedented harmony between the minds of individuals. Such a prospect may have authoritarian or liberal overtones; indeed, the mixture of individual subordination and fraternal intimacy that it involves might be said to exist at the vanishing-point where 'total democracy' equals 'totalitarianism'. As long as the harmony that is attained is founded on the recognition of scientific truths, the achievement of a state of collective mind is, according to Wells, the ultimate goal of science itself.

Science fiction, as a genre, is not devoted to collectivism. Some of its best-known writers, such as Robert A. Heinlein, are right-wing individualists whose heroes stand out by virtue of their individual courage, expertise and contempt for the herd. Nonetheless, SF has repeatedly given expression to the dream of mental harmony, most strikingly in its use of themes of telepathy or 'mindspeech'. Whether brought about by a form of religious discipline (as in Ursula K. Le Guin's novels) or by the simple mechanical expedient of connecting two brains together (as envisaged by J. D. Bernal), telepathy may be looked upon as a form of biological mutation which would release us from the prison of our individuality. A sharp distinction should be drawn here between SF which portrays telepathy as a further stage of human development, as most memorably in Olaf Stapledon's *Last and First Men* (1930), and the mass of fantasies which make it magically available to selected characters in the here and now. Where they are not put in the service of sheer escapism, telepathy and 'psi' powers can be one of the most subversive elements in the scientific outlook. The materialization of the idea of collective mind not only involves a radical evolution of human nature; it may be one of science's most far-reaching contributions to the dream of the brotherhood of man.

III

The major champion of the twentieth-century scientific world-view was H. G. Wells. Though enormously influential in its day, this aspect of his work is now enshrined for the most part in little-read books, written after the completion of his major SF cycle around the turn of the century. The concept of collective mind, for example, was introduced in *First and Last Things* (1908, and subsequently revised in 1917 and 1929), and finally elaborated in the D.Sc. thesis that Wells completed in 1944, two years before his death. The development of new social structures and the emergence of world government also play a major role in Wellsian thought. Other themes, such as space travel, alien intelligence and the detailed projection of further biological evolution, belong much more to his science fiction. It was the combination in Wells of the visionary and the untiring practical prophet that made him recognized by his contemporaries as the representative spokesman of the scientific world-view.

Among SF writers, his closest intellectual disciples are probably Olaf Stapledon and Arthur C. Clarke; though his wider influence is felt from Brian Aldiss, who has called him the 'Shakespeare of science fiction', to Jack Williamson who has recently devoted a critical book to him. Less familiar, and more difficult to trace, is the impact of Wells and 'Wellsian' thought among twentieth-century scientists themselves. This impact was strongest on the generation of British scientists who came to world-wide prominence between the two wars.

One of the main concerns of Wells and his associates was with popular scientific education (a cause which was also furthered by SF magazine editors such as Gernsback and John W. Campbell). Wells's famous *The Outline of History* (1920) was followed by his surveys of contemporary biology, *The Science of Life* (with Julian Huxley and G. P. Wells, 1930), and of sociology and economics, *The Work, Wealth and Happiness of Mankind* (1931). To these may be added *Mathematics for the Million* (1936) and *Science for the Citizen* (1938) by Wells's admirer Lancelot Hogben. At a more essayistic level, the scientific outlook was propagated by J. B. S Haldane in widely read books such as *Daedalus: or Science and the Future* (1924) and *Possible Worlds* (1927). The classic exposition of the world-view of science is, however, J. D. Bernal's first book *The World, the Flesh and the Devil* (1929). Haldane's main work was to lie in genetics, while Bernal was a physicist and the author of standard books on the history and social function of science; but they are probably best remembered as the two most eminent Western scientists to have devoted a major part of their lives to international Communism. After the mid 1930s their interest in the visionary horizons of science was obscured – though not obliterated – by commitment to the Communist cause. Both men were invited to address the British Interplanetary Society in the 1950s, and a utopian novel from the same period, found among Haldane's posthumous papers, has recently been published as *The Man with Two Memories* (1976).

The detailed connections between scientific thought and the SF of the inter-war period are still awaiting full investigation. Haldane and his friend Julian Huxley (later to become the first Director-General of UNESCO) were both occasional writers of science fiction. Huxley's story 'The Tissue-Culture King', first published in the *Yale Review* in 1927, was quickly reprinted in *Amazing Stories*. Haldane's 'The Last Judgment' in *Possible Worlds* – a description of the end of the world as witnessed by human colonists on Venus – has frequently been acknowledged in SF circles. Haldane and Bernal directly influenced such writers as Stapledon, James Blish and C. S. Lewis, as well as Arthur C. Clarke (who has dignified one of Haldane's characteristic statements of the queerness of the universe with the title 'Haldane's Law'). Bernal's *The World, the Flesh and the Devil* may have had a wider importance as a source of ideas for the American pulps, since it contains concise technical descriptions of rocketry, weightlessness and the construction of space stations in addition to speculations about man's ultimate destiny.

Bernal's 'space stations' are, in fact, celestial cities of up to 30,000 inhabitants made out of hollowed-out asteroids. Each space station is a self-contained ecosystem, so that all waste matter has to be recycled. It is in one of these vessels that the first group of men would venture outside the solar system – a journey taking hundreds of years and only to be accomplished by the remote descendants of the original adventurers. In speculating as to who these explorers will be, Bernal suggests that mankind may eventually divide up into two species, the scientists and the others. The scientists would colonize the heavens, but would continue to regard their earthbound inferiors with a 'curious reverence': 'The world might, in fact, be transformed into a human zoo, a zoo so intelligently managed that its inhabitants are not aware that they are there merely for the purposes of observation and experiment.'

The combination of technical hand-book to space-flight and dream of a scientific élite makes *The World, the Flesh and the Devil* remarkably close to the outlook of SF in the 1930s and 1940s. Where Bernal differs from Gernsback and his heirs is in his insistence on the moral, physical and intellectual transformation of humanity which must accompany space exploration. Ultimately his vision is of a Stapledonian breaking-down of the barriers of individuality:

Finally, consciousness itself may end or vanish in a humanity that has become completely etherialized, losing the close-knit organism, becoming masses of atoms in space communicating by radiation, and ultimately perhaps resolving itself entirely into light. That may be an end or a beginning, but from here it is out of sight.

It is difficult to think of a more startling embodiment of Darwin's conception of 'endless forms most beautiful and most wonderful' than this.

Bernal was aware that the prospect of a dissolution of individuality, however poetic in expression, must prove abhorrent to many people. He admits the extent of the 'distaste and hatred' that have been caused by the present stage of the technological revolution, and believes, as we have seen, that the conflict between 'humanizers' and 'mechanizers' may eventually lead to a dimorphism of the human race. This is an ingenious attempt to patch over a basic contradiction of the scientific world-view – that, despite its promises, it cannot possibly be adequate to fulfil the hopes of *all* men. This underlying contradiction may account for the failure of any of Haldane's and Bernal's successors as scientific popularizers to display a comparable degree of intellectual authority and visionary confidence. It may be (as Fred Hoyle has claimed) that contemporary science itself is in decline, its great age having been the first thirty years of this century. As early as *The Social Function of Science* (1939), Bernal was noting a general loss of enthusiasm for scientific progress.

Two groups who did not share this loss of enthusiasm were, firstly, the 'hard core' of American SF writers, and secondly the ruling élite in the Soviet Union. In America Gernsback, John W. Campbell and their 'stable' of writers saw it as part of their role to convert their mainly adolescent readers to science and the scientific attitude. Of all the writers for the magazines it is Isaac Asimov who has written most prolifically in this cause. While Asimov's robot-stories are deliberate attempts to counteract the Faustian view of technology as inherently self-destructive, his numerous books and essays on popular science often read like a vulgar-scientific parody of Haldane and Bernal. Despite his Ph.D. in biochemistry, his outlook is that of a pragmatic, self-confident entrepreneur rather than a biologist or physicist.

In *View from a Height* (1963), for instance – a collection of essays reprinted from *The Magazine of Fantasy and Science Fiction* – Asimov discusses the most efficient means of exploiting the planets and asteroids of the solar system. Jupiter, he suggests should be colonized, both for its helium and because it could contain life which might turn out to be edible! The radioactive ash-disposal problem on earth is to be solved by creating an 'off-limits' area of space for dumping poisonous wastes. Eventually, the planets should be broken up into asteroids to produce the maximum surface-area of real estate for potential settlers. The earth itself might be left intact as a museum (an echo of Bernal?), or, if the 'Progressives' outvoted the 'Traditionalists' on this issue, it too would be blown apart. The book concludes with the vision of a cosmic work-fleet advancing to accomplish this operation, all in the name of scientific progress; such was the image of 'enlightened' technological thinking that was being fed to Asimov's magazine readership not so long ago.

If Asimov's 'science' is a prop for ruthless free enterprise, Bernal and Haldane tried to combine the scientific outlook with social justice by turning to Soviet Marxism. Both men became active Communist supporters in the 1930s, in response to the rise of Fascism, and both became embroiled in the post-war Lysenko controversy, which revealed the extent to which Soviet scientific research, like all other forms of intellectual work, was subject to Party control. Though committed to the ideal of a classless society, the works of Bernal and Haldane show a suppressed tendency towards scientific élitism, to viewing the scientist as a member of a privileged caste. (In Haldane's case, his personal struggle with élitism was dramatically manifested in his emigration to India in the last years of his life.) The deep attraction that 'Soviet science' held for them was the misguided result of their recognition of the contradiction in the scientific world-view that has already been pointed out.

IV

Behind the barrage of early twentieth-century prophecies of space travel, eugenics and the prolongation of life lay the implication that these things were intrinsically desirable, and those who opposed them Luddite reactionaries. This was still more true of the popularization of the scientific world-view in the SF magazines. The 'hard' SF of the 1930-60 period often gives an impression of mindless technology-worship. At the same time, this fetishism of technology has been accompanied by its opposite, an anti-scientific fantasy literature using the settings and situations of SF, but resorting to magic and sorcery to resolve any difficulty. This split in popular science fiction, which has lately become increasingly obvious, is significantly reflected in the little-known controversy between J. B. S. Haldane and the writer, scholar and Christian apologist C. S. Lewis in the mid 1940s.

Lewis's space trilogy, *Out of the Silent Planet* (1938), *Perelandra* (1943) and *That Hideous Strength* (1945), was intended as an attack on 'scientism' – the term he uses to denote uncritical acceptance of scientific aims and methods as good in themselves. Lewis's brilliant imagination of alien worlds is the redeeming feature of a sequence in which plot and characterization are, for the most part, heavily didactic. Corresponding to the three volumes of the trilogy there are three stages in his unmasking of contemporary science and scientists. In *Out of the Silent Planet* the physicist Weston is a Machiavellian figure in league with big business to destroy both liberty on earth and the culture and ecology of any planet he may visit. He justifies this by his fanatical belief in the overriding glory of human destiny as foreseen by science – a belief which is simply a new form of imperialism. In *Perelandra*, Weston abandons this doctrine of 'human racism' for belief in a Wellsian 'finite God' which can be identified with the cosmic process of nature. (In keeping with Lewis's general thesis of diabolism, this change of front is the result of possession by the Devil.) *That*

Hideous Strength turns back to the human world to show scientists, administrators and the popular novelist Horace Jules (H. G. Wells) as collaborators in a sinister research establishment, N.I.C.E., dedicated to a form of social control which amounts to Fascist oppression. What is remarkable about this (in some ways very silly) novel is its anticipation of some of the most popular themes of more recent fantasy. Lewis's reduction of social history to a struggle between two immemorial secret conspiracies, and his reliance on the beneficence of occult forces mediated through a small community of ordinary and apparently defenceless people in a pastoral setting, are features which could be paralleled many times over. Both the form and the substance of Lewis's attack on scientism have turned out to be surprisingly prophetic.

Haldane's sense of the damage it could do to the scientific cause led him to attack the Lewis trilogy in an article in the *Modern Quarterly*, the Communist Party theoretical journal, in 1946. His scorn for the reactionary posturings involved in Lewis's accusation of devil-worship is reflected in the title of his essay, 'Auld Hornie, F.R.S.' He has little difficulty in exposing the pseudo-scientific expedients of Lewis's plots and the hostile caricatures of individual scientific morality that the books contain. Lewis did not choose to defend himself against these charges, but an unpublished 'Reply to Professor Haldane' was included in his posthumous collection of essays, *Of Other Worlds* (1966). Here Lewis argues rather feebly that Haldane had misunderstood his intentions, and defends the use of pseudo-scientific concepts in SF so long as they do not contravene the 'folk science' necessary to secure the ordinary reader's suspension of disbelief. (Here it may be noted that his practice – such as, for example, describing the canals on Mars – has the almost unanimous endorsement of SF writers.) For his major point, however, the reader is referred back to *The Abolition of Man* (1943), a book in which Lewis set out the philosophical position underlying the trilogy. The commitment to the subjugation of nature fundamental to modern science, Lewis argues, is necessarily a commitment to the subjugation of 'man' as well. In answer to the technologists' programme of human 'abolition', Lewis dreams wistfully of a 'regenerate science' which resembles the most extreme yearnings of present-day ecologists. Such a science, he writes, 'would not do even to minerals and vegetables what modern science threatens to do to man himself'. Lewis's ideal is not even 'pastoral' – since it threatens the very existence of agriculture – but, unfortunately, absurd; it would mean the elimination alike of nature and of human history.

Lewis's appeal to literary and religious values against those of science is in some ways reminiscent of a later and much better publicized British *cause célèbre*, the quarrel between C. P. Snow and the literary critic F. R. Leavis in the early 1960s. While the debate that it provoked has little relevance to science fiction, Snow's lecture *The Two Cultures and the Scientific Revolution* (1959) was a memorable statement of the scientific world-view by a novelist who is very much a disciple of men like Wells and Haldane. However, in terms of the history that we have been tracing in this essay, one of the most striking features of Snow's lecture is its belatedness. Snow argues that Western intellectual life is polarized between literary and scientific 'cultures', but it was only in a later essay, 'The Two Cultures: A Second Look' (1963), that he noted the imminent emergence of a 'third culture' of social scientists taking as their province the human effects of the scientific revolution. It is the growing dominance of the so-called 'software' sciences, together with widespread alarm at the human consequences of a century of technological progress, that has upset the close relationship of SF and the scientific world-view that lasted, by and large, to the end of the 1950s.

V

The shift of emphasis to the social sciences and the development of intrinsic methodologies for these sciences (notably, those methods which come under the umbrella of 'structuralism') have taken place in a context of disillusion with natural science. For someone like Snow, social science is largely the *application* of the attitudes and techniques of natural science in the field of human society; for example, modern agricultural technology may be used to feed the world's hungry. Yet scepticism about the benevolent intentions of a scientific élite (Snow's 'intellectual Luddism') is probably as old as science itself. In an age when Huxley and Haldane were dominant figures it is not surprising to find Adam Fenwick-Symes clutching his 'Huxlane–Halley bomb (for the dissemination of leprosy germs)' in the lurid future-war scene which ends Evelyn Waugh's *Vile Bodies* (1930). What is much more startling is the recent spread of 'anti-scientific' attitudes among science-fiction writers and, to some extent, among scientists themselves.

At the beginning of his brilliant history of the atomic scientists, *Brighter Than a Thousand Suns* (1956), Robert Jungk records a conversation with a central European scientist at Los Alamos in 1949. 'What an extraordinary and incomprehensible thing!' the scientist said. 'My whole youth was absolutely devoted to truth, freedom, and peace; and yet fate has seen fit to deposit me here where my freedom of movement is limited; the truth that I am trying to discover is locked behind massive gates; and the ultimate aim of my work has to be the construction of the most hideous weapons of war.' Scientists in the early Cold War years responded to the growth of the military–industrial complex with a campaign to enlighten the public about the dangers of nuclear energy. Some, like J. Robert Oppenheimer, became victims to the rising tide of anti-Communist hysteria, but they did not lose faith in science itself. The science-fiction magazines became a forum for debate about the social control of science, as T. A. Shippey's essay in this volume shows so fully. Once again, their scepticism had not yet developed into a reaction against scientism as such.

Nevertheless, 'atomic doom' stories began appearing in the magazines less than a year after the destruction of Hiroshima and Nagasaki, and by 1948 John W. Campbell felt obliged to tell his writers that such stories were no longer wanted.[2] H. G. Wells himself gave way to despair in his last book *Mind at the End of its Tether* (1945) – written, in fact, *before* the A-bomb became public knowledge – in which he states bluntly that man has failed to adapt to his environment, and must shortly perish. It was not until the 1960s, after the vogue for 'realistic' novels and films of nuclear catastrophe such as Nevil Shute's *On the Beach* (1957), that the generation of SF writers loosely known as the 'New Wave' began to exploit post-nuclear nightmares as a way of expressing cynicism about the scientific enterprise as a whole. Though examples might be taken from Samuel Delany, Harlan Ellison, Philip K. Dick and several others, the most influential writer in this mode, and the one who seems most deliberate in his reaction against the scientific outlook, is J. G. Ballard.

Ballard in his early work is the poet of the scientific world-view in decline. While he has run through the gamut of science-fictional prophecies – from tomorrow's disasters to the ultimate achievement of union with the cosmos ('The Waiting Grounds', 1967) – he has often argued that SF's futures are merely extrapolative, a projection of essentially contemporary wishes and needs. Several of his stories envisage the failure of the Space Age. 'The Cage of Sand' (1963) shows a group of fugitives infected with a dangerous Martian virus lurking in an abandoned and quarantined Cape Canaveral. 'Thirteen to Centaurus' describes an earthbound spaceship whose crew have been tricked into believing they are on a 100-year voyage to Alpha Centauri. 'What began as a grand adventure in the spirit of Columbus', Ballard moralizes, 'has become a grisly joke.' The tone of hard-boiled disillusion with science is the stock-in-trade of these stories.

Ballard's deliberate inversion of the scientific outlook may be seen by examining one of his favourite metaphors, the 'terminal beach'. As an apocalyptic symbol this presumably comes from Wells's *The Time Machine*, where the narrator travels forward 30 million years to a beach which is the last stronghold of life as it regresses back to the sea. Ballard's beaches belong to the immediate future. Typical of them are the half-submerged landscape of London in *The Drowned World* (1962), the beach crowded with sunbathers waiting for a satellite launching in 'The Reptile Enclosure' (1964) and the post-nuclear wasteland of Eniwetok Island in 'The Terminal Beach' (1964). Biological regression is hinted at in all these stories. The fauna and flora of the Triassic Age are re-created in *The Drowned World*. In 'The Reptile Enclosure', infra-red radiation from the satellite sets off 'innate releasing mechanisms' inherited from man's Cro-Magnon ancestors which drive the sunbathing crowds like lemmings into the sea. And Eniwetok is a source of pilgrimage for the 'possessed' – like Ballard's character Traven – who find it an 'ontological Garden of Eden'. But although the theory of evolution is used as an adjunct to Ballard's visions of present-day environmental disaster, it is clear that the main 'scientific' background for these stories is not biology, as it was for Wells, but Jungian psychology. The sea towards which life regresses stands for the womb, just as outer space stands in Ballard's work for inner space. He is, in a sense, correct in implying that the concern with the very long-term future found in Wells and his successors is a sublimation of present-day anxieties. However, the cumulative effect of Ballard's fictions is reductive in the extreme. The more he extends his range to new areas of social experience, whether those of the car crash, the high-rise apartment block or the concrete deserts of the modern city, the more he eliminates the sense of wonder. Ballard's fiction is a progressive subjugation of every feature of external reality to the demands of the 'collective unconscious'.

The monotony of his characteristic titles (*The Drowned World*, *The Crystal World*, 'The Illuminated Man', 'The Overloaded Man', 'The Subliminal Man', etc.) reflects the basic determinism of his universe. Wells's Time Traveller discovered a comparable determinism, but his invention left him free to travel across the range of earth history and, as the epilogue of *The Time Machine* suggests, to find his own preferred resting-place within it. Perhaps Ballard's SF illustrates not so much a debasement of the potentialities of the universe as a debasement of the hero, who becomes no more than a trapped spectator sharing some of his creator's relish for the aesthetics of decay and destruction.

Ballard seems to have been keen to associate his early work with the anti-nuclear protest movement. The Penguin editions of his books that appeared in the 1960s proclaim his view that SF is 'the apocalyptic literature of the twentieth century, the authentic language of Auschwitz, Eniwetok, and Aldermaston'. The experience of disaster is the goal of each of his fictions, and it is this which makes him such a representative figure among the writers of his generation (he was born in 1930). It is now a commonplace that SF in England and America since 1960 – where it has not been swept up in a current of drug-sustained, quasi-mystical euphoria – has been largely pessimistic.

Why is this, it may be asked, when most SF writers are middle-class citizens of affluent societies, and the prospects for the world as a whole have not grown noticeably bleaker in the last twenty years? In a recent discussion of 'Discontent in American Science Fiction', Gérard Klein explains the near-universal distrust of science and scientists in contemporary SF, not in terms of the inherent nature of science itself, but of the particular fate of the social group – the 'technologically oriented middle class' – to which most SF writers and readers belong. After going through periods of expansionist optimism (pre-1940) and of 'confident scepticism' (1940-60), the technological middle class now finds itself increasingly in the position of a proletariat. Scientists and technicians are essential to the working of modern industry, yet they are further than ever from assuming the political and economic control of affairs which Wells and his disciples demanded. Science, it is now clear, is not a revolutionary force in society, but a servant of big business and the international corporations. Recent SF reflects this change, while at the same time enjoying an unprecedented popularity. As Klein says, 'When SF was the bearer of a scientific messianism, it was mocked.' The seriousness with which it is regarded today is a measure of its expression of (and, in many cases, its ability to lull) the latent anxieties of large classes of people who sense a future of growing servitude.

Though Klein's thesis must remain speculative, the pessimism of recent SF and its loss of faith in scientific horizons are undeniable. If propagandists like Haldane and Bernal have found few successors it is not because their scientific predictions have been disproved, but because their confidence that humanity can draw the maximum benefits from its own technical resourcefulness now seems discredited. Technological change is now generally seen as something imposed from outside, not that we bring about. (The so-called 'alternative' or people's technology, on the other hand, is frequently regressive in character.) This dehumanization of change is reflected in the cold-blooded perspectives of American 'futurology', and in the popularity of books like Alvin Toffler's *Future Shock* (1970), which are concerned not with the desirable directions of change as such, but with ways of softening the psychological impact of uncontrolled change on the individual. This tendency to concentrate on the individual psyche as the key social unit ('psychologism') is shared by advocates of 'behavioural engineering', on the one hand, and by the anti-rationalists and neo-mystics on the other. Despite the dangers of unthinking 'scientism', our dependence on the shared accumulation of science and technology for survival is frequently overlooked in today's climate.

VI

In Philip K. Dick's science-fantasy *Galactic Pot-Healer* (1971), the force of unyielding entropy is finally opposed by the efforts of a single, isolated artist, Joe the pot-healer. Similarly, this essay must end by noting the widespread fragmentation of the scientific world-view that has been sketched, and the efforts of individual writers to come to terms with this fragmentation and to go beyond simple acceptance or rejection of scientistic attitudes.

Since SF did so much to anticipate the Space Age, it is ironic that contemporary physics has tended to accentuate the difficulty and – some would say – the impossibility of star travel. For all their spectacular successes, the US/USSR space programmes have demonstrated both the subordination of 'pure' science to power-politics, and national prestige, and the enormous cost of venturing even a little way out into the solar system. Despite the moon landings, man is still, today, a virtual prisoner of this earth.

It would be difficult enough to reach the stars in a static universe – but what about a universe in which the galaxies are inexorably rushing apart? The 'expanding universe' theory is one of several aspects of modern cosmology that SF writers tend to ignore because, if taken seriously, they would lead to despair. Can science fiction do any more than to purvey consoling myths about a universe of which a contemporary physicist, Steven Weinberg, has written that 'the more [it] seems comprehensible, the more it also seems pointless' (*The First Three Minutes*, 1977)? Whether optimistic or pessimistic, SF has always made its cosmological and futurological perspectives seem more meaningful to the individual reader than, perhaps, they really are. Hence a cosmos populated by aliens and robots who talk and behave like recognizable beings, an intergalactic politics which closely resembles terrestrial politics, the various kinds of 'space-drive' and 'hyper-drive' to cross the apparently insuperable barrier of the speed of light. Today it is increasingly difficult to sustain the genre's 'domestication' of the universe without resorting either to stale conventions or to a blatant use of pseudo-science.

For example, American science fiction has long resorted to the idea of cosmic anomalies to make faster-than-light travel possible. As the hero explains in Heinlein's *Starman Jones* (1953), 'if it weren't for the anomalies, there never would have been any way for us to reach the stars; the distances are too great. But looking back, it is obvious that all that emptiness couldn't be real – there *had* to be the anomalies. That's what my uncle used to say.' The idea that these benign anomalies are there just waiting to be found is a lot less credible now than it may have been in 1953; yet the air remains thick with speculations about harnessing the most destructive and least understood forms of natural energy, such as that of the 'black holes'.

A number of strategies are open to SF writers who are not content with a simple repetition of yesterday's dreams, and yet remain concerned to counteract the entropy which afflicts the scientific world-view today. It is possible to write SF which recognizes the inherent destructiveness and limitations of science's Promethean quest for knowledge. Alternatively, the writer can introduce an 'anthropological' view of Western civilization in which science and (especially) space travel appears as a cultural aberration or a new form of religion. Or one can endorse the belief that space travel and further evolution are proper goals for mankind, while showing them as the expression of societies essentially different from ours, in which life has been revolutionized and the 'inner demons' have been brought under control.

The most important writers to have adopted such pot-healing strategies appear to me to be Stanislaw Lem and Ursula K. Le Guin. Some brief indications of the relevance of their work are all that is possible in the present context. Lem is distinguished by his epistemological scepticism and his very literal endorsement, in novels like

Solaris (1961) and *The Invincible* (1963), of Haldane's Law that 'the universe is not only queerer than we suppose, but queerer than we *can* suppose'. The weird behaviour of the incomprehensible, oceanic intelligence of the planet Solaris produces irreconcilable differences of opinion between the three scientists isolated on the planet's research station, each of whom represents a particular aspect of science's institutional morality. The hero, Kelvin, both achieves a new understanding of the discipline of Solaristics and becomes enthralled by the mystique of contact with the ocean, so that he is quixotically unable to admit that further research is futile and the research station ought to be abandoned. The novel leaves it open whether he is a great scientist in embryo, or merely an emotional simpleton tragically deluded.

While Lem is by no means the first SF writer to explore an intellectual dilemma through the form of character-biography, his concentration on the history of Solaristics and the growth of Kelvin's understanding of its problems is exemplary, and forms part of a growing tendency for SF to show scientific values as circumscribed by a broader humanism. A similar development can be found in Ursula K. Le Guin's work, although where Lem's early writings showed the imprint of orthodox scientism, Le Guin has been deeply influenced by traditional romance and heroic fantasy. Nevertheless, her cycle of future histories, which runs from heroic adventure-tales such as *Rocannon's World* (1966) to the biography of a theoretical physicist in a soberly realistic parallel world in *The Dispossessed* (1974), incorporates all the elements of the classic scientific world-view. Twentieth-century nuclear catastrophe is averted at the last minute, in *The Lathe of Heaven* (1971), by the arrival of the Hainish, the first of the alien races who will eventually join together in the Ekumen or League of All Worlds. (The universe, in fact, was populated during a prehistory of space travel in which all known worlds were seeded experimentally by the Hainish.) The institution of the Ekumen is made possible by the discovery of the ansible, or instantaneous communication device, in *The Dispossessed*. Meanwhile, further evolution is presaged by the discovery of 'mind-speech' or telepathic communication on Rocannon's World, and of the discipline of 'foretelling' on the planet Gethen in *The Left Hand of Darkness* (1969).

The Dispossessed, discussed in Raymond Williams's essay in this volume as a Utopia, takes this future history out of the domain of romance and anthropology and sets it in a context of modern ideology and politics. As the story of the physicist Shevek, discoverer of the ansible, it implies an inevitable conflict between scientific research and almost any society, no matter how egalitarian. Anarres, Le Guin's anarchist Utopia, cannot help setting constraints on the work of an individualist genius, and it is only by entering – and, in turn, escaping from – the Fascist society of Urras that he can become one of the outstanding benefactors of 'greater humanity'. The story is in several respects a political parable of East and West, and the career of Shevek (whose only needs are the means of life, a private room, a library and a desk computer) resembles today's dissident writers as much as its practising scientists.

If the scientific world-view is really in decline, science fiction may yet be split between a popular fantasy-literature weaving a mythology out of disparate, 'magical' elements of the scientific vision (a category which is, of course, as old as SF itself), and a minority of serious writers such as Lem and Le Guin struggling to expose the scientific outlook to psychological, epistemological and ideological scrutiny. Gone, in other words, would be the large body of popular writing which, in the last fifty years, has simply endorsed and propagated scientific values on the assumption that they embodied a coherent, challenging and imaginatively satisfying world-view. Such a development would probably mean the disappearance of SF as a separate genre. Yet, if there is a natural reluctance to write off SF in this way, still less is it feasible to write off the tradition of scientific thought. Science is still one of the most basic attributes of civilized humanity, however sceptical we may have become of nineteenth-century views of historical evolution and of nineteenth-century aspirations to galactic imperialism. The question of the future of some form of the scientific world-view is, very probably, the question of human survival itself. A new synthesis of scientific ideology, modified to meet men's changing perceptions and definitions of their real needs, would provide the best guarantee of a healthy and flourishing science fiction. In the future, as in the past, SF writers themselves could do much towards the emergence of such a synthesis. It may well be that this, rather than the cultivation of 'style' and literary respectability, is their most urgent task.

Notes

1. See: Paul A. Carter. *The Creation of Tomorrow*. New York: Columbia U.P., 1977, p. 11.
2. See: Carter, op. cit., pp. 250-1.

Bibliography

The most relevant works of H. G. Wells, J. B. S. Haldane and J. D. Bernal to the definition of the scientific world-view are those mentioned in the text (Section III above). A wider sample of Haldane's writings would include *The Inequality of Man and Other Essays* (London: Chatto and Windus, 1932), his essay 'Biological Possibilities for the Human Species in the Next Ten Thousand Years', in *Man and His Future*, ed. Gordon Wolstenholme, (London: J. & A. Churchill, 1963), and his lecture on 'Biological Problems of Space Flight', reported by A. E. Slater in *Journal of the British Interplanetary Society* 10 (July 1951), 154-8. In addition, Haldane, Julian Huxley and H.

G. Wells all contributed to a series of BBC talks reprinted as *Reshaping Man's Heritage: Biology in the Service of Man*, (London: Allen & Unwin, 1944).

The standard exposition of H. G. Wells's political and social ideas is W. Warren Wagar's *H. G. Wells and the World State* (New Haven: Yale U.P., 1961). The H. G. Wells Society, with its journal *The Wellsian*, continues to propagate these ideas. Haldane's life and work is the subject of a full-length biography, Ronald W. Clark's *J.B.S.* (London: Hodder and Stoughton, 1968). Julian Huxley recalls his collaboration with Wells and Haldane in *Memories I* (London: Allen & Unwin, 1970). J. D. Bernal's *The World, the Flesh and the Devil* has been reprinted (London: Jonathan Cape, 1970) with a new Foreword by the author.

Arthur C. Clarke's non-fictional writings include 'The Challenge of the Spaceship', *Journal of the British Interplanetary Society,* **4** (Dec. 1946), 66-78; *The Exploration of Space* (rev. edn, Penguin Books, 1958); *Profiles of the Future* (London: Gollancz, 1962); and *Report on Planet Three and Other Speculations* (London: Gollancz, 1972), which includes a brief essay on Haldane.

Olaf Stapledon's version of the scientific outlook is best encountered in his science fiction, especially *Last and First Men* (1930) and *Star Maker* (1937 repr. Harmondsworth and New York, Penguin, 1972, 1973). For discussions of SF and science by writers of a different generation see Brian W. Aldiss's *The Shape of Further Things* (London: Faber, 1970), and also George Hay's symposium *The Disappearing Future* (London: Panther, 1970).

C. P. Snow's essays on science and culture were collected as *The Two Cultures: and A Second Look* (Cambridge: Cambridge U.P., 1963). Snow has compared British scientism and American technocracy in 'Engineering the Future', a review in the *Times Literary Supplement* (16 Dec. 1977), p. 1465.

Gérard Klein's 'Discontent in American Science Fiction' appeared in *Science-Fiction Studies*, **4** Part 1 (Mar. 1977), 3-13.

For a consideration of SF and the new cosmology, see Stanislaw Lem's essay 'Cosmology and Science Fiction', *Science-Fiction Studies*, **4,** Part 2 (July 1977), 107-10.

The criticism of particular writers in this essay is indebted to David Pringle's essay 'The Fourfold Symbolism of J. G. Ballard', *Foundation*, No. 4 (July 1973), 48-60, and Ian Watson's 'Le Guin's *Lathe of Heaven* and the Role of of Dick', *Science-Fiction Studies* **2,** Part 1 (Mar. 1975), 67-75. Franz Rottensteiner surveys Lem's work in his essay in the present volume. There is a fuller discussion of *Solaris* and *The Dispossessed* in Patrick Parrinder, 'The Black Wave; Science and Social Consciousness in Modern Science Fiction', *Radical Science Journal* No. 5 (1977), 37-61.

Although their approach is very different from mine, the reader will find certain points of convergence between the present essay and Robert Scholes and Eric S. Rabkin's *Science Fiction: History, Science, Vision* (New York: Oxford U.P., 1977), especially their sections on C. S. Lewis and on 'The Sciences of Science Fiction'. Paul A. Carter's *The Creation of Tomorrow* (New York: Columbia U.P., 1977), is a valuable guide to the treatment of a number of scientific themes in magazine SF.

Part III

Science fiction today: aspects of a contemporary literature

The cold war in science fiction, 1940-1960

T. A. Shippey

The literary critic, sociologist, or other outsider venturing to cast his eye over science fiction is likely to be struck almost immediately by two facts. One is the intensely participatory nature of the readership's inner core, something which reveals itself in passionate correspondence in the magazines, in a high proportion of amateur writing, and in the ritual of massive and enthusiastic conventions. The other is that all science fiction incontestably contains some datum known not to be true to the-world-as-it-is. The easiest conclusion to jump to is that the two facts are related: the charge that 'fans' get from science fiction is one of irresponsibility, freedom from restrictions. 'The trouble with these here neurotics is that they all the time got to fight reality. Show in the next twitch', to quote the psychologist from C. M. Kornbluth's 'The Marching Morons' (*Galaxy*, 1951). This is an irritating thesis, and one which does no justice to the often intense self-scrutiny of many science-fiction writers and readers. Nevertheless, it does pay *some* attention to observable facts; and this cannot be said of a style of criticism common enough, and easily forgivable, among the fans themselves, but too often reflected back at them by fan-spokesmen venturing into criticism, and by professional critics who should know better.

It is the distinguishing mark of this second critical style to confuse chronology with history and personalities with explanations. Thus, it is certainly true that the first commercial magazine designed to publish nothing but science fiction was *Amazing Stories*, edited from April 1926 till early 1929 by Hugo Gernsback. Gernsback, then, in many accounts becomes the 'father (or founder) of modern science fiction'. All histories of the genre contain some reference to him; the 'Hugo Awards' for the year's best novel, short story, magazine, etc. are called after him; comment on him approaches the hagiographical. Yet in one sense Gernsbackian priority was an accident. He himself might easily have started a science-fiction magazine earlier than 1926, and it is inconceivable that someone else would not have spotted the market opportunities at most a few years later. To see science fiction as led by Hugo Gernsback is therefore a theory of complete naïvety. One might say the same even of John W. Campbell Jr, the editor of *Astounding Science Fiction* from 1938 to 1971, and a much more familiar and dominant personality, whose stimulation many authors even now remember and acknowledge. Surely if anyone 'shaped' modern science fiction, it was him! Yet, though it is an unanswerable question, one might consider for a moment what would have happened if he had opted for a different career. Many novels and stories would no doubt have come out different. Still, they would have come out. In the face of the millions of words published by scores of magazines and thousands of authors between 1926 and now, one is forced to conclude that even individuals at the centre of the field cannot have exerted more than a certain gravitational influence. Listing dates, titles, anecdotes, and conversations is, in short, an established mode of 'fanzine' chatter. But the real question is not who led science fiction on, but what force generated so many willing followers? Allied to that is the question of whether the compulsive element in science fiction is at all reducible by the conventions of ordinary literary criticism. These are the questions which the essay that follows tries to answer.

I have to admit immediately that, in my opinion, rather detailed demonstration is needed to make any answer convincing. For this reason I have confined myself here to one theme alone, a large and a typical theme, but one which has no direct connection with Asimov's *Foundation* or Bester's *Demolished Man* or Blish's *A Case of Conscience*, or any of a hundred other 'classic' stories even from the period with which I am centrally concerned. Furthermore, that period is a relatively short one, in essence the mid-1950s, though with reference as much as a dozen years either way. The reason for *that* is that I think the questions posed above are probably unanswerable without a certain 'life experience', a memory at least of personal involvement. Magazine science fiction was, from the 1930s to the 1960s (when market forces began to destroy it), almost a collective mode, and one structured, like Dickens's novels, by the expectation of monthly appearances. Authors at any time knew what had been published in the last issue of *Galaxy* or *Astounding* or *Fantastic*; they might indeed be writing in reply to it. Readers simultaneously appreciated cross-references, argument, parody, in an almost subliminal way. This sense is hard to recover from the stacks of libraries. I try to regain it from the time when I read magazines by the month, and collected 'back issues' with a feeling of being in touch with a dialogue that had not yet stopped: i.e. roughly, 1952-60. This was not, according to many, the real 'Golden Age' of science fiction (which was the 1940s, or the 1930s or whenever the commentator's youth happens to have been). It was, however, a period when all the major authors *of* that 'Golden Age' were established, mature, writing at what ought to have been the height of their powers. It was also a time when science fiction, for reasons I discuss, was getting over the nervous defensiveness and 'news-stand orientation' of the early years. Finally, it was a time when science fiction actually had some political and ideological influence. '*We* put the man on the moon', yelled convention posters in 1969. They were wrong; nevertheless many in NASA had read *Astounding* for formative years. With that reflection it is possible to return to the point made at the start: that all science fiction contains some element known not to be true to the-world-as-it-is. An initial insight can be derived by noting that one cannot always be sure which element that is.

Consider, for instance, the first four statements from 'Solution Unsatisfactory', a story by 'Anson MacDonald' (really Robert A. Heinlein) published in *Astounding Science Fiction* in May 1941.

In 1903 the Wright brothers flew at Kitty Hawk.
In December, 1938, in Berlin, Dr Hahn split the uranium atom.
In April, 1943, Dr Estelle Karst, working under the Federal Emergency Defense Authority, perfected the Karst—Obre technique for producing artificial radioactives.
So American foreign policy had to change.

The first two statements are, of course, science fact; everybody knows about the Wrights, and everybody ought to know about Dr Hahn. The third is science fiction; it is the major technological datum of the story. What is the status of the fourth? In context it, too, is science fiction, the story's major *non*-technological datum. With hindsight, though, it becomes hard to take it quite so simply.

For what happens in Heinlein's story is this: Dr Karst accidentally develops, in a still-neutral USA of 1943, a radioactive dust of unprecedented deadliness. The American government supplies this to Britain to use on Hitler's Berlin; and is then faced with an appalling and unforeseen problem. For the secret of the dust is not beyond rediscovery, the example of using it has been given, and there is an immediate prospect of many nations using it on each other out of fear or revenge. The 'unsatisfactory solution' of the title is to ground all aircraft, so that there are no delivery systems, and then institute a multinational 'Peace Patrol' of dust-carrying bombers to make sure no one evades the embargo. But who is to guard the guardians? The story ends with deliberate uncertainty, feelings of guilt and defeat: Dr Karst inhales her own dust, the 'I'-narrator mentions that he is dying of cumulative radiation poisoning acquired during his delivery of the stuff to the Royal Air Force.

Now, much of this story is irrevocably dated. It has no Pearl Harbor, no Hiroshima, no atomic bomb, while the first sneak-attack of its new era comes from the 'Eurasian Union' (a euphemism for the USSR). On the other hand, its non-technological prophecies are almost uncanny: a nuclear weapon, used by the Allies, ending one war, and starting something else – a state of threatened peace whose major premises are a deadly secret, a short-lived technological lead, and the temptation to use both in a manner totally inhumane, but nevertheless in a sense comprehensible, born of the fear that someone else will do the same thing first. This is, in short, the 'Cold War', predictable and predicted in 1941. However, to return to the last sentence of the passage quoted above, the point is not that for once a science-fiction author guessed right, nor that he foresaw more than the existence of a new technology. It is that even in 1941, when no one could be in doubt as to which statements were factual and which fictional, Heinlein was trying hard and deliberately to make, through fiction, a true statement about the nature of his own society: that *if* technology changed, its foreign policy *would* change, would have to change, and its morality and constitution and everything else with it. The power of his story is indeed a factor of two separate things: the provocative nature of the future he shows, and the force with which its premises are made to seem irrefutable – 'unpredictability' and 'plausibility', one might say, multiplied together.

An underlying (and highly provocative) belief is that history and politics are by-products of scientific research. The A-bomb, of course, appeared to prove this. Diplomacy became 'atomic' (or so one thesis put it), and Western society for a while seemed traumatized – not so much, one thinks, from the sheer destructiveness of the new weapon nor from moral doubts about its employment, as from its unpredictable quality, the way it was (unlike aeroplanes, rockets, or radar) related to no previously familiar principle. 'If one shock like that can come out of the laboratories', many people must have thought, 'how can you tell what's left inside?' The nervousness produced was expressed by many American politicians, writers, military correspondents. Science-fiction authors, however, remained largely immune. For one thing they liked weighing speculative possibilities, for another they could feel that the world was at last conforming to their notions of how things ought to be, with the scientist firmly established at the top of the totem pole and politics calculable in terms of research and development. Besides, many years of painful scorn for the fantastic element in science fiction ('Horsemarines, Dan Dare, and bloody Martians', to quote a character from John Wyndham's *The Kraken Wakes*, 1953) were being most satisfactorily repaid. For a while aficionados liked to recall the incident of the visit of Military Intelligence to the offices of *Astounding* in 1944, prompted by Cleve Cartmill's otherwise undistinguished U-235 story 'Deadline' (*ASF*, Mar. 1944).[1] That *showed* science fiction had to be taken seriously! If only the rest of America had realized in time!

And yet the genre contained its own drive towards making statements about society-as-it-is, which prevented too long a rest on Cartmill and Heinlein's laurels. It prevented also the sort of simple 'extrapolation' of present into future which was in practical terms exemplified by the 'arms race' – A-bomb, H-bomb, cobalt bomb, strategic bomber, submarine missile, ICBM, and so on. Stories about these might work, but they would lose in 'predictability' what they gained in 'plausibility'. Something more had to be done. So, while it was no doubt a great achievement to predict the Cold War from 1941, a much more broadly based reaction was to express itself in stories written from within the Cold War itself, after 1945. Society as a whole was adjusting gingerly to the possibility of nuclear extinction, and developing the sort of controls only hinted at in 'Solution Unsatisfactory'. But once again science fiction was groping for the second-order phenomena beyond the immediate horizon of reality: How would people react to these controls? Could anyone afford to *let* scientists remain at the top of the totem pole? Was there a way out of deterrents? These and other questions litter the science-fiction magazines from the very start of the 1950s. In them reality and fantasy intertwine; without that intertwining science fiction would have lost half its fascination.

The elementary strategy of extrapolation was, of course, tried, and not without success. The United States might find itself in an atomic war: Judith Merril's *Shadow on the Hearth* (1951) combined incongruity with probability by relating the event to an American commuter suburb full of housewives. 'But the war's *over*', says the heroine at the end, as she finally realizes that her little girl's illness comes from her deadly cuddly toy, left out overnight in the radioactive rain. The new phenomenon of 'half-life' is integrated with the new indivisibility of war and peace. Of course the United States could engage in such a war and *lose* (or just not win): this prospect was explored best by Wilson Tucker's *The Long Loud Silence* (1952). Least thinkable of all, the United States, for all its 'minuteman' traditions, could in the new conditions of mass destruction be forced to surrender and face occupation: this was outlined in C. M. Kornbluth's *Not This August* (1955, retitled *Christmas Eve* in the UK). But Kornbluth's novel incidentally demonstrated why all these varieties of 'hot war' might be missing something out. For one of his accepted data – of course Hiroshima-derived – is that if one side gains a sufficient technological lead (e.g. by launching an A-bomb-armed satellite) the other side's fleets and bombs and armoured divisions are all immediately reduced to a value zero. This realization leads to a further point: if technological lead is so important, the drama lies in achieving it, not exploiting it. Wars are now information wars, they are fought in filing cabinets. Or, to quote a character from Eric Frank Russell's *With a Strange Device* (1964), 'In this highly technological age, the deadliest strike one can make against a foe is to deprive him of his brains, whether or not one acquires them oneself.'

By an interesting semantic shift, 'brains' in that quotation has become a count-noun, its singular being 'a brain', and meaning 'a scientist capable of furthering weapons research'. The last clause of the quotation further indicates a long-standing popular phobia, especially in America (though Russell is British); for one could hardly fail to notice either the part played in the development of nuclear fission by German emigrés (Einstein, Frisch, and in rocketry von Braun), or the belief of many that the Russian A-bomb of 1949 came from the same source, with a fillip from Western traitors (such as Fuchs, Nunn May, Greenglass). 'Brains', then, were valuable but treacherous. Russell actually does not develop these notions in this book; the 'strange device' of its title is simply a gimmick, a means of 'automated brainwashing' which makes scientists think they have committed murder and must flee from their jobs, the police, their friends in Military Intelligence. Still, the clashes between state and individual, security agent and scientist, are there in potential in a single sentence. If one combined them will the all-politics-is-science belief and the technological-leads-are-total theory, one had a basic plot of intense importance and even human interest. All of it, furthermore, could be felt, like Heinlein's 'foreign policy' statement and Russell's sentence just quoted, to be fictional but also in essence *true*. These hints and implications were best exploited by Algis Budrys's famous novel *Who?* (1958, expanded from a short story in *Fantastic Universe,* Apr. 1955).

Its central character is Lucas Martino, a scientist working on something called 'the K-88' – Budrys's firm rejection of the 'gimmick' strategy is shown by the fact that we never find out what this might be. It is enough to know that (like anything else from the laboratories) it might turn out to be the one vital thing, the thing that decides all human futures. But Martino's lab in West Germany near the border – this was before the Berlin Wall – blows up, and a Soviet medical team obligingly whisks him off to hospital. What they return is unrecognizable, a man half-metal. Is it Martino, or a Soviet agent trained to impersonate him? If the latter, then Martino is the other side of the wire, and the K-88 may turn out Soviet. One of these days, muses the American Security Chief at the start, his opposite number is going to outwit him critically, 'and everybody's kids'll talk Chinese'. One 'brain' (in this scenario) can outweigh the efforts of the rest of the world. But ever since Korea it had been accepted that everybody cracked, that 'brainwashing' was as certain as a surgical operation – see the *Oxford English Dictionary* entry under 'brainwash' in the *Supplement* of 1972, and further Frederik Pohl and C. M. Kornbluth's story 'The Quaker Cannon' from *ASF* (Dec. 1961 (B.)). Finding out who the metal man is thus becomes very much a fulcrum of destiny. But of course he himself does not see things this way. While *Who?* is in one way a story about technological leads, it is also about the discrepancy between subjective and objective knowledge, about the incapacity of states and security systems to control, predict, or even understand the intelligences on whom their existence depends.

So the FBI dog Martino's every step, try furthermore to find out every detail from his past, to check the one set of actions against the other and determine the presence or absence of a consistent pattern. Their massive filing-cabinet thoroughness is almost a parody of the way scientists are supposed to work, inductively, accumulating facts and waiting for the right truth to emerge. But of course induction by itself never pays off. Though Martino is inductive – he 'couldn't ignore a fact. He judged no fact; he only filed it away' – he also works largely by hypothesis, a habit which often leads him directly to the right conclusion via the traditional 'flash of genius', but which also leads him, in youth, to scores of blind alleys and false structures. These are never discarded entirely: 'Another part of his mind was a storehouse of interesting ideas that hadn't worked, but were interesting – theories that were wild, but had seemed to hold together. To a certain extent, these phantom heresies stayed behind to colour his thinking.' They mean that when it comes to the K-88, he cannot be replaced. They also mean that, in personal terms, the actions of Martino before or after his accident may be perfectly logical to him (and to the reader who shares his mind); to the watchers and investigators, though, they are random, inexplicable.

This thesis keeps *Who?* from dating, even though many of its assumptions have been overtaken by events. It also shifts the story in the direction of fable or parable, stressing the element of general truth contained in the setting of particular fantasy. The central scene of the book is the one in which the metal Martino returns to visit one of the two girl-acquaintances of his youth, Edith, now a widow with one son. All through his adolescence the peculiar logic of his mind has made it hard for him to form ordinary relationships. Now his half-metal body reflects and magnifies his inner strangeness. Can he get back to one of the few people he ever understood? The FBI men on their microphones wait with baited breath. But the answer never comes, for though Martino and Edith seem for a moment to recognize and understand each other, her little son, waking up, sees only a nightmare monster. Pursued by his screaming, Martino leaves, collides with a girl, sees in her (momentarily and erroneously) his *other* girl-acquaintance, tries to introduce himself – and terrifies her, too, into panic. Driven by his mechanical heart, he rushes away down the street, the FBI trailing behind him in an ineffectual and (for one of them) fatal attempt to keep up. Their exhaustive enquiries afterwards never reveal what happened, nor (since naturally they cannot see the girl's resemblance to the now-forgotten Barbara) what triggered Martino's reaction. His phrase of self-introduction – *'Barbara — e io — il tedeschino'* – becomes a personal analogue of the K-88, forever beyond explanation except in Martino's mind.

The interpretation of this 'Frankenstein's monster' scene is evident enough. Martino is an image of the scientist post-1945. Both are figures of enormous and world-changing power; yet both remain mortal, isolated, vulnerable. Both would like to be loved, and yet both terrify people through no fault of their own; they are bitterly hurt by ordinary reactions. Martino's clumsily powerful rush down the street, one might think, is a kind of image of the 'arms race' itself. Meanwhile the security men who watch with increasing bafflement and impotence, who are always trying to catch up and never to head off (because they never know where Martino is going), *they* represent the attempts of average men and normal politics to come to terms with the technology they have sponsored, though not created. Naturally, putting it all in these allegorical terms seems over-complicated and may not have been 'designed in' by the author. Still, it is in general there, in essence

understood. Budrys rubs several of the points in by a sequence of
ironies at the end of the book.

For the metal man *is* Martino. He ought, then, on the 'brainwashing'
hypothesis, to have cracked during the period he was in Soviet hands.
He did not simply because so much of him was then non-organic.
However, the Soviet security chief did indeed have a scheme to replace
him with another manufactured double from Martino's past, his old
roommate from MIT. This would give him time to complete the
cracking, to steal the K-88. The plot failed because it depended on a
'sleeper', an American turned traitor by his own emotional vulnerability. But people like that are *ipso facto* weak, unreliable. The
'sleeper' reneges, the double drowns, the plot fails. Martino is returned
in what ought to be a moment of Western triumph. 'A man is more
than just a collection of features', he thinks, as he approaches safety in
the last, 'flashback' scene, 'I haven't lost anything.' He is of course
completely wrong. Where Soviet security inadequacies stop, American ones take over. Endemic suspicion and the inability to clear him
totally mean that Martino never works again. Genius is crushed, pure
science castrated by fear, incompetence, inductive thinking. The moral
of *Who?* is that in scientific matters security systems are counter-
productive (as useless as the descent of Military Intelligence on
Astounding back in 1944). Admittedly, the fear that generates them is
entirely explicable too, so there may be no cure. Still, the G-man and
the genius are now yin and yang, growing out of each other but
fundamentally opposed. In a sense the most daring theme to which
science-fiction authors were attracted during the 1950s was that of
inner treason: the obligation to resist at once the Federal government
and constitutional processes.

For there had been more than one 'Cold War' going on within the
United States. The true date of hell's birthday – according to a character in Wilson Tucker's *The Time Masters* (1953, also published in
abridged form in *Startling Stories*, 1954) – was neither 6 August 1945
(Hiroshima) nor 16 July 1945 (Alamogordo), but 8 March 1940. On
or about that date 'the President set up the National Defense Research
Committee; both the Manhattan District and our organization grew
out of that'. What 'our organization' is never appears clearly, but
Tucker is thinking of such events as the creation of the CIA in July
1947, the Bill for FBI investigation of Atomic Energy Commission
applicants in August 1949, the ban on sending technical publications
to the Soviet bloc in March the same year, and a series of other moves
in the direction of tight control over atomic power. All this was highly
illiberal. But the complaint voiced by Tucker and other science-fiction
writers was that it was unrealistic, too. They knew that whatever its
etymology 'science' was not the same as 'knowledge'; the 'Deadline'
affair had shown there was no need of a security leak to tell people
about U-235 and critical mass. So you could not keep 'secrets' this side

of the Iron Curtain just by restricting the passage of information. To quote Tucker again: 'There are only two kinds of men in all the world who still believe there are keepable secrets in modern science! One of those men is the blind, awkward and fumbling politician. . . . The other man is a jealous researcher. . . . Realistic secrecy in modern science is a farce.' The new exemplar of the clown, one might add, is the security agent trying to censor references to data which can be revealed by experiment.

There is no doubt here that science fiction was correct, nor that it was opposing a powerful orthodoxy. J. Robert Oppenheimer ('the father of the atomic bomb') had said 'you cannot keep the nature of the world a secret', and Eisenhower in 1945 had agreed with him, suggesting that the USA should make a virtue of necessity and share nuclear information, so aborting the arms race. But both were readily out-voted. By November 1945 the US had decided not to share nuclear technology with Britain and Canada, who had helped to develop it. Because it was thought that this decision settled matters many politicians were horrified by the Russian nuclear explosion of 1949. An easy explanation was treason. Loyalty investigations got fiercer, and the Rosenbergs were sentenced to death in March 1951. Meanwhile the real secret of the hydrogen bomb had been revealed on television by a US senator trying to educate the nation in security![2] By a final irony Oppenheimer himself (who appeared in 'Murray Leinster's' *The Brain Stealers* (1947) as the head of a security system dedicated to keeping nuclear technology safe) had been tried and convicted in a case seen by many as a trial of the United States. The phobia over nuclear security was there before Senator McCarthy, and went straight back to the unpredictability-trauma of 1945. Its development showed once more the split between those who felt science was still a human endeavour and those who saw it as a djinn to be stuffed back in the bottle. As McCarthyism advanced, science fiction became increasingly angry and sarcastic.

One can, for instance, turn over the pages of *Astounding* during the worst of the arms-race years and see one story after another about security: 'Security Risk', by Poul Anderson (May 1957 (B.)), 'Security', by Ernest M. Kenyon (Mar. 1956 (B.)), 'A Matter of Security', by W. T. Haggert (July, 1957 (B.)). Others present the theme under less obvious titles. In Poul Anderson's 'Sam Hall' (Aug. 1953), the Major in charge of Central Records in a near-future state broods over the 'Europeanization of America: government control, a military caste . . . censors, secret police, nationalism and racism'. All this has been created by a Third World War the US lost, with a consequent *revanche* in the Fourth World War leading to world domination. The Major himself has a relation arrested by Security. To protect himself he rubs him out of the records, then creates a fictitious rebel 'Sam Hall' as a kind of therapy. The fiction comes to life (not in any supernatural sense) and cannot be caught because Security itself breeds rebels and traitors – as it has done with the Major. The point of the story is again the self-fulfilment of fear. Analogous or complementary points are made by the other stories listed. They insist that the United States has no moral or natural right to its technological leads, and that attempts to impose the contrary opinion will lead only to stagnation and totalitarianism. Security systems are the delusions of people who had not understood the nature of scientific discovery before 1945, and had learnt nothing since. Science is a tool, not a (dammable) reservoir of knowledge.

Following on this, or overlapping with it, came a further point about the nature of discovery: if science is not the same as knowledge, it is also not to be identified with truth. To put it another way, science does not progress additively any more than discovery works by induction. To advance, one has to discard. The true obstacle to development may then be that what needs discarding is deeply integrated in personalities and academic systems, too familiar to be challenged. In this view, the intellectual equivalents to security chiefs may well be senior researchers – both groups are committed to the *status quo* which has brought them eminence. A basic plot along these lines is given in Raymond F. Jones's novelette 'Noise Level' (*ASF*, Dec. 1952).

This begins, conventionally enough, with Dr Nagle, the expert in electronics, sitting in the anteroom of the Office of National Research while his colleagues try to get him security clearance to attend the vital conference to which he has been summoned. The first few paragraphs make clear Jones's lack of faith in the FBI and the 'bureaucrats' who think they can 'button up the secrets of nature which lay visible to the whole world'. But the concept of 'visibility' (or 'audibility') gets more thoughtful treatment in the rest of the story. For this conference has been called by the Office of National Research to inform senior physicists that antigravity has been discovered and demonstrated; there are films, tapes, and eye-witness accounts to prove it. Unfortunately, an accident has killed the inventor and mangled his apparatus before the secret could be disclosed. The physicists' job is to make the rediscovery. But there is a distracting factor: the original inventor was close to madness, with a compulsive belief in levitation, mysticism, astrology, etc. and a reluctance to accept convention of any kind. Clues to his invention may lie in one of the 'mad' areas rather than one of the 'sane' ones.

'This was a project in psychology, not physics', observes its controller at the end. His physicists have in fact polarized. One faction, represented by Nagle, has accepted the real-life data offered and concluded that, since antigravity is ruled out by the state of scientific knowledge, something in that knowledge must be wrong: they identify Einstein's 'postulate of equivalence' as the root error, and by rewriting it manage to produce a feeble, clumsy, hundred-ton antigravity device (their films had shown a one-man flying harness). At the other extreme Dr Dykstra of MIT insists that the whole thing – and especially the stuff about levitation! – cannot be true, eventually retreating into madness himself when his premises become untenable. The irony is that Dr Dykstra is in a practical sense right. The whole thing *has* been a fraud, concocted by the Office of National Research, its mainspring being the notion that invention is checked not by ignorance but by prior assumptions. To give the analogy of the psychologist-director: (1) all information can be expressed in a series of pulses, and is therefore contained in 'pure noise'; (2) 'there must be in the human mind a mechanism which is nothing but a pure noise generator, a producer of random impulses, pure omniscient noise'; (3) and somewhere else in the human mind there is a filtering mechanism set by education to reject 'all but a bare minimum of data presented by the external universe, and [by] our internal creativeness as well'. Nagle has managed to override the filter; Dykstra has had in the end to shut out all the noise.

This story evades some vital issues (such as the propriety of driving professors mad so the US can have antigravity), and its sequels 'The School' (*ASF*, May 1955 (B.)) and 'The Great Grey Plague' (*ASF*, June 1962 (B.)) are not inspiring. One might note, though, that just as Algis Budrys in some ways paralleled the ideas of Karl Popper, so 'Noise Level' anticipated the central thesis of Thomas Kuhn's later much-admired book *The Structure of Scientific Revolutions* (1962), offering a proto-structuralist view of science as an activity in practice culture-bound, though in potential (science fiction's fundamental loyalty) infinite. In one form or another, discrepancy between this potential and this practice became a staple of science-fiction plotting: the characters embodying one side tended to be government officials, senior professors, security agents, and politicians, those on the other crackpots, engineers, social misfits, and businessmen – anyone, in short, more interested in results than explanations. The theme is a good one; it relates to reality as well as to wish-fulfilment; perhaps the main criticism one can make of it is that, in the 'participatory' world of science-fiction magazines, it leads easily to a kind of paranoia, in which the underlying statements about the world and those who run it turn sour and strident. One can see the dangers in two series of stories by Mark Clifton (some all his own work, others, rather bewilderingly, in collaboration with either Alex Apostolides or else Frank Riley).

The more attractive of these is the sequence about the problems at 'Computer Research Inc.', in which the hero is not a scientist at all, but a personnel manager – another embodiment of the good or pragmatic paradigm. Much to his horror, he finds himself (in 'What Thin Partitions', *ASF*, Sept. 1953) controlling an antigravity device – a bagful of curious cylinders. But he needs a poltergeist to activate any more, and he has done his job too well in curing the one he began with. At the end of the story he sends the US Army (who are interested in antigravity) a requisition in proper form for six more poltergeists, assuming that will be the end of it. Unfortunately, at the start of 'Sense from Thought Divide' (*ASF*, Mar. 1955) the Army's Division of Matériel and Supply proves equal to the task – it delivers a swami, a fake, they admit, but nevertheless one who can sometimes do more than is theoretically possible. Production problems begin once again. The basic principles of this series, note, are exactly those of 'Noise Level': orthodoxy has built-in limits; frauds may contain an element of truth; real advance comes from amateur initiative plus professional finish. But the whole argument is handled with grace and humour. In an *Astounding* serial, however, *They'd Rather Be Right* (Aug.–Nov. 1954), Clifton and Riley put a similar thesis much more aggressively. The novel's plot need not be summarized, but in its central scenes an organic computer offers human beings health, beauty, rejuvenation – in exchange for their abandonment of 'single-valued logic', all belief-structures of any kind. Very few, in the authors' opinion, could pay such a price; the unexpressed concluding words of the title are '. . . than go on living'. This might be acceptable, even true, if not for the ominous word 'they'. Readers of *Astounding* were evidently encouraged to see themselves as the leaven and the rest of America as the lump – something they appear to have enjoyed, since the 13th World Science Fiction Convention of 1955 voted the book the 'Hugo' award as best science-fiction novel of the previous year. The 'ghettoizing' of science fiction was not entirely imposed from without. If general readers, even after the A-bomb, kept on thinking of science-fiction fans as 'escapist' or 'unrealistic', many writers and readers inside the genre responded equally thoughtlessly by regarding the bulk of their own society as mistaken, ill-informed, and probably ineducable. They had a point, in the 1950s. But they took it too far.

A better-judged example of the same reaction can be seen in James Blish's in retrospect highly courageous book *Year 2018!* (British title *They Shall Have Stars*, published first in 1956, in Britain, but going back in outline to two more *Astounding* novelettes, 'Bridge' (Feb. 1952) and 'At Death's End' (May 1954)). The audacity of this is shown by the fact that even the earlier version contained a perfectly recognizable caricature of Senator McCarthy in the guise of 'Senator Francis Xavier MacHinery, hereditary head of the FBI.'[3] The expanded version began, furthermore, with two Americans deliberately plotting treason: one, Senator Wagoner, the other, Dr Corsi, senior member of the American Association for the Advancement of Science, 'usually referred to in Washington', remarks Blish in evident allusion to the Oppenheimer affair, 'as "the left-wing triple-A-S" '. The speakers' discussion dovetails neatly into a joint politico-scientific opinion: the USSR has *won* the Cold War (this is Wagoner, by the end of the book), and it has done so because 'scientific method doesn't work any more' (Corsi, at the start). As another quasi-true statement this aphorism is particularly provocative: scientific *method* is supposed to work everywhere. But it's not a natural law, argues Blish/Corsi, only 'a way of sifting evidence', a new kind of syllogism. The reasons it need not work in the twenty-first century are, first the control of technical information, and second the low quality of those drawn to government research (familiar notions in science fiction, as has been said), but third, the nature of the facts eventually under investigation – increasingly subtle ones, to be proved only by experiments of increasingly fantastic cost. This view (not entirely without prophetic force, as one can see from the NASA experience) means that Manhattan District Projects will have to stop. It is the crackpot ideas that must be winnowed now, the rejected hypotheses, the notions that are not senseless but out of style. The rebellions that Wagoner and Corsi lead are against scientific method and the 'McCarthyite' US. Behind them lie deeper loyalties to empiricism and to Western tradition, labelled though these may be (in 2018 or 1957) as treason and folly.

The projects set up finally eventuate as the 'gravitron polarity generator' or 'spindizzy' and the 'anti-agathic drugs' which halt old age; the two between them make interstellar flight a possibility. They also lead to disaster within the world of the novel. The impact of anti-agathics will destroy the West, and the Soviets only marginally later. The fact that such initiatives have been concealed will give power to MacHinery and his associates, whose suspicions (like Dr Dykstra's) will for once turn out to be true. Both originators of the new initiative will die by torture, Dr Corsi without knowing what he has brought to life, and Wagoner by the standard treason-penalty of immersion in the waste-dump of a radioactive pile. 'It's a phony terror', says Wagoner. 'Pile wastes are quick chemical poisons; you don't last long enough to notice that they're also hot.' Still, the macabre vindictiveness of the notion offers a final opinion on the 'decline of the West' that Blish foresees, on the long-term effects of victory at Hiroshima, on the way the Cold War could be fought and lost. It took courage to offer such a picture of America in the mid-1950s, when the Korean War was over, the Vietnamese one not yet on, and when the Strategic Air Command still held more than the balance of power. Even more daring, though, was the rejection of 'scientific method' and official physics so soon after their most apparent triumph. Science-fiction authors have often been accused of letting themselves be mesmerized by mere technology. *Year 2018!*, however, shows one of them shaking off the glamour of nuclear power and the Manhattan Project while the rest of America was still trying to adjust to it. The rejection is as creditable, as implausible, as Heinlein's equally unnoticed predictions only a decade and a half before.

All the stories discussed so far have their root in a critique of the relationship between science and society. The latter either cannot control the former (as in 'Solution Unsatisfactory'), or else breaks it in the attempt at control (as in *Who?*), or else provokes it into rebellion (as in *Year 2018!*). Failure of comprehension is embodied in the two emasculating theses of science as a body of information (some of it 'classified'), and of science as revealed truth to be dispensed through the educational system by the proper authorities. And yet in spite of all these antagonisms science was much more deeply integrated with society than the latter liked to admit. In science fiction this last notion is expressed by the aphorism 'steam-engine time'. 'When a culture has reached the point when it's time for the steam-engine to be invented', lectures a character from Raymond F. Jones's 'The School' (*ASF*, May 1955 (B.)), 'the steam-engine is going to be invented. It doesn't matter who's alive to do the inventing, whether it's Hero of Greece, or Tim Watt of England, or Joe Doakus of Pulaski – the steam-engine is going to get invented by somebody. Conversely, if it's not steam-engine time nobody under the sun is going to invent it no matter how smart he is.'

This opinion contradicts a popular stereotype of the Great Inventor, promoted in the movies about Young Tom Edison which attract Budrys's scorn, and in the 'rituals of mass entertainment' pilloried in one of the epigraphs to *Year 2018!* – the 'hero-scientist . . . discovered in a lonely laboratory crying "Eureka" at a murky test-tube'. But the *raison d'être* of that stereotype is that it makes it easy to fix responsibility on single men or single events. 'It is steamboat time', says someone at the end of Harry Harrison's *In Our Hands, the Stars* (*ASF* serial, Dec. 1969-Feb. 1970); but he says it sadly, because the deadly and plausible image of science as one man's secret has led the security agents of many nations (the US and Israel prominent among them) to join in a multiple fatal hijacking of the new spaceliner built by Denmark and employing the 'Daleth Effect'. The irony is that the secret was no secret all along. The discoverer's data were freely available. Once other scientists had the clues of knowing what had been done and who had done it, they could duplicate his work and even make his 'Effect' commercial; they were about to do the latter just as the hijack started. 'Steamboat time' means that the deaths were all pointless. And this is not just a fantasy, Harrison insists (via his character). The Japanese independently re-invented radar, magnetron and all, in this way during the Second World War; and as Wilson Tucker had said much earlier, Russian production of the A-bomb followed exactly the same pattern. 'Stimulus diffusion' is a fact of the modern world, not merely an anthropologists' curiosity. But people prefer to think of science as a kind of magic controllable only by individual adepts, because it gives them idols/scapegoats – Einstein, or Oppenheimer.

So what *is* the mutual responsibility of the individual innovator and the society that makes his innovation possible? Several approaches to this question are visible in 1950s science fiction. One could consider *Astounding*'s long and quarrelsome discussion, in stories, articles, and letters, of patent law – something felt to symbolize and encapsulate America's ambiguous relationship with the inventor. On a much broader scale one might reflect that the many social satires or 'dystopias' published during the period tend to share one opinion, which is that the self-images of society are so powerful and so delusive that they channel rebellion just as much as they channel innovation. The heroes of Frederik Pohl and C. M. Kornbluth's *The Space Merchants* (1953, originally serialized in *Galaxy* as 'Gravy Planet', 1952) and of Kurt Vonnegut's *Player Piano* (1952) both start as agents of the system, and have to be virtually excommunicated from it before they can think of going into opposition. Deep in the core of the former book's assumptions, too, is the argument that just as the 'Consies' or Conservationists are necessary scapegoats of the consumer society, so the 'Commies', or forever-rumoured, forever-invisible American Communist traitors of the McCarthy era, are figments of the capitalist imagination, part of a drama which American society has written for itself, and into whose villain-roles weak characters are drawn or thrust. However, full consideration of that issue would lead us away from weapon-makers and towards weapon-users. It is a point that the two are related: the A-bomb was publicly accountable, even if secretly produced. But *next* time that something like the A-bomb came up, where would a future Einstein's duty lie? It is this narrower question which underlies the Harry Harrison novel just mentioned; and also, more surprisingly, many of the 'telepathy' stories published during this period in *Astounding* and elsewhere.

Signs of it can be seen even in such an apparently low-level story as Eric Frank Russell's *Three to Conquer* (1956, serialized in *ASF* as *Call Him Dead*, Aug.–Oct. 1955). This opens with a man, a telepath, 'hearing' in his mind the dying call of a shot policeman. He goes to help, tracks down evidence of what seems to be an interrupted kidnapping, and then, when he comes on the 'kidnapped' girl, shoots her dead. Her mind was projecting alien gabble; her body had been taken over by a parasite-organism from space. The rest of the story is devoted, very naturally, to fighting off the invasion. Yet it is, queerly, almost comic in tone, marked by the habitual irreverence of its hero, Wade Harper. He never obeys orders, always answers back, takes deliberate pleasure in waving at generals when he should salute them. Childish behaviour, especially for a telepath? The story itself insists that it is not. During the first few pages, for instance, we keep hearing, over the radio, of the apparently unrelated battle going on between the US government and the 'Lunar Development Company'. 'According to the latter the government was trying to use its Earth–Moon transport monopoly to bludgeon the L.D.C. into handing itself over complete with fat profits. The L.D.C. was fighting back. It was the decades-old struggle of private enterprise against bureaucratic interference.' One might note, again, the characteristic switch from definite fiction to hypothetical fact. What has this to do with Harper? Nothing immediate: but he sees himself analogously as a man under threat, one who will (from his job as a microforger) become 'federal property the moment war breaks out'; and will become it even sooner if they know he can read minds! The Venusian emergency makes him declare himself, but nothing less would have. And his continuous irreverence is a form of protest against government infringements of liberty.

There is something slightly crazy about this, even (much worse in science-fiction criminology) contra-survival. After all it is sheer chance that the one telepath in the US crosses the invaders' trail right at the outset. The odds were against it, they were even more against Harper as private citizen being able to undo the effects of (say) Soviet tele-pathic espionage managed by their more autocratic government. Surely Harper should know his public duty, indeed his duty to science. But Russell suppresses this obvious line of argument in favour of appeal to anti-government sentiment, and – traditional *Astounding* train of thought – to a continuing equation of government with social repression, conservatism, scientific orthodoxy. Harper's conversations with scientists are punctuated by their cries of 'Impossible!' 'Unthink-able!', while the FBI repeatedly let him down through their rigid obedi-ence to orders. Both groups, though, are only manifesting an attitude which Harper (and Russell) see as essentially human – fear of the unknown, a wish to shut it out or deny its existence rather than make it a part of one's world. 'At the ripe age of nine', we are told, Harper 'had learned that knowledge can be resented, that the means of acquiring it can be feared.' So he is secretive as well as irreverent. At the end of the story it is presented as a triumph that he has contacted and married a female telepath without letting his watchers realize – if they did, of course, children of the union would probably become 'federal property' too. Harper is 'in hiding'. That's where innovators ought to stay.

The 'in hiding' theme relates closely to the 'noise level' one and that of 'stimulus diffusion', as well as to the stories about the failure of Security. They all assume that education is essentially education in acceptability, that society acts as a governor on human minds to prevent them realizing their full potential, and that some similar mechanism triggers hate-and-fear reactions in those who detect novelty. 'In Hiding' itself is a story by Wilmar H. Shiras, published in *ASF* (Nov. 1948), and one of the many examples of amateur authors articulating one classic theme and never succeeding – or trying – again. It deals with the discovery of a super-intelligent child by a sympathetic psychologist, rather like Olaf Stapledon's *Odd John* thirteen years before. But Miss Shiras's Tim is a 'mutant' created not by Darwinian chance but by the exposure of his parents to radiation. He is also non-competitive, conscious above all of his own vulnerability to the hate-and-fear reaction. Sequels to the story in *ASF* (Mar. 1949 and Mar. 1950) recede into blandness. Other variants, like Mark Clifton and Alex Apostolides's 'Crazy Joey' (*ASF*, Aug. 1953, and the fore-runner of the *They'd Rather Be Right* serial) take a grimmer view. However, the most thorough development of the theme – the book is dedicated to 'Paul Breen, wherever he may be hiding' – comes in Wilson Tucker's *Wild Talent*, serialized in *New Worlds* (Aug.–Oct. 1954): Superman versus the government.

The central irony of this book is that Paul Breen, the telepath, the 'new man', is by nature a loyalist. Like Russell's Wade Harper, he first displays his telepathic talent by hearing the call of a dying man – in this case an FBI agent or G-man (symbolic figure!) shot by the villains he is pursuing. But Breen, unlike Harper, is still only a boy, still 'in hiding'. With complete confidence, however, he writes down what he knows and posts the letter, covered in fingerprints, to:

> The President,
> The White House,
> Washington, D.C.

Eleven years later, in 1945, they get him. Drafted into the army, he has his fingerprints checked against the FBI's files with the massive, routine thoroughness then (as in *Who?*) ascribed to this organization. His secret penetrated, he too becomes 'federal property'. But they don't like him. If 'brains' are valuable but potentially treacherous, 'brain-readers' are bound to be a good deal worse.

The 1945 date is of course a vital factor in all this. 'What's an atomic bomb?' asks Paul casually, having picked the phrase from the mind of a passer-by. The panic that ensues determines the official view taken of telepathy: (1) it is something which shatters security (for if Paul were a Russian agent no screen could stop him); (2) but it might make security 100 per cent effective (for as long as Paul is not a traitor he can be a traitor-detector); (3) further, it is a potentially aggressive development (for Paul can mastermind a spy-ring himself).

The mixture of exploitation and anxiety mirrors reactions to the A-bomb itself. Its compulsive nature provides a sort of excuse for society; but then one is needed, for in an obvious way *Wild Talent* is a story of disillusionment. Its hero begins as a normal go-getting teenager riding the rails to the 1934 Century of Progress Exhibition in Chicago. By the end he has chosen exile, alienated by the collapse of all his early father-figures (the President, the FBI), and even more by his government's disregard of his own rights, the continuous 'bugging' by no means compensated by occasional pandering. And yet in a sense the American ideal remains intact. Mutant and superman himself, Breen nevertheless retains a respect for some of his associates, and a deeper, undevalued feeling for the *mores* of his youth – thrift, work, privacy, 'dating', and so on. 'We can't come here again', he says regretfully to his telepath fiancée at the end, as they wait for the escape boat. But she disagrees, and has the final word. To translate back into real-life terms, Tucker seems to be arguing that though contemporary societies are not fit to be trusted with new powers (whether nuclear or telepathic), this may nevertheless be a temporary phenomenon sprung from fear and militarization, not a universal law. Hate-and-fear reactions should not be provoked – and that is why Superman goes 'into hiding' – but may be overridden. Of course in the case of telepathy 'stimulus diffusion' is not imposing a panic-breeding time-limit.

Not all science fiction was as balanced as this in its view of the merits and demerits of nationalism. In 1957, Sputniks I and II (with the ominous 2,000 lb. payload of the latter) created something of a Pearl Harbor mentality, reflected in *Astounding* by several flights to familiar icons – Yankee inventiveness, teenage secret weapons, and the like. 'Murray Leinster' produced a totally reassuring 'History of World War III' for *ASF* (Oct. 1958 (B.)), while 'Darrell T. Langart' (or Randall Garrett) contributed a success-oriented reprise of *Who?*, 'What the Left Hand was Doing', to *ASF* (June 1960 (B.)). Yet even Garrett a little later wrote a novel in which the FBI lets the US collapse sooner than start the Last War – *Occasion for Disaster*, *ASF* (Nov. 1960–Feb. 1961), this time in collaboration with L. M. Janifer and under the pen-name 'Mark Phillips'. Probably the most creditable sign of science fiction's detachment from and immunity to the worst crazes of the Cold War lay in its reaction to Vietnam involvement. Its authors were on the whole completely unsympathetic to the anti-industrial and 'technophobe' bias of many of the war-protestors, and showed as much in many stories (such as James Blish's bad-tempered 'Skysign' from *ASF*, May 1968, or Wade Curtis's sarcastic 'Ecology Now' and 'Power to the People' in *ASF*, Dec. 1971 and Aug. 1972, respectively). However, as early as 1959 John W. Campbell Jr. – *Astounding*'s editor, son of a Daughter of the American Revolution, and a man addicted to neat but callous solutions – was explaining in an editorial (*ASF*, Feb. 1960 (B.)) why attempts to impose democracy overseas were unlikely to be successful, and why Communism was probably the best option for members of some developing nations. The area he had particularly in mind was South-East Asia. And the editorial was called 'How to Lose a War'. Campbell had the grace to refrain from saying 'I told you so' ten years later, but he had provided one more example of a certain flexibility of mind producing better results than professional evaluations based on professional prejudices

However, the value of science fiction and the science-fiction magazines during this period is not to be quantified in hits and misses. What should have emerged from this essay is that the fantastic elements of the stories were a cover, or a frame, for discussion of many real issues which were hardly open to serious consideration in any other popular medium: issues such as the nature of science, the conflict of business and government, the limits of loyalty, the power of social norms to affect individual perception. It is this which science-fiction fans felt they could not get anywhere else; this which accounts for the horde of 'willing followers' shoving writers and editors on. Of course a great quantity of science fiction was *not* about these themes, but dealt with robots, mutants, aliens, starships, asteroids, time-travellers, or any one of twenty other plot motifs. It would be a mistake, though, to think that even these did not contain a high proportion of serious thought, with a reference to real life not beyond recovery. Even more than most literature, science fiction shows a strong conventional quality which makes its signs and symbols interpretable only through familiarity; to instance only matters touched on above, it was a provocative act to polarize *Odd John* into 'Crazy Joey', while after so many novels (*The Space Merchants*, *Wild Talent*, *Year 2018!*) had ended with innovators escaping from governments, it was a striking move by Harry Harrison to make *In Our Hands, the Stars* start with the same scene – and with the innovator's knowledge that his government was going to come after him. It is this conventional quality which makes literary criticism difficult, and foredooms to failure the search for isolated fictional pearls. But the same stylization makes it possible to see much science fiction of the 1940s and 1950s, and later, as a 'thinking machine' for the convenience of people largely without academic support or intellectual patronage. This view further explains and excuses the attitude of the thousands of fans to whom the genre appears to be Bible, King's Regulations, and Constitution all in one. Does it allow science fiction to qualify as 'literature'? Possibly not. Nevertheless, it does ask questions as to what one means by literature, and as to whether the conventional categories of criticism can afford to leave out so much material uniting such vitality with such serious enquiry. To these considerations professional educators have not yet framed an adequate or accepted reply.

Notes

1. *Astounding Science Fiction* changed its name to *Analog: Science Fact/Science Fiction* in Jan. 1960, an interesting fact in itself. References to either title are abbreviated in this essay as *ASF*. A further difficulty is caused by the fact that up to Sept. 1963 the American edition of this magazine was followed a few months later by a slightly different British one. References are given to the American edition where possible; those to the British edition are marked (B.).
2. For a lengthier account of these events, see: D. F. Fleming. *The Cold War and its Origins, 1917-1967* (2 vols.) London: 1961, esp. Vol. I, pp. 315, 321, 411, 525.
3. He is 'D. O. MacHinery' in the magazine version. The change to 'Francis Xavier' three years later points the finger more definitely at McCarthy, whose connections with the Order of Jesus were well known. On the other hand, in the British edition of Oct. 1954 (I have not been able to see an American edition) 'MacHinery' appears in one place as 'McCarthy', a slip which quite likely goes back to authorial typescript.

Bibliography

Commentaries on magazine science fiction tend to be attracted towards one of two opposite errors: the amateur ones are exact but uncritical, the professional ones highly selective and so out of touch with the conventions and private symbolism of the medium. Thus Alva Rogers's *A Requiem for Astounding* (Chicago: Advent, 1964) is avowedly 'a labor of love', and a great help in locating stories, penetrating pseudonyms, and demonstrating the total effect which magazines (letters, artwork and all) could have on representative readers. It is, however, incapable of generalization, and the work of someone uninterested in literature as a whole. The same involvement and fiercely partisan quality is found in the books by Damon Knight and 'William Atheling Jr' (actually James Blish), respectively *In Search of Wonder* (1956, 2nd edn, Chicago: Advent, 1967) and *The Issue at Hand* (1964, 2nd edn, Chicago: Advent, 1973). Both consist of essays for the most part printed first in 'fanzines' or amateur magazines with a small coterie circulation. The authors know exactly what they are talking about. Unfortunately they also know the *people* they are talking about; objectivity is not felt to be a virtue. Blish also published *More Issues At Hand* under the 'Atheling' pseudonym, Chicago: Advent, 1970. James Gunn, a distinguished science-fiction writer turned academic, manages to distance himself more successfully in *Alternate Worlds* (Englewood Cliffs, N.J.: Prentice-Hall, 1975). His chapters on 'The Birth of Mass Magazines', 'The Rise of the Pulps', etc. provide an excellent historical outline.

Deeper and narrower studies are made in Chapters 7 to 9 of Brian W. Aldiss's *Billion Year Spree* (London and New York: Corgi and Doubleday, 1973) and in Paul A. Carter's thematically organized *The Creation of Tomorrow: Fifty Years of Magazine Science Fiction* (New York: Columbia U.P., 1977). An attempt at providing a theory for the genre is made by Robert Scholes, in a book with the significantly nervous title of *Structural Fabulation* (Notre Dame, Indiana: Univ. of Notre Dame Press, 1975), followed by *Science Fiction: History, Science, Vision*, by the same author and Eric S. Rabkin (New York: Oxford U.P., 1977). Darko Suvin's *Pour Une Poétique de la Science-Fiction* (Montreal: Presses de l'Université de Quebec, 1977) is more powerful than either of the preceding, but almost entirely confined to the genre's late nineteenth-century precursors. Finally, an indispensable guide (and another labour of love) is Donald H. Tuck's *The Encyclopaedia of Science Fiction and Fantasy Through 1968* (Vol. I 'Who's Who A-L', Chicago: Advent, 1974; Vol. II 'Who's Who M-Z', Chicago: Advent, 1978).

Science fiction, religion and transcendence

Tom Woodman

In an article in *Books and Bookmen* for February 1971, J. G. Ballard stated that science fiction was 'totally atheistic'. Darko Suvin's important article 'Science Fiction and the Genological Jungle' (*Genre*, Fall 1973) has argued the theoretical case for this viewpoint: the conceptual frameworks of science, the real basis of the genre, forbid any dabbling with religion beyond its purely historical or anthropological interest. Yet Samuel R. Delany has written that 'Virtually all the classics of speculative fiction are mystical' (*Extrapolation*, May 1969), and Arthur C. Clarke is reported to have called *2001* the world's first 'billion dollar religious movie'. The list of Hugo and Nebula award winners includes various novels and stories on religious themes. Anyone's list of famous science fiction would have to include C. S. Lewis's trilogy, Blish's *A Case of Conscience*, Miller's *A Canticle for Leibowitz* and the works of Philip K. Dick, and all of these have religion as a central theme, treat it seriously and become the vehicle for metaphysical and even theistic speculations.

If we look to the history of the genre for light on the question we see that several of its important antecedents were written by bishops or Jesuits like Godwin, Wilkins and Kircher. Later Jules Verne was to receive the papal blessing. It is true that the science fiction of the later nineteenth and early twentieth centuries often reflects the preconceptions of 'scientism' (the view that science has now explained away religion and indeed replaced it as the agent of man's salvation). The religion found in the pulp magazines is usually an exotic or barbaric magic, a caricature of pagan cults, like the gods encountered by Flash Gordon and Buck Rogers. The conscious view of religion here is that it is a base and primitive phenomenon, though an unconscious fascination with religious archetypes is also evident, as well as vague metaphysics in some stories. In the same period the epics of David Lindsay and Olaf Stapledon embody the genuine metaphysical searching that is often endemic to the genre.

After the Second World War critiques of scientism are much more common. An intellectual resurgence of Christian orthodoxy occurred in the 1940s and early 1950s, and this is reflected in C. S. Lewis's and Walter Miller's attacks on scientism in the perspective of man as fallen. James Blish reveals a fascination with the intellectual problems of orthodoxy and science. The 1960s are the period in which the recognition that science had failed to provide values becomes widespread. The themes of science fiction begin more and more to overlap with religious aspirations rather than dismissing them. At the same time the writers of the 'New Wave' regard science itself as a mythology. Reflecting a movement in the culture at large, an undifferentiated quest for 'mystical' or spiritual experience takes the form of a new interest in non-Christian religions, as in Zelazny's *Lord of Light* (1967), and a new Californian gnosticism, the harbinger of which is Heinlein's *Stranger in a Strange Land* (1961). Philip K. Dick's work reflects the interest in the mysticism of drugs, at the same time as providing an early critique of it in *The Three Stigmata of Palmer Eldritch* (1965), and his and Vonnegut's black comedy is frequently the medium for metaphysics,

So a brief survey of the history of the genre provides little support for Professor Suvin. Yet his purism is surely an essential start. The formulaic fertility gods and goddesses of the pulp magazines are magic in a disguised modern form with no necessary connection with science fiction. Suvin is prepared to concede that since religion is a scientifically observable human phenomenon, its history and anthropology are legitimate subjects for science fiction. However, if you explore the future of man you may explore the future of his religions, though Marxist social science of course foresees no real future for religion at all. But many writers have treated the subject, and there seems no reason to doubt the legitimacy of a topic like the future of religion, at least if it is seen as a fictional and speculative extrapolation from history, and not as a factual prediction.

Catholicism, as a large institutional Church with a powerful cultural impact, has been the favoured religion for such treatment, witty, irreverent or agonized. Brian Moore's *Catholics* (1972) is a moving study of the tension between a post-Vatican IV progressive papal authority and a pocket of conservative Catholicism in Ireland. Various writers use their understanding of the Church's historical attitude to science as a basis for predicting the suppression of scientific activity by an all-powerful reactionary Church of the future, as in Edgar Pangborn's *Davy* (1964). Alternatively, one may envision an empire of the enlightened, who persecute Christians. This is the theme of an anonymous early novel, *In the Future* (1875), and also of several modern stories of which the best is Barry N. Malzberg's 'In the Cup', a dignified account of a future Christian martyr. Roger Ellwood's anthology *Signs and Wonders: Science Fiction Stories for the Christian Reader* (1972) puts Malzberg's story together with another on the same theme, Eando Binder's 'All in Good Time', in which an anti-Christian technocratic society is converted by seeing on a time-viewer that its own future is Christian. God has intervened through the technology by which man attempts to control the future to show that it is in fact in his hands. An interesting early presentation of the twin alternatives, triumphant Church and triumphant scientism, occurs in the Catholic priest Robert Hugh Benson's *Lord of the World* (1907) and *The Dawn of All* (1911). Recent writers have been more interested in witty speculations, like George Zebrowski's idea that the future world religion will be a mixture of Christianity and Teilhard de Chardinism ('Heathen God', 1971). (De Chardin's *The Phenomenon of Man* remains the most ambitious modern attempt at a synthesis of scientific and religious values, and it is not surprising that references to this famous Jesuit and evolutionist crop up in several recent science-fiction writers.) In *Deus Irae* (1976) Philip K. Dick plays with the idea of 'teilhard de chardin' birds that mutate forward, and envisages a post-holocaust conflict between Christianity and a religion worshipping the 'God of Wrath', the man who pressed the button. Various of these fantasies go beyond futurological extrapolation from the history of the Church as a human phenomenon. Robert Hugh Benson's are, of course, wedded to the idea of a divinely activated future, but several of the others also have a genuine theological content.

The same is often true of the classic science-fiction theme of encounters with other planets and aliens. (According to *Time* magazine for 24 April 1978, some theologians even consider this as a special branch of their discipline, namely 'exotheology'). Admittedly, this theme is sometimes the means of setting up a purely anthropological contrast with human religion. The religious practices of the aliens may serve as an allegorical representation of the absurdities of our religiosity, as in John Robert King's *Bruno Lipshitz and the Disciples of Dogma* (1976), where an earth-controlled space station is invaded by a group of canine missionaries, who worship the great canine god called 'Dogma'. The satire is funny if unsubtle and the point presumably is to show how we create gods in our own images. The new perspective on our religions provided by other planets is often used in the interests of relativism. How parochial we are! How presumptuous of us to assume we know the secrets of the universe! The argument for relativism is intelligently put in Robert Lowndes' *Believers' World* (1961), which deals with three planets, each run by a different theocracy derived from basic teachings identical on all three worlds. Each planet grimly maintains that the religions of the other two are heresies. Brian Aldiss's brilliant *The Dark Light Years* (1964) adopts a genuinely anthropological perspective. Earthmen encounter aliens to whom excremental functions are sacred. In a hideous scene they perform vivisection experiments on the gentle creatures and later destroy them. Aldiss's point is, of course, more than purely anthropological. Our contact with these alien creatures shows up our deficiencies: 'By the standards of another species . . . our culture might merely seem like a sickness' (Ch. 7). Life on earth is a hell, which is what drives men out to other planets in the first place. The book hints at a religious outlook in its insistence that men need a less rational and more reverent attitude towards reality (Ch. 4). A similar example of a story that begins as anthropology and ends as a kind of religious statement is Chad Oliver's 'Guardian Spirit' (1958), where a scientist on Mars is converted to a tribal religion there which clearly has the author's sympathy too.

One of the wittiest stories about the religions of other planets and their relationship with earth religions is Winston P. Sanders' 'The Word to Space' (1960). Earth establishes communication with a star, but all that is beamed out by its inhabitants is abstruse religious propaganda. A Jesuit sends back casuistical queries about this religion, so that its theologians lose their faith, and then the communication of scientific truths can occur. The story's real presupposition seems to be that religion is nonsense, but the Jesuit is at least technically proficient in it. Many stories deal with the sub-theme of earth's missionary endeavours in the galaxy. In Harry Harrison's 'An Alien Agony' (1962) an earth missionary tells the story of Christianity to an innocent people who crucify him to see if he will rise again. On the face of it, as Brian Aldiss explains in his introduction to *More Penguin Science Fiction* (1963), the presupposition of the story is that the introduction of an earth religion to an alien society only causes damage. But another reading is also possible: the missionary is a martyr who brings a knowledge of sin to these people and hence the possibility of redemption. He is a true Christ figure as well as a parody of one. Of course, various straightforwardly Christian stories have been written to suggest that Christianity is relevant outside an earth context. In Lawrence Yep's 'My Friend Klatu' (1972) an alien is converted, and in Roger Lovin's 'Apostle' (1973) a whole planet. The same happens in Philip José Farmer's 'Prometheus' (1961), but this is a much cleverer and more sceptical story on the theme than most. Its scepticism is a virtue not because it is the opposite of faith (the story is not concerned to call its hero's Christian preconceptions into doubt), but because it leads Farmer to examine with real intellectual agility the theological and practical problems that the inhabitants of other planets would create for Christianity. The hero, a Catholic monk-scientist called Carmody, whom Farmer involves in fascinating exploits with the wholly fictional Manichaeist religion of Bontoism in *Night of Light* (1966), is shown in the earlier story as reluctant to try and convert the strange birdlike creatures until they start asking questions about the after-life. He teaches them the rudiments of both Christianity and technology, aware that both may be perverted, before he leaves them by starship in a well orchestrated parody of the Ascension. He also has to deal with ethical questions like their practice of eating their own eggs. Murder? Birth control? As in Blish's brilliant *A Case of Conscience* (1958) theology is the subject-matter of a skilful science-fiction equivalent to a chess problem.

The theological problems involved in the existence of life on other planets are dealt with at a more serious level in Ray Bradbury's beautiful story 'The Fire Balloons' (1951). Two missionaries on Mars encounter a race of intelligent beings that look like spheres of blue fire. They are sinless, and live blissfully in God's grace. They have no need of Christian revelation for there is a truth on that world and a truth on this. As if in deliberate debate with Bradbury's famous story, R. A. Lafferty, who described himself as an orthodox Catholic Thomist in a 1973 interview, has a story called 'Name of the Snake' (1970) in which original sin has infected the ostensibly sinless beings on another planet, and they eat the missionary.

If space travel raises concrete theological issues that can make amusing or serious themes for science fiction, then the same is true for the ethical or theological implications of various other scientific achievements, fictional or real. In Dick's *Ubik* (1969) the dead are kept in a state of suspended animation by cold-pack technology, and the hero announces that the 'half-life' experience has made theologians of them all, since it necessarily touched on the issues of life after death, resurrection and the nature of the soul. Genetic engineering in John Boyd's *The Last Starship from Earth* (1968), behaviourism in Anthony Burgess's *A Clockwork Orange* (1962), contraception in Lester del Rey's *The Eleventh Commandment* (1962) – these are just three examples of novels whose themes involve specific scientific techniques and which, playfully or not, discuss these issues directly as they relate to the Church's moral theology.

If you have a religion then it must be a cosmic one, says C. S. Lewis. The cosmic Christ who reigns over the whole universe is a vision of the Pauline epistles, the early Church Fathers and, recently, of Teilhard de Chardin. In Bradbury's 'The Man' (1949) Christ goes as Messiah from planet to planet, though the earth spacemen always just fail to see him. The same writer's 'Christus Apollo' (1969) hymns the cosmic Christ, and Jeff Duntemann's 'Our Lady of the Endless Sky' (1974) ends with the cosmic vision from the Book of Revelation of the woman clothed with the sun, the moon and stars at her feet. Obviously science fiction, as Lewis argues, can explore these themes, seriously or for fun, whether the product be the grandeur of Duntemann's vision or a savage satire on our blinkered presumptuousness.

The ultimate theme of the genre of science fiction is man's attempt through science to come to terms with the cosmos he inhabits. Implications that go beyond a purely anthropological or sociological approach to religion may well develop out of the fictional exploration of science as a human activity or as technology, the main focus of earlier writers. The ethics of scientific activity may be examined by religious criteria or a look at the claims of scientism may involve its conflict with religion. Science fiction has always had another aspect to its central theme as well, and from the early sixties on writers have increasingly moved away from science as an external activity towards considering it as a body of knowledge and a methodology. If the older prevailing mode was humanist and ethical, the other interest is almost contemplative, emphasizing the greatness of the cosmos that man comes to know. Writers present a fictional imitation of the methodology of science to make quasi-cognitive assertions about the cosmos. So they imitate the way science inevitably overlaps to some extent with religion in making such statements. The study of the cosmos has always induced metaphysical speculations and is the source of what is traditionally called 'natural theology'. In some recent writers this theme has taken the very different form of critical agnosticism about science as a means of knowledge, so that the critique has led on to the assertion of a universe the incomprehensible richness of which transcends man's mind altogether.

The great epic of man's scientific endeavours is simplified into a hymn to scientism, assuming its values without analysis, in much fiction of the 1920s and 1930s. Asimov's 'Trends' (1939) is a touchstone, with its story of religious oppression trying to crush space travel until enlightenment finally triumphs. Lester del Rey's 'Evensong' (1967) is a late, almost mythic, account of the pride and achievement of scientism. By science men have become the superiors of God, whom they usurp and put in exile. The presupposition that religion is the enemy of scientific enlightenment is found in a whole set of novels involving parallel worlds like Keith Roberts's *Pavane* (1968) – where there is a papal encyclical entitled *Petroleum Veto* – or Kingsley Amis's *The Alteration* (1976). In Keith Roberts's novel it finally appears that the Church's reason for withholding science from man is paternalistic but well intentioned, but Amis's novel is a curiously dated assertion of anti-religious prejudices, including the view that science would have disproved God if the Church had not crushed it. Other writers also reflect the idea that science has explained religion away. In Heinlein's 'Universe' (1941) he provides the aetiology of a religion: the descendants of abandoned astronauts in a space-ship invent one to explain their situation. In Brian Aldiss's 'Heresies of the Huge God' (1966) mankind projects divine characteristics on to a mass of galactic debris that has fallen on to earth causing disaster. In various novels we are shown religious 'miracles' that are really powered by science, as in Fritz Leiber's *Gather Darkness* (1950), where a guild of scientists has grown afraid of the diffusion of knowledge. They establish a 'religion' that works miracles by scientific tricks. With the genuine spread of technology a golden age would have come, but the scientist-priests keep the serfs in ignorance by fostering superstition. Philip K. Dick parodies the view that science has explained away religion in *Our Friends from Frolix 8* (1970), where it is announced that God's carcase was found in space several years before the action of the book began.

In 'scientism' science becomes a new religion, providing salvation, and worshipped with the same fervour as other gods. Scientists are the true 'priests'. In various novels by A. E. van Vogt the religion of the worship of atomic energy is the determinant of the action, a religion served by a guild of priest-scientists. The central symbol for the whole theme is the machine. Raymond F. Jones's hero in *Renaissance* (1951) is told:

Teach the people to build and dream of greater and greater machines until they can reach the stars. The Machine is man's poetry and his music and all his art.

It can also become his religion. In John W. Campbell's 'Last Evolution' (1932) the evolution into machine is seen as the final stage of perfection. So machines become God, as in H. G. Wells's prophetic 'The Lord of the Dynamos' (1894). In John Brunner's 'Judas', (1967) a robot is God, and in Frederick Brown's clever 'Answer' (1954) all the computers in the world are linked up to answer the question 'Is there a God?' The reply that comes, of course, is, 'There is now!' In John Boyd's *The Last Starship from Earth* (1968) there is a computer as Pope, and in Robert Silverberg's award-winning 'Good News from the Vatican' (1971) a robot.

The implicit argument behind scientism is that science has genuinely conferred the saving benefits that the old religions could not bring. So in Blish's *They Shall Have Stars* (1957) the religious group called 'The Witnesses' prophesy that some men shall achieve immortality. This is indeed the case in the novel, but through medical technology, not religion. In Richard Ashby's *Act of God* (1951) a pseudo-religion based on science grows up. Its priesthood has possession of a medical elixir that confers immortality, and the heroes are real scientists who try to analyse the substance to give its benefits to mankind as a whole. One of the cleverest treatments of the theme of science as true religion is Robert Silverberg's *To Open the Sky* (1967). A religion based on the adoration of the atom and on immortality through technology has developed. It fails because it is too secular and makes no proper provision for man's religious instincts. It is overcome by a sect based on the same beliefs but using a highly developed religious mythology to express them. Silverberg assumes that man's religious instincts are inveterate, as indeed the religious trappings surrounding scientism might suggest. The religion based on science will be as genuinely 'religious' as one based on fertility gods. So Silverberg's central figure

saw that the time was ripe for an eclectic, synthetic new creed that dispensed with the mysticism of the former religions and replaced it with a new kind of mysticism, a scientific mysticism. (Ch. 3)

Stanislaw Lem likewise suggests in *Solaris* (1961) that the science of Solaristics has become a new religion epitomizing man's desire to make contact with the unknown.

A more sympathetic and sophisticated method of 'explaining away' religion within a framework of scientism is the view expressed by several writers that religious phenomena are the products of parapsychology. It is announced in Frank Herbert's *The Godmakers*

(1972) that the wise man prays once a week and practises 'psi' every day. The whole vast Mohammedan-style religion that dominates the same author's *Dune* (1965) has been set up by an order of clairvoyants and psychics, who sow prophecies about the coming of the messiah who is the hero of the book. In *The Godmakers* we see the process by which psychic gifts can be developed so that the protagonist becomes like a god in awareness and power. Similarly, in Clarke's *Childhood's End* (1953) it is suggested that the traditional mystics had experienced a foretaste of 'breakthrough' into the next *gestalt* stage of human consciousness. Unfortunately, they had translated their insights into dogma. So, though this approach seems sympathetic to religion and depends on para-science (which is legitimate for a fictional genre) it does continue to carry the implication that religious phenomena are not valid in their own terms.

The same is true of the writers of the New Wave when they interpret religion rationalistically, though not unsympathetically, through a sci-entifically based interest in the structures of mythologies. But they see science, too, as a mythological structure of thought-patterns, which they test against more traditional mythic structures, and so the critique of scientism is a major aim. As Glogauer, the hero of Michael Moor-cock's *Behold the Man* (1967), puts it,

It was not conviction that had led him to defend religion against Monica's cynical contempt for it; it was rather lack of conviction in the ideal in which she had set her own faith, the ideal of science as a solver of all problems. He could not share her faith and there was nothing else but religion, though he could not believe in the kind of God of Christian-ity. (Ch. 18)

Glogauer has a masochistic religious neurosis. He travels back to the time of Christ, who turns out to be a simpleton. Glogauer becomes Christ instead and is crucified. He makes the myth a reality for himself, transcending his neurosis, and vindicating the Jesus myth against sci-entism. Aldiss's hero in *Barefoot in the Head* (1969) assumes the paradigms of the Christ model, and Roger Zelazny works through the Hindu pantheon in *Lord of Light* (1969). Some critics have argued that myth is anti-historical, and so inappropriate for treatment in science fiction, but I do not see how this applies to these sophisticated fictional explorations of the psychological truth of traditional mythic structures and the comparison of them with the paradigms of science.

The more usual perspective for the critique of a science that is trying to dislodge religion is that of Christian orthodoxy. Mary Shelley's *Frankenstein* (1818) presents the possibility that the scientist is usurp-ing the role of God in trying to create life. This is a frequent archetype, seen, for example, in J. R. Fearn's 'Before Earth Came' (*Astounding Stories*, 1934) where a group of experimenters plan to create a new solar system. It all goes wrong, and the Chief Scientist says that the reason is that they are trying to usurp the Creator's power. Nor can fallen man create Utopias through technology, as we see in R. A. Lafferty's *Past Master* (1968), where St Thomas More is taken to a utopian planet. But the inhabitants attempt to stamp out belief in a beyond, and he has to become a martyr again. The world is condemned to repeat the pattern of trying to create new Edens and then destroying them again in *A Canticle for Leibowitz*. The most famous and popular orthodox critique of scientism is, of course, C. S. Lewis's trilogy *Out of the Silent Planet* (1938), *Perelandra* (1943) and *That Hideous Strength* (1945), and James Blish takes up Lewis's linking of scientism and the demonic when he envisages the megalopolis created by post-industrial technocratic man not as a new Eden but a new hell (*The Day after Judgement*, 1971).

Ursula Le Guin's *The Lathe of Heaven* (1971) offers a thorough-going attack on scientism from the perspective of Taoist philosophy. The universe, as she has beautifully conveyed elsewhere, is a system of dualities held in balanced harmony. Man is a part of the whole, and his fulfilment comes from the acceptance of this. Utilitarian technology, as symbolized by Dr Haber, is man's attempt to set himself above the universe and to tamper with it. Haber goes beyond utilitarianism into scientism when he boasts of a technological revolution that will trans-form men into gods and this world into heaven.

The Lathe of Heaven is anti-science science fiction, just as much as C. S. Lewis's, though Ursula Le Guin's other work often shows more sympathetic attitudes to science. This novel exemplifies how the critique of scientism often leads on to more general themes in the relationship between science and religion which are legitimate topics for fictional treatment within the genre. The novel deliberately sets out to associate Haber's world-view with the Judaeo-Christian tradition. So a curious situation has occurred in the fictional presentation of the relationship between the Church and science, one that reverses the preconceptions of many other writers. Despite the prejudices against science that the Church has often revealed and despite the anti-Church values of scientism, Ursula Le Guin's view is probably closer to the truth. Ernan McMullin argues in *New Blackfriars* (March 1969) that Christian revelation, which sees the universe as God's creation, and believes that God works through the historical process, is hospitable to science in a way that the Eastern religions are not. This is not to deny the special analogies between the highest levels of Eastern mysticism and modern physics that the physicist Fritjof Capra has pointed to. But the answer that *The Lathe of Heaven* gives to Haber's claim that technology will one day make a heaven of earth is to say that it is a heaven already if we could only see it. Marxism, Judaeo-Christian revelation and scientism all agree in saying that this world is not yet like heaven. Christianity agrees with Marxism, too, in seeing technology as one means that will help in the transformation. Thus, a tradition of theology, which Milton, Hartlib and Bacon were only developing, affirms, as in Hugh of St Victor, that the sciences were given by God to help man overcome the effects of the Fall, ignorance and infirmity.

Historically, this is the main Christian tradition; the more negative one that sees science as Faustian self-assertion is only secondary.

Several writers do in fact treat the theme of the relationship between science and religion by presenting the Church as favourable to science, as in Philip José Farmer's parallel-world story 'Sail On, Sail On' (1952), where there is a clerical order of scientists called after 'St Roger Bacon'. The Jesuit scientist who is the hero of Blish's *A Case of Conscience* (1958) comes finally to realize that there is no ultimate conflict between his science and his religion. The same happens in a charming Ray Bradbury story of 1949 in which an elderly conservative priest comes to see that rockets are the 'Machineries of Joy' of the title, and can help man to know more of God's handiwork and so praise him better.

In some stories a religious reversal of the theme of the machine as God is used to point to what the authors see as a better version of the relationship between science and religion. In Arthur C. Clarke's 'The Nine Billion Names of God' (1953) Hindus use a computer to spell out all the possible words which could be God's name, and so bring about the end of the world. So religion uses technology for its own ends, as also in Michael Davidson's *The Karma Machine* (1975), where a computer is linked up with Eastern wisdom to produce Nirvana. The ultimate pro-religious twist to the theme is Anthony Boucher's clever 'The Quest for St Aquin' (1951), which tells of the conversion of a robot to Thomist Catholicism. The preconceptions behind Boucher's story are the Thomist ones that science deals with secondary causes which lead, when properly interpreted, to God. The end of *A Case of Conscience* is a very sophisticated presentation of the same teaching about the relationship between scientific and religious values. Blish makes use of the Thomist theology of science as the realm of secondary causes to provide a clever conclusion to the novel. At the same time as the priest exorcizes the planet he has come to see as a demonic delusion it is accidentally blown up by the scientists who wish to exploit it for armaments. So the author leaves us to make up our minds whether we want to believe supernatural or natural explanations, or whether both coexist, as in the Thomist view that God works out supernatural purposes through the natural order, which preserves its own logical autonomy.

In theological terms the most sophisticated novel on the relationship between science and religion is Walter Miller's *A Canticle for Leibowitz* (1959). The book is a marvellous imaginative invention describing the time after the nuclear holocaust when a monastic order is the sole preserver of scientific knowledge. Miller creates fine comedy out of the monks' naïve reverence for pre-holocaust science and their superstitious misunderstandings of the monster 'Fallout'. But the book contains an implicit argument. It is, after all, true that it was the monks who preserved scientific wisdom in the early Middle Ages. After the nuclear disaster a movement called 'The Simplification' had blamed science, and tried to stamp it out. Miller's point is that the

Church cannot set herself against any real truth, for all truth bears some relationship to the Logos (Ch. 17). It is not science that is wrong but men's hearts. But scientism, the opposite extreme to 'The Simplification', is equally wrong. Leibowitz, the scientist-founder of the religious order, came to see that 'Great knowledge, while good, had not saved the world' (Ch. 18). The whole book is dominated by the idea of the Fall. This is the basis of its impressive black comedy and of the genuine tragic vision which gives it, despite a rather dated view of Catholicism, a sombre power. Science has been given to help man. It is a means of overcoming the effects of the Fall. But in itself it cannot bring back the lost Eden. Science's Utopia is a blasphemous and unsatisfying parody of man's true fulfilment, which is brought about by God's grace alone, in radical disruption of this world's order:

Too much hope for Earth had led men to try to make it Eden, and of that they might well despair until the time toward the consumption of the world. . . . The closer men came to perfecting for themselves a Paradise the more impatient they seemed to become with it and with themselves as well. (Ch. 25)

On each occasion that man seems about to break through into a new Eden of science a terrible fall occurs, yet the book is ultimately optimistic. Though the earth itself is to be destroyed in the final holocaust, a new human creature is revealed without Original Sin, manifesting the 'preternatural gifts of Eden – those gifts which man had been trying to seize by brute force again from Heaven since first he lost them'. So the effects of the Fall are reversed only by God's grace. But the representatives of the Church leave the earth on a spaceship, and they decide to take the 'memorabilia' of scientific learning with them. The hope for man is assisted by God-given gifts of science, though these in themselves cannot bring about the new Eden which scientism claims: 'It was no curse, this knowledge, unless perverted by man, as fire had been, this night . . .' (Ch. 25).

A Canticle for Leibowitz achieves an epic centrality in the genre by the way it confronts types and prototypes of science and its aspirations, whether as medicine versus euthanasia, or as the monk-scientist versus Thon Taddeo, who washes his hands of science's ethical implications. It explores the ethics and aspirations of science, which it tries to differentiate from scientism, and it suggests the grounds for a reconciliation between science and religion. Certainly it deals, in Darko Suvin's terms, with the anthropology of religion and with a future extrapolation from the history of the Church's relationship with science. It also goes beyond these into an exploration of theological themes, providing a brilliant theological critique of scientism which is firmly embodied in a fictional narrative.

If, as I have argued, fables of the territorial claims, conflicts and reconciliations of man's scientific and religious activities are a legitimate subject for science fiction, it is also true that reflections on the nature of the cosmos revealed by science often have religious and metaphysical implications. Here we are in vaguer areas than direct treatments of future clashes between the Church and scientists. But the inventive and wondering exploration of the cosmos is as much at the heart of the genre as the fictional study of the science which makes such knowledge possible. Often, it will be agreed, the primary interest is not, for example, the rockets that transport us to strange new worlds but the new worlds themselves. Of course if the scientific content of the work is purely a vehicle for fantasy then we would not wish to call it science fiction. But science is a methodology and a body of knowledge as well as a technology and a profession. A simple interest in stars and planets, an awe at the immensity of the cosmos, is clearly a part of the 'sense of wonder' that Damon Knight sees as the main impulse of the genre. Often this has been specifically religious. The night sky is seen as a manifestation of God's power and design. 'The heavens declare the glory of God', says the psalmist (Psalm 19); 'He decides the number of the stars/And gives each of them a name' (Psalm 147, *Jerusalem Bible*). God's transcendent power, constantly turning matter into energy and energy into matter, has been most cearly symbolized for modern writers as well as ancient in the beauty of the stars, which come to stand also for the 'otherness' of transcendence, for what Olaf Stapledon calls 'the cold light of the stars, symbol of the hyper-cosmical reality' (*Star Maker*, 1937). For the priest-hero of Blish's *A Case of Conscience* each new planet is another manifestation of God's power. In Ursula Le Guin's *The Left Hand of Darkness* (1969) the impulse to form a confederation of galaxies is 'for the greater glory of God', which is more and more revealed as the splendour of the cosmos is seen to be of greater and greater complexity and as it grows in communication and harmony. For one of Ray Bradbury's characters space is 'a cathedral' (*The Silver Locusts*, 1951). For C. S. Lewis in *Out of the Silent Planet* the world we call 'space' is not at all the emptiness that terrified Pascal's atheist, but is better described in the classical formulation of 'the heavens'. It is through the 'Yoga of Space' that the astronaut in the title story of Robert Silverberg's *The Feast of St Dionysius* (1975) encounters the divine. He explains that in outer space he has the sense that

there may be real forces just beyond my reach, not abstractions but actual functioning dynamic entities, which I could attune myself to if I only knew how to find the key. You feel stuff like that when you go into space, no matter how much of a rationalist you are . . . I want to feel it again. I want to break through . . . I want to reach God.

R. A. Lafferty 'theologizes' further on these lines with his speculations about space as the real beatific vision. An old man explains in his unpublished novel *Archipelago* that:

Space is the tapestry of Heaven, the real Heaven of the Beatific Vision where we go when we die, and also where we are now. The Infinity of Space was not made for a game: it is the real infinity rolling in the real eternity. But we see this tapestry now only from the reverse side. We see only the tangled thread behind: we have not the vision of the face of the picture itself. . . . There are multitudinous emanations, and sight is only one of them which is given us here in the childhood of the soul. But it is all Out There, Hell and Purgatory and Heaven, all there: or here, for we are also in the middle of Out There. And there is a time before time, and a time after time, a space beyond space, and a space inside space. They talk now of re-entrant space, which is the attempt to see infinity. I talk also of re-entrant time which is the attempt to see eternity. (The Alien Critic, Aug. 73)

So, as Lafferty's old man shows, a sense of awe at the stars can lead on to metaphysics and to ideas of transcendence, to a sense of how limited we and our visions of reality are, and to speculations about eternity and time.

The theme of creation may also follow on from a consideration of the stars. Many writers play with the topic, from the beautiful reworking of traditional Judaeo-Christian ideas in Eric Frank Russell's 'Second Genesis' (1951) to the nihilist view of a galaxy created from the debris of the cosmos that we find in Silverberg's *The Masks of Time* (1968). Several writers explore the idea that the galaxy was created not directly by the Christian God but by a demiurge, well intentioned but weak, who makes several mistakes. George Zebrowski's 'Heathen God' (1971) makes fine use of this theme. The demiurge was loving, and has left a loving spirit among men. The ultimate God figure, the creator of all reality, recedes further and further away as the story continues, and the priest-hero realizes that the demiurge has no knowledge of such a God. All we can do is to live with the hope of perpetuating the demiurge's benevolence. The story translates Christian ideas of the Holy Spirit into its own terms. But 'Heathen God' is so complex that, despite its anthropocentric emphasis, it might also intimate the possibility at least of a benevolent creator on a vastly grander scale than the god directly responsible for this world in the story.

The interest in other planets and their possible inhabitants raises specific theological problems discussed earlier. In a much more general sense it evokes the whole mystery of man's relationship with the alien and the Other. The strangeness of bizarre forms of life in the galaxy can be an imaging of the frightening aspects of what is transcendent to the individual ego and its controls. As J. Robert King has pointed out, these aliens from other planets are often projections of father and god figures. They may also embody man's yearning to transcend his own isolations and limitations. Lord Running Clam in Dick's *Clans of the Alphane Moon* (1964) is a spore clam that sacrifices itself for the hero. There is something consoling and moving in the idea of being cared for by a creature so different from man. In Karl Barth's theology God is the wholly Other, to whom man must yet relate himself in love if he is to be made whole. Man fears Otherness at the same time as he needs it to complete himself. This theme is brilliantly explored in Dick's *The Three Stigmata of Palmer Eldritch* (1965), where the alien is a terrifying possessor who yet, because transcendent to man, is a part of God or an analogue of God. A similar speculation occurs in Lem's *Solaris*. One of the novel's central themes is man's urge to communicate with what is beyond himself, and Lem is manifestly aware of there being religious implications to this impulse.

The cosmic viewpoint that arises naturally in science fiction, the interest in ideas about the creation, and the reflections of relativity theory all evoke a special interest in the theme of time. Vonnegut's *Slaughterhouse-Five* (1969) utilizes quasi-scientific concepts to explore the difference between an earthly sense of time and an eternal perspective, as the hero is snatched out of this world to the planet Tralfamadore. The cosmic viewpoint of the inhabitants encourages quietism and determinism, which Vonnegut seems half to urge and half condemn. In *Perelandra* C. S. Lewis discussed man's deluded sense of time, which Simone Weil, like Lewis, sees as one of the primary results of the Fall. Science fiction can make us aware of this delusion by manipulating our ideas of time, by contrasting our time with a cosmic perspective, by fictionalizing versions of true science, and by using pseudo-scientific motifs like time travel. The cosmic perspective and the motif of time-travel also leads science fiction writers to the same themes as Milton's bad angels, who debated:

> Of Providence, Foreknowledge, Will and Fate,
> Fixt Fate, Free Will, Foreknowledge Absolute,
> And found no End in wandering Mazes lost.

If our time can be seen from an eternal perspective, then is there free will? Or are we involved in a predestined cosmic plot? The heroine of the comic strip *Misty* (1973) finds out she is involved in a cosmic war with a character called Godd, the evil master of the International Destiny Machine. Themes of determinism fascinate Vonnegut. In *The Sirens of Titan* (1959) we discover that the whole of human history is part of a plot to send a message from one part of the galaxy to another. But Vonnegut implies, through the person of Beatrice, that this does not destroy human dignity. She argues in her book *The True Purpose of Life in the Solar System* (Epilogue) that

those persons who have served the interests of Tralfamadore have served them in such highly personalized ways that Tralfamadore can be said to have practically nothing to do with the case.

Charles Harness's *The Ring of Ritornel* (1968) investigates the same metaphysical theme. Here the central conflict is between a religion based on predestination and eternal recurrence and one based on a celebration of the principle of random chance. The two apparently antithetical principles seem to blend in the book's universe, as predestination and free will blend in Augustinian theology. The motif of time travel provides the most popular way of introducing these metaphysical issues. Is the past fixed? Or can we go back and alter it?

What changes will alterations of the past produce in present worlds? If our sense of time is a delusion then do all possibilities coexist? Are there parallel worlds? Is it possible to alter salvation history, too, going back, as in Boyd's *The Last Starship from Earth* and Moorcock's *Behold the Man,* before the time of Christ and tampering with the events of his life? Boyd's novel is a virtuoso piece of intellectual playfulness on these themes as well as on the relationship between the Church and science. The plot is too complex for adequate summary here, but basically it deals with a future world dominated by sociology, genetic engineering and the Church, whose head is a computer Pope. Deviants from this world are sent to a planet called Hell, but this turns out to be a place of hedonistic love rather than of punishment. The hero is sent back in a time machine as part of a plot by the deviant forces to kill Christ and so to stop the Church developing. Instead he drugs him and sends him back in a starship to 'hell' (an echo of the traditional harrowing of hell). The hero is left wondering at the end whether

he had sidetracked history or derailed it when he laid the hissop-drugged body of Jesus into the one-seater right after the crucifixion.

Would the hero bring about Armageddon by causing the 'final merger of the ultimate thesis with the ultimate antithesis' or would he have to wait, marooned in a different time band, until the Second Coming? This novel is a fine example of the way science-fiction writers sometimes use religious concepts solely for the possibility of witty and semi-blasphemous theological speculation, especially on the ways in which science and religion interweave, or on ways in which scientific developments might drastically alter religion. These writers are latter-day metaphysical poets using theology, and for that matter science, irreverently, and for fun, though they, like their predecessors, also spark off genuine insights. As Philip K. Dick has explained, ideas about God are, as subject-matter for the science-fiction writer, 'intellectually exciting' (Afterword to 'Faith of our Fathers', 1967).

Another very popular science-fiction motif that has religious implications is parapsychology. When writers like Frank Herbert, Arthur C. Clarke and Robert Heinlein explain religious phenomena in terms of parapsychology they are revealing in a disguised form, as I have suggested, the preconceptions of scientism. There is, of course, an overlap between mysticism and parapsychology, but the two are not identifiable. Catholic theology, for example, teaches that these are '*preter*natural gifts', natural to man before the Fall, rather than supernatural. They have often been associated with the lives of the Saints, as Brian Inglis shows in *Natural and Supernatural* (1978), which is what might be expected in those for whom the effects of the Fall have been reversed and who have become 'new creations'. But these gifts can also be abused for power, becoming the means of ego-assertion rather than of the subjection of the ego to a greater and other power, as is the case with all true mysticism, even the non-theistic mysticism of which

Ursula Le Guin writes. Science-fiction writers rarely seem to exercise the spiritual virtue of discernment in this context. Often they write out of an eclectic California-style fascination with all forms of the psychic, the occult and the quasi-mystical, and sometimes such work ceases to be genuine science fiction at all. Even with a major work like Heinlein's *Stranger in a Strange Land* (1961) we feel ambivalent. Though the hero uses his psychic powers with generosity and creativity, it is suggested that only about 1 per cent of the population possess them and that they make us gods. The élitism and the dangers are extreme, as the well-known cultural side-effects of the book suggest.

As if to echo the theological tradition various writers link the preternatural psychic powers with man's time before the Fall, and with his recovery of the lost Eden. In Robert Silverberg's *The Feast of St Dionysius* (1975) the astronaut learns that before the Fall we were all one entity. He gets involved in an ecstatic religion that preaches self-loss through orgies and wine leading to reunion in the Ocean of God. His longings for this experience of oneness were stimulated, as we have seen, by the 'Yoga of Space'. A common idea is that man will develop his telepathic powers and break through into a new stage of human evolution in which he becomes one consciousness, 'Homo Gestalt'. This is the theme of Theodore Sturgeon's *More than Human* (1953) as well as of Arthur C. Clarke's famous *Childhood's End* (1953). William Irwin Thompson compares this new stage of human consciousness to the idea of the mystical body of Christ. The effects of the Fall are reversed. Theologically Christ becomes *The New Adam*, a title which Stanley Weinbaum takes up (1939), the first mutant of the new stage in evolution. He draws mankind through the threshold in fellowship with him. George Zebrowski's *Omega Point* (1972) explores the concept of the merging of consciousness in the terms of Teilhard de Chardin. R. A. Lafferty's enthralling *Fourth Mansions* (1970) discusses these developments using the criteria of St Theresa of Avila's *The Interior Castle*, the classic guide to the discernment of true and false mysticism. He describes the conflict between a sinister web-like group of mutants with a unified consciousness and his hero, who becomes the true and benign mutant at the close.

The theme of telepathy and parascience in science fiction often turns into a reworking of religious concepts and a wider discussion of the future of the whole human species. This is only one aspect of the radically future-orientated nature of the genre, which is bound to produce general theological implications. For, like science fiction, theology is future-orientated. A famous book by the theologian Father Schillebeeckx is called *God, the Future of Man*. Judaeo-Christian revelation sees the whole of history converging to its divine fulfilment. Much science fiction envisages a future brought about by increasingly rapid technological change, or extrapolates one from the present by imaginative sociology. But it has often shown itself fascinated by theology's visions of the future, and how they overlap with and differ from science's. The relevant distinctions have already been made by the critics, especially David Ketterer in *New Worlds for Old*, so I shall only refer briefly to them here. Some writers present a scientific 'Utopia', alien to the Christian vision of the future, and brought about entirely by man's own efforts. They may criticize this from a theological perspective, showing it not to be a Utopia at all, or celebrate it if they believe in the creed of scientism. Other writers follow the same method as H. G. Wells often does, using the symbolic structures of Christian apocalyptic or eschatology, but purely for literary effect. Others again, like Clarke in *Childhood's End*, retranslate theological ideas into a new, but still theological form, so that his version of the human future is controlled by a divine impetus. Finally, various writers are interested in exploring for their own sake the Judaeo-Christian ideas of the end of the world, as in Silverberg's novella *Thomas the Proclaimer* (1972) or Mark Geston's terrifying *Out of the Mouth of the Dragon* (1969), a parody apocalypse, which cannot actualise itself.

Lester del Rey (Afterword to 'Evensong', 1967) has written that:

A writer who thinks seriously about his craft must surely find himself more and more engaged with the ancient problems of philosophy — good and evil, and causality — since these lie deep within every plot and character. As a science-fiction writer, trying to scan the patterns of the future, I find myself also inevitably concerned with the question of teleology; is there a purpose and design to the universe and man?

I have tried to suggest certain ways in which science-fiction writers have legitimately tended to go beyond what Professor Suvin regards as the boundaries of the genre. Metaphysics and theology have arisen naturally out of the genre's common themes, the limits and ethics of science, time, eternity, creation, and out of its radically future orientation. At the furthest limits of this development towards theology, a very specific 'theologizing' occurs; that is, the exploration of a range of speculations about the nature of God, from the mad god of Dean Koontz's *A Darkness in My Soul* (1972), through the imperfect deity of Lem's *Solaris*, and the incompetent one, powerless to bring about the end of the world in Mark Geston's *Out of the Mouth of the Dragon* (1969), to the majestic but impersonal and indifferent *Star Maker* (1937) of Olaf Stapledon. Philip K. Dick is a good example of a recent and prestigious writer who explores theistic ideas of varying degrees of bizarreness or orthodoxy such as the god whose carcase is found in space in *Our Friends from Frolix 8*, the evil god of the paranoid vision in 'Faith of Our Fathers' (1967), and the totally Augustinian theodicy that we find in *Counter-Clock World* (1967, Ch. 20):

Evil is simply a lesser reality, a ring farther from Him. It's the lack of absolute reality, not the presence of an evil deity.

Here St Thomas Aquinas, St Augustine and Erigena are quoted to back up the presentation, through fictionalized technology, of an 'after-life' experience which brings you into touch with the divine.

Various scientists and theologians have been suggesting for some time now that the views of modern science are much more compatible with religion than those of the older science. Teilhard de Chardin's is only the most ambitious attempt at a synthesis. Harold Schilling, Emeritus Professor of Physics at Pennsylvania State University, claims in *The New Consciousness in Science and Religion* that modern science acknowledges its inability to grasp in its fullness a reality that is seen as inexhaustible. Scientists now tend, in Professor Schilling's view, to see man as part of a universal creative process, not inaugurated by us and to which we must humbly submit. The word 'transcendence' is interpreted by Schilling as referring not to 'a spatial beyond but to the "infinitely more than" anything observable directly in us or the cosmos'. (This sense of science's cognitive limitations is a strong theme in *Solaris*.) The implications of various aspects of the new science for theological concepts are considerable. The idea, for example, of the continuum of energy and matter is an amazingly fruitful one for theological speculation, as when one of James Blish's characters in *The Day after Judgement* (1971) points out that evil spirits must be real energy foci with a particular atomic structure. (Indeed, the idea of purely non-material fields of force now seems acceptable in science.) Philip Josè Farmer's *To Your Scattered Bodies Go* (1971) plays with the idea of a matter–energy converter machine that brings about the General Resurrection of the Dead! Of course Farmer is translating theological concepts into pseudo-scientific ones solely for fun, but the interchangeability of matter and energy is relevant to the theology of resurrection, as Professor Thomas Torrance explains in *Space, Time and Resurrection*. He points out some of the implications of Christ's Resurrection as a redemption of time–space reality, and shows that the Risen Christ must have entered into an entirely new relationship with matter. St Paul writes (1 Corinthians 15, 41-4, *Revised Standard Version*):

There is one glory of the sun, and another glory of the moon, and another glory of the stars; for star differs from star in glory. So it is with the resurrection of the dead. . . . It is sown in weakness, it is raised in power. It is sown a physical body, it is raised a spiritual body.

A. R. Peacocke rephrases the Pauline insight in scientific terms in *Science and the Christian Experiment* (p. 168):

How 'matter is organized', to use our usual terms, when in the form of resurrected human persons in the 'presence' of God, we have no means of describing.

These ideas, like the whole concept of the cosmic Christ and the Pauline aspects of Teilhard de Chardin's theology, which develop from them, could well be treated in science fiction, as Zebrowski has tried to do in *Omega Point*. There seems no reason why a science-fiction version of the *Merveilleux Chrétien*, once recommended for epic poets, should not succeed, as indeed at times it already has, in, for example, Dick's imaging of Christian concepts through pseudo-scientific drug phenomena in *The Three Stigmata of Palmer Eldritch*, or in places in the first two volumes of the Lewis trilogy. 'Fictional' because imagined and speculative, these ideas can also be 'scientific', and can both spring from and contribute to theological insights.

What finally links religious aspirations and the best science fiction is a common interest in transcending our present reality. Both have a cosmic dimension. Both have a common focus on the future of man, an interest especially built into Judaism and Christianity. Cosmic awe, the perspective that comes from contemplating the stars, makes us realize our littleness, as Troilus looks down from the eighth sphere at the end of Chaucer's poem and smiles at the triviality of our concerns. Science fiction relates us to vast cosmic forces. It is the opposite as a genre to what D. H. Lawrence once called 'wearisome sickening little personal novels'. Our earthly viewpoint is bound to be narrow and half-blind, and the epistemological sophistication of modern science confirms this: 'We see through a glass darkly', writes Philip K. Dick, quoting St Paul, and as the critic Bruce Gillespie explains, Dick's aim is not to give us an ecstatic religious vision but to show us the frailty of our reality and the intimations of another. Father Simon Tugwell says that our world and our present human status are 'provisional'. He cites St Thomas Aquinas's view that genuine religious prophecy needs imagination, a gift for seeing that things could be other than they are, a gift of seeing from God's viewpoint. We are not to be 'conformed to the present age' (Romans 12, 2). He also explains that transcendence is more a temporal than a spatial concept. In the future man will be radically different from what he is now, conformed not to the present age, but to Christ, the 'first fruits' of the new humanity:

It does not yet appear what we shall be, but we know that when he appears we shall be like him, for we shall see him as he is.
(1 John 3, 1-2, *Revised Standard Version*)

The genre of science fiction can help shatter the complacencies of our present views of reality, and make our imaginations enjoyably receptive to new visions of the future. Obviously the great mass of work in the genre is formulaic. Its material is of interest to the psychologist, the sociologist and even the theologian as a record of man's aspirations and prejudices. It can entertain us and soothe us with predictable futures and safe horrors. But it bears the same relationship to the greatest achievements and potential of the genre as a British country-house detective novel of the 1920s bears to *Crime and Punishment*. The idea of transcendence creates a common ground between aesthetic criteria for evaluating science fiction and a degree of theological interest that goes beyond the purely diagnostic. For, in the best science fiction with theological implications, we are startled in some way. It may merely be that shock of newness which is essential for the effect of a witty or even blasphemous manipulation of religious ideas. It may be the playful shock of an intellectual puzzle in which a tired dogma is confronted with a facet of reality that tests or breaks it. Or the aesthetic shock may come from the comedy or the tragedy of man's attempts to transcend himself through science and technology. Religious science fiction might condemn the attempt as futile by the standards of a different transcendent vision altogether, or it might even celebrate it as an epic, God-given and marvellous creative struggle, as Teilhard de Chardin does. But the aesthetic shock to our complacencies that the best science fiction brings is *cognitive*, a reminder of our provisional status. We get the sense in Olaf Stapledon's *Last and First Men* (1930) that our present humanity is only a brief stage in the titanic mental and spiritual mutations that man must undergo. Science fiction from a committedly religious point of view will fall into stale pieties unless it can present old doctrines prophetically, in the challengingly cosmic and futurist dimension which is of their essence. The best science fiction from an agnostic or atheistic point of view has often indicated, like Stapledon's, that the inexhaustible creativity of man and the cosmos utterly transcends our present experience.

Bibliography

The topic of 'transcendence' is helpfully discussed in *Transcendence*, ed. Herbert Richardson and Donald R. Cutler (Boston: Beacon Press, 1967). Simone Weil's *Waiting on God* (Eng. trans. London: Putman, 1951) contains a view of fallen man which I have found valuable. The first volume of *Prayer* (Dublin: Veritas Press, 1974) by Fr Simon Tugwell O.P. is full of brilliant insights, some of which are especially relevant to science fiction. Two other Dominicans, Fr E. Schillebeeckx in *God, The Future of Man* (Eng. trans. London: Sheed and Ward, 1969) and Fr John Orme Mills in *New Heaven? New Earth* by S. Tugwell, G. Every, J. Orme Mills and P. Hocken (London: Longman, Darton and Todd, 1976) have filled in the contexts of Christian eschatology, apocalyptic writings and theology's radically future orientation.

Various theologians have written on the relationship between science and religion. Tielhard de Chardin's *The Phenomenon of Man* (Eng. trans. London: Collins, 1965) is the most famous recent synthesis. Other interesting studies are Thomas Torrance's *Space, Time and Resurrection* (Edinburgh: Handsel Press, 1976), Harold K. Schilling's *The New Consciousness in Science and Religion* (London: SCM Pr., 1973) and A. R. Peacocke's *Science and the Christian Experiment* (London: Oxford U.P., 1971).

Scientists and popularizers of science whose work contains suggestive religious implications include Fritjof Capra, *The Tao of Physics* (London: Fontana, 1976), Brian Inglis, *Natural and Supernatural* (London: Hodder and Stoughton, 1978), Arthur Koestler, *The Roots of Coincidence* (London: Hutchinson, 1972) and William Irwin Thompson, *Passages About Earth* (New York: Harper and Row, 1974).

There is finally a body of material specifically on the theological implications of science fiction. C. S. Lewis's essays in *Of Other Worlds* ed. Walter Hooper (London: Geoffrey Bles, 1966) are an obvious starting point, as is *The Issue at Hand* by William Atheling Jr [James Blish] (1964 2nd edn. Chicago: Advent, 1973). Good surveys of the whole area of science fiction and religion are found in *The Visual Encyclopaedia of Science Fiction* ed. Brian Ash (London: Pan Books, 1977). Ray Bradbury has discussed 'The God in Science Fiction', in *Saturday Review* (10 Dec. 1977). David Ketterer has argued in *New Worlds for Old* (Bloomington, Indiana: Indiana U.P., 1974) that various forms of apocalypse are central to the genre, and that religious implications are therefore almost inevitable. Helpful brief essays are those by J. Norman King, 'Theology, Science Fiction and Man's Future Orientation', in *Many Futures, Many Worlds*, ed. Thomas D. Clareson (Kent, Ohio: Kent State University Press, 1977); Mayo Mohs, 'Introduction: Science Fiction and the World of Religion', *Other Worlds, Other Gods* ed. Mayo Mohs (1971, n.e. London: New English Library, 1976); Carol Murphy, 'The Theology of Science Fiction', *Approach* (Spring 1957, No. 23); and George Zebrowski, 'Introduction: Whatever Gods There Be: Space-time and Deity in Science Fiction', in *Strange Gods* ed. Roger Elwood (New York: Pocket Books, 1974). Lois and Stephen Rose's *The Shattered Ring: Science Fiction and the Quest for Meaning* (Atlanta: John Knox Pr., 1970) has some pointers. Two critics on Philip K. Dick, Bruce Gillespie in *Philip K. Dick: Electric Shepherd* (Melbourne: Norstrilia Press, 1975) and Angus Taylor in *Philip K. Dick and the Umbrella of Light* (Baltimore: T-K Graphics, 1975) help to elucidate that writer's interest in religion. R. A. Lafferty's interview (with Paul Walker) in *The Alien Critic* (Aug. 1973) is an extremely interesting exploration of his orthodox theological beliefs by a brilliant science-fiction writer. Finally, though I have argued against him, it is obvious that I have found Darko Suvin's essays stimulating, especially 'Science Fiction and the Genological Jungle', *Genre*, Fall 1973).

Characterization in science fiction: Two approaches
1. The disappearance of character

Scott Sanders

I

Science fiction is a home for invisible men and women. One is hard put to name half a dozen memorable characters in all the annals of the genre, to recall any science-fiction protagonist who hangs in the mind with the weight of Raskolnikov, say, or Stephen Dedalus or Quentin Compson. Even the celebrated *rapprochement* between SF and mainstream literature during the past fifteen years, whatever it has added by way of stylistic and metaphysical complexity to the genre, has added little to the rendering of character. Critics weaned on the traditional novel frequently use this weakness of characterization as a bludgeon for attacking the genre. Even sympathetic commentators concede the point, then either apologize for it or move quickly on to discuss the genre's strengths. Thus David Ketterer writes in *New Worlds for Old* (1974) that apocalyptic literature – which by his definition includes most SF – 'involves a certain magnitude or breadth of vision which militates against an interest in detailed characterization'. Kingsley Amis argues in *New Maps of Hell* (1961) that SF must deal in stock figures because it ponders our general condition rather than the intricacies of personality. Theme replaces character as the organizing principle of the genre, he maintains – a view summarized in his terse formula, 'Idea as hero.' In sketching the distinctive features of the genre, Joanna Russ claims that 'the protagonists of science fiction are always collective, never individual persons (although individuals often appear as exemplary or representative figures)'. It is this dealing in types rather than individuals that has led critics such as Robert Scholes and Darko Suvin to claim for SF a cognitive function analogous to that of science.

Wherever you find the matter of characterization in SF discussed at all, you will only discover versions of the same circular argument: character is neglected because something else – such as ideas or situation or plot – commands the writer's attention.

But why should such a narrative form flourish in our century? The answer, I believe, is primarily sociological. In its treatment of character science fiction reproduces the experience of living in a regimented, conformist society, within which the individual has become anonymous: persons are interchangeable, relating to each other through socially defined roles; actions are governed by procedure, and thus do not characterize the actor; emotion is repressed in favour of reason; the individual is subordinated to system. Science itself, increasingly bureaucratized and collectivized, has fostered an impersonal model of knowledge which, however ill-suited to the actual work of scientists, has become the most influential epistemology in industrial civilization.

In other words, weakness of characterization in SF is not the accidental consequence of attention to other things. On the contrary, I would argue that *in the twentieth century science fiction as a genre is centrally about the disappearance of character*, in the same sense in which the eighteenth- and nineteenth-century bourgeois novel is about the emergence of character.

'Character' was the focus of the bourgeois novel, at a time when the individual was the kingpin of liberal ideology, and when the economic system of capitalism was still primitive enough to make such an ideology convincing. During the nineteenth century the middle classes of Western Europe and America were still persuaded that the individual was an autonomous creature, the true unit of value, capable of determining his own destiny. This faith has been progressively eroded by the growth of cities and industries, which dwarf the individual, by the impact of technology, by war, by the transformation of capitalism into a world corporate economy, by the acceleration of social change. Even in the nineteenth century the working classes never fully accepted the notion of the autonomous individual, since it was false to their experience of society. This scepticism was reflected in the literary forms most popular among the working class, especially melodrama and romance, in which character was subordinated to plot.

Belief in the autonomous individual – belief in what D. H. Lawrence called 'the old stable *ego* of the character' – was likewise abandoned in the modernist novel. Writers such as Lawrence and James Joyce and André Gide retreated further and further into the psyche in search of a layer of the self which remains free of social domination. The interest in the intricacies of character, the romance of psychology, which animates the modernist novel is the dialectical opposite of the typological, generalizing interest that has sustained SF since the 1920s. While writers such as Franz Kafka, Robert Musil, and Samuel Beckett have recorded the dissolution of character under the pressures of recent history, SF begins by assuming that dissolution, and explores the causes. SF deals, in other words, with the same social and intellectual developments whose intimate effects on personality have been explored in modernist fiction; the two literary modes examine the outside and inside of the same phenomenon.

We find a paradigm of this split between fiction of the inside and fiction of the outside in the famous dispute between Henry James and H. G. Wells over the scope of the novel. James urged Wells to leave off his social preaching and explore instead the subtleties of personality. Wells replied that close scrutiny of character is only possible when the social frame remains constant. In his own time, Wells argued, the acceleration of social change, under the combined impact of scientific discovery and industrialization, had made the frame itself part of the picture. (As long ago as 1848 this constant revolution in the material and ideological conditions within industrialized society had seemed a commonplace to Marx and Engels, who wrote of it in *The Communist Manifesto*.) The modernists generally sided with James in this dispute, probing ever deeper into the vein of consciousness while progressively ignoring the social realm. With few exceptions, and those fairly recent, writers of SF have sided with Wells, creating a genre in which, not character, but the framework within which character acts out its destiny, is at issue.

Hence the SF novel offers an extension and restatement of the central problem with which the modernists wrestled – namely, the fragmentation and anonymization of the self in modern society – although SF usually presents that concern in a displaced form. Whether this displacement occurs by means of extrapolation or analytical model-building, as Darko Suvin has suggested, or by world-reduction, as Fredric Jameson has argued, it creates the effect which both Suvin and Jameson, following Bertolt Brecht, have called *estrangement*: we are not led to identify with the characters, as we would be in a bourgeois novel; instead we are invited to reflect critically on our own social, ecological, and metaphysical situation, in light of the fictive system.

Character is not merely neglected in SF; it is subverted. The very idea of complex, autonomous, unique individuals – the idea at the heart of the Continental and Anglo-American novel from the eighteenth until the early twentieth centuries – is undermined in SF. The primacy of system over individual appears formally in the genre in the subordination of character to plot; in the use of stereotypic figures; in the preference for technical and discursive (and therefore anonymous) language. The threat to identity appears implicitly in the figures of androids, robots and zombies, in the spectres of totalitarian computers, in the celebration of supermen and superwomen as the only rebels in a world of drones, in the themes of invasion and possession, in the visions of apocalypse. In the following section I will examine these various expressions of the disappearance of character in SF, drawing most of my examples from the period since 1945, the period in which social pressures towards anonymity have grown most intense.

II

The nightmare of losing one's identity within a totalitarian society haunts the protagonists of our century's most famous speculative fictions, from the numbered citizens of Yevgeny Zamyatin's *We* (1920) and the hapless supplicant of Kafka's *The Castle* (1926), to the furtive rebels of Aldous Huxley's *Brave New World* (1932), George

Orwell's *Nineteen Eighty-Four* (1949), and Thomas Pynchon's *Gravity's Rainbow* (1973). Such fictions often transpose into the future, or into a fabulous non-time, images of repression with which we are painfully familiar from the history of this century. Zamyatin could turn for models of his dystopia to the early experiments in social engineering conducted by the Bolsheviks, and to the militarization of England during the First World War; Huxley, to that same era of regimentation in England, extending through the strikes in the 1920s; Kafka, to the rusting machinery of the Habsburg bureaucracy. Orwell and Pynchon could model their dystopias upon several actual societies – Hitler's Germany, Mussolini's Italy, and Stalin's Russia being only the most spectacular expressions of a totalitarian impulse which also surfaced in Spain and Japan during the 1930s, in Britain during the Second World War, and in the United States during the Cold War.

The crushing of self by system, the denial of individuality, is nowhere more savagely illustrated in our recent history than by the Second World War, especially by the concentration camps, and is nowhere more painfully recorded than in the literature of the holocaust. Memoirs such as Elie Wiesel's *Night* (1958) and novels such as *One Day in the Life of Ivan Denisovitch* (1962) by Alexander Solzhenitsyn describe the camps as places where identity is stripped away and humans are reduced to knots of hunger and fear. The documentary film by Resnais, *Night and Fog* (1955) – through its pictures of warehouses stuffed with human hair, buckets heaped with gold fillings, pits choked with the bulldozed carcases of nameless victims – reveals the ultimate anonymity of the furnaces and mass graves. We find in these records of historical experience many of the images which recur in post-war SF: the numbered inmates, the uniformed bodies, the suffocating routine, the omnivorous machinery of death.

As their architects proudly declared, the camps were death factories, embodying the same ideals of precision and efficiency that manufacturers of automobiles and radios had already perfected in their own spheres of production. Hitler choreographed these ideals into his Nuremburg rallies, as we can see from Leni Riefenstahl's film, *Triumph of the Will* (1934-6). Those endless rows of identical soldiers goose-stepping past the camera, those high-angle shots of faceless multitudes ranked like wires in a printed circuit, those boots stamping in unison – all dissolve the individual into the collective. The rallies themselves were a physical expression of the mental conformity which every dictator seeks. Goebbels declared that all Germans must think with one mind; and through the use of terror and mass propaganda he did his best to achieve that goal. In *The Plague* (1947), an allegorical novel about the impact of the war, Albert Camus suggests that this experience of anonymity was not by any means confined to the dictatorships:

Some . . . contrived to fancy they were still behaving as free men and had the power of choice. But actually it would have been truer to say that by this time . . . the plague had swallowed up everything and everyone. No longer were there individual destinies; only a collective destiny, made of plague and the emotions shared by all.

In such a state, common citizens enjoy little more individuality than soldiers or prisoners.

No one familiar with the history of our time should be surprised, therefore, that visions of totalitarian futures have become a staple of SF since the Second World War. We find such visions in Ray Bradbury's *Fahrenheit 451* (1954), where a ruling party reminiscent of those described by Huxley and Orwell burns books for fear of subversive knowledge; in Philip K. Dick's 'Faith of Our Fathers' (1967), where a drugged populace cringes beneath the omniscient gaze of the Great Benefactor, a thinly disguised *alter ego* of Mao Tse-Tung; and in Ursula Le Guin's *The Dispossessed* (1974), where several autocracies share dominion over the planet Urras, rivalling each other in methods of repression. (In the same novel Le Guin projects an alternative planet, Anarres, organized along the lines of anarcho-communism, which, though preferable to the tyranny of Urras, offers equally grave challenges to identity.) Often writers provide social explanations for the rise of their fictional tyrannies, the most common ones, understandably, being war, over-population, and environmental degradation. Thus Isaac Asimov in *The Caves of Steel* (1953), Brian Aldiss in *Earthworks* (1966), and John Brunner in *The Sheep Look Up* (1972) all present us with societies which have been overwhelmed by collective pressures. Scene after scene portrays anonymous crowds, waiting for medical care or heaped on stairways for sleep, crowds fleeing from the scoops of government trucks sent to quell a riot, crowds of the dead reprocessed for food.

The narrator of *Earthworks*, one in a long line of science-fictional rebels against authority, sounds the complaint which is echoed by all the citizens of these regimented dystopias: 'In me grew that weary sense of lack of identity that was itself an identification.' We hear the same dread of anonymity voiced by a character in *Fahrenheit 451* (Part I), who laments that

We must all be alike. Not everyone born free and equal, as the Constitution says, but everyone made *equal. Each man the image of every other; then all are happy, for there are no mountains to make them cower, to judge themselves against.*

Conformity, homogeneity, loss of identity: these are the obsessive fears in each of the tales I have mentioned. We can readily link such fears to the experience of totalitarianism, since all of these fictional dystopias reproduce the grisly outlines of historical tyrannies. But the dread of anonymity also takes on subtler forms in post-war science fiction, forms whose links to our social experience are less clear but no less strong.

III

While society as a whole grows more rationalized, the experience of living within it grows more alienated. In proportion as the complexity of social organization increases, the power of the individual to comprehend or affect the world dwindles. The reigning institutions of modern society – technological production, bureaucracy, cities, mass media – so regiment and fragment the social world that the individual is thrown back upon his island of subjectivity in search of meaning and coherence. In response to this fact, as I have already suggested, modernist writers have burrowed ever deeper into the self, while writers of SF have projected images of the self as puppet, robot, or automaton. The characters in much SF written since the war are manipulated creatures; they are citizens of an administered world.

In his *Foundation* trilogy (1951–3), Asimov presents us with an entire cosmos governed according to impersonal laws which are incomprehensible to those caught up in the historical process. Although various human agencies conspire to shape history, the real shaping influences, the trilogy assures us, are 'the deeper economic and sociological forces' that 'aren't directed by individual men'. Drawing upon the crudely deterministic version of Marxism which served as a scarecrow during the 1930s and during the Cold War, Asimov invented for the purposes of his novels a new discipline called psychohistory (*Foundation and Empire*, Ch. 3):

Without pretending to predict the actions of individual humans, it formulated definite laws capable of mathematical analysis and extrapolation to govern and predict the mass action of human groups.

Hari Seldon, the pre-eminent psycho-historian in the trilogy, succeeds in explaining history by dissolving psychology into physics, by treating humans as if they were elementary particles (*Foundation*, Part III, Ch. 2):

He couldn't work with individuals over any length of time; any more than you could apply the kinetic theory of gases to single molecules. He worked with mobs, populations of whole planets, and only blind *mobs who do not possess foreknowledge of the results of their own actions.*

Governments, armies, multi-national corporations, insurance companies – all large institutions do in fact treat individuals as if they were elementary particles, statistically defining humans in terms of markets, services, life-expectancies.

New disciplines such as motivation research and behaviour modification have arisen in response to the desires of advertisers to manipulate customers, industrialists to manipulate workers, politicians to manipulate citizens. B. F. Skinner, whose behaviourist theories have influenced American schools and prisons, has argued doggedly since his *Walden Two* appeared in 1948 that the notion of individual freedom of the will must be abandoned. He sees no reason why human behaviour should not be manipulated as thoroughly as the behaviour of pigeons or rats. Of course historians and psychologists have searched in vain for the mathematical laws which Asimov invokes; yet whether such laws exist in reality or not, within the *Foundation* trilogy they express the individual's sense of being manipulated by forces which he cannot resist or understand. Whatever name is given to the governing influence – the laws of history, aliens, computer, government, Big Brother – the psychological root of the matter is the same.

There is another common motif in post-war SF which seems to contradict this vision of an administered society, and yet which registers the same feeling of the self's isolation and impotence: this is the spectre of ungovernable social and technological change. All those encounters with mutants, with aliens, with berserk computers and self-propagating monsters speak of a fear that the material world, and the creatures who populate it, have slipped the reins of reason and grown strange to us. One of the most vivid examples of this motif is offered by Michael Crichton's *The Andromeda Strain* (1969) in which an extraterrestrial form of matter, lethal and benign by turns, mutates and multiplies faster than even the most highly trained scientists can cope with. In the film version of this tale, experts watch in helpless bewilderment as images of the self-transforming Andromeda strain flash into incomprehensible new forms upon a screen.

Computers carry on a similar self-transforming mutation in Fred Hoyle and John Elliot's *A for Andromeda* (1962) and in the film, *Colossus: The Forbin Project* (1970). In the latter, two machines speak to each other in mathematical language which, like the Andromeda strain, bewilders experts who are supposedly in control of the phenomenon. Gathered about the computer printer, the scientists watch helplessly as the cybernetic dialogue accelerates into higher mathematical spaces where no human can follow. Monsters of other sorts commonly propagate themselves in post-war SF, multiplying as ruthlessly as dandelions. For example, every shred of tissue hacked from the Carrot Man – who is the featured monster in a film entitled *The Thing* (1951) – will, if nurtured with human blood, produce a new mobile carrot, as if by cloning. The aliens in Jack Finney's *The Body Snatchers* (1954), who duplicate human bodies and then discard the originals, work through their town of victims with the accelerating pace of a chain reaction.

In numerous other fictions written since August 1945, mutants and aliens confront us with threatening images of transformed humanity. Of course creatures with two heads and glowing eyes play upon our fears of radiation-induced monstrosities; berserk computers play upon our fears of machinery; mysterious poisons, upon our fear of ecological catastrophe. But mutation also represents a historical leap, a change so radical and swift that ordinary people cannot accommodate it. Long before Hiroshima, H. G. Wells arranged to have his Martians bring a red weed with them when they invaded earth in *The War of the Worlds* (1898). Once loosed on England, this weed spread with a frenzy to blanket the countryside and choke the streams. Only earth's inhospitable bacteria called a halt to this maniacal vegetation, as they put an end to the Martians as well. (After the bombing of Hiroshima and Nagasaki, weeds in fact did grow rampant over the ruins.) In 'Nobody's Home' (1972), Joanna Russ presents a future earth on which transportation has become so rapid that our own nomadic life has been supplanted by an even more feverishly mobile existence, within which individuals jostle around as aimlessly as dust particles in Brownian motion. The self does not live in continuous relation to other persons or to place, but instead is subjected to quantum jumps, in time and space.

In each of the examples I have sketched, the object of the mutation – Andromeda strain, computer language, vegetation, and so on – is less important than the *fact* of mutation. The effect of all these encounters with hectic growth and accelerating change is to enforce our sense of living in an age in which social and technological processes have escaped human control. Just such a quantum jump in the rate of social change led, according to Georg Lukács, to the emergence of the historical novel in the wake of the French Revolution and the Napoleonic Wars.

One can find evidence for this new, urgent awareness of historical change in writers outside SF. In *What is Literature?* Jean-Paul Sartre, for example, discussing the 'Situation of the Writer in 1947', argued that the violent global events of the previous two decades had forced upon himself and his contemporaries a keen awareness of their historicity:

From 1930 on, the world depression, the coming of Nazism, and the events in China opened our eyes. It seemed as if the ground were going to fall from under us, and suddenly, for us too, the great historical juggling began.

The form of that awareness, according to Sartre's description, is similar to the view of history I have been tracing in post-war SF:

. . . our life as an individual which had seemed to depend upon our efforts, our virtues, and our faults, on our good and bad luck, on the good and bad will of a very small number of people, seemed governed down to its minutest details by obscure and collective forces, and its most private circumstances seemed to reflect the state of the whole world. All at once we felt ourselves abruptly situated.

During the past three decades, many writers of SF have felt themselves situated in just this fashion. Even though their tales are usually displaced in time or space, and thus appear to evade history, they convey by form and theme the historical awareness of which Sartre speaks: manipulated by 'obscure and collective forces', the self dissolves.

IV

Wordsworth looked forward to a time when poets could embrace machinery in their writings as readily as they had always embraced stars and flowers and trees. He would be disappointed on this score with all of modern literature except SF, for in this genre alone has machinery – and technical invention generally – become a dominant source of imagery. The significance attached to machinery in SF has shifted in response to our experience of technology in modern society. During the 1930s and early 1940s, when technology seemed to offer the firmest hope of escaping the Depression and defeating fascism, writers of SF generally honoured inventors, scientists, and their creations. In its crude form this attitude was expressed as a fascination with gadgetry, in its sophisticated form as a vision of society modelled on the laboratory. Precedents for each manner of honouring science – as a collection of ingenious devices or as a habit of mind – could be found in Jules Verne and H. G. Wells, respectively. The early tales of Isaac Asimov, Robert Heinlein, and Theodore Sturgeon display this generally benign view of science, and of science's technical machines.

Since 1945, however, machines have increasingly become the objects of dread in SF. Just as the Second World War provided writers with models for totalitarian nightmares, so it demonstrated the powers of destruction lurking in technology. Death had been mechanized on a fantastic scale, not only in the concentration camps and in the atomic bombings, but in routine military operations. Since the war, weapons have become more devastating, automation has cheapened labour, devices such as the automobile have transformed and often degraded our environment, and industrial pollution has begun poisoning all life on the planet. Taken together, these social developments help explain why machines, once the objects of fascination, have become a focus of dread in post-war SF. In particular, machines have frequently come to stand as both cause and symbol of the threat to identity.

Before computers were more than a gleam in the eyes of technicians, writers such as John Campbell in 'Twilight' (1934) and E. M. Forster in 'The Machine Stops' (1909) imagined entire civilizations given over to the control of machinery, in the face of which individuals withered into anonymity. As long ago as 1916, D. H. Lawrence wrote in 'The Industrial Magnate' chapter of *Women in Love* about the mining industry as a vast machine which annihilates the personality of all who work within it. More recently, in Michael Frayn's *A Very Private Place* (1968), machine-dependence has been pushed so far that humans actually become captives inside their apparatus. The ruling families dwell in mechanical castles, dealing with the enslaved classes through projected images, enjoying (or perhaps suffering) a narcotized existence. Hermetically sealed inside their machines, cut off from nature and each other, they are prodded into every sensation from orgasm to meditation by chemicals.

Since the onset of the cybernetic revolution in the 1940s, computers have provided writers with a symbol for rationalized society, the electronic wizards frequently taking on the dictatorial powers of human autocrats. In Kurt Vonnegut, Jr's *Player Piano* (1952), for example, a computer presides over every detail of society, from market-place to kitchen sink, becoming a kind of mechanical fate which is as impersonal and inescapable in its operation as any fate ever conceived of by theologians. As a result of automation, challenging work has been transferred to machines, humanity has been divided between a managerial élite and the disenfranchised masses, the countryside has been depopulated, and life has been given over to the consumption of trinkets lacking all human purpose. Individuals have been reduced to the status of cyphers in the books of corporations and in the memory-banks of the computer. The scenario is a familiar one, both inside science fiction and outside, in industrialized society. Arthur Clarke carries the rule of the computer to its logical extreme in *The City and the Stars* (1957), where a whole society, from skyscrapers to fingernails, is projected by a central machine. Individuals are assembled atom-by-atom from the personality patterns stored in the memory-banks; each is given a life-time of 1,000 years and then retired again into the computer. Until a freak emerges, who becomes the familiar rebel-against-conformity, every last detail of society, every least human gesture, is foreordained by the machine.

Totalitarian computers, and the threat to identity which they symbolize, have become as commonplace in films as in novels. Television viewers are familiar with maniacal machines from *Star Trek*, and viewers of film from productions such as *2001* (1968) and *Colossus*. In the latter film, Americans turn over control of their military system to an invulnerable computer, which links with its Russian counterpart and proceeds to govern the world, subordinating all human existence to its own cybernetic ends. A computer named HAL (an acronym removed one alphabetical notch from IBM) usurps power over a spaceship in *2001*, dispatching one-by-one the humans with whom it was designed to cooperate. Both films are typical of the genre in the mesmerized attention they pay to the running of machinery. Cameras dwell upon dials, switches, tape reels, and data displays. Gadgets contrived at great expense by the special-effects crew perform modernistic functions. Humans become the appendages of machines, dancing like men and women entranced through procedures which are more important than the characters themselves. A good deal of SF cinema is *about* machinery and procedures – one could cite examples ranging from *Things to Come* (1936) to *Star Wars* (1977) – rather than about the fates of characters (a fact generally reflected in film budgets), registering our own experience of subordination to impersonal systems in factory or office or university.

Like *Player Piano* and *The City and the Stars*, both films pit a lonesome hero against the mechanical wiles of the computer, just as

Orwell and Zamyatin pit rebels against their autocrats. The parallel is an exact one, because the totalitarian computers, while of course reflecting the dominant machinery of a cybernetic age, also stand for the governmental and technological system as a whole. The individual confronts the computer as he confronts any bureaucracy: it obeys rules he cannot fathom, manipulates him in ways he cannot appeal, speaks a procedural language he cannot understand.

V

While loss of identity is represented on the social level by totalitarian computers, it is commonly represented on the individual level by the figures of robots, cyborgs, androids, and zombies. These automatons are the husks of human beings, devoid of feeling and free will, mere contraptions for the carrying-out of functions which are programmed from the outside. In his famous robot stories of the 1940s, Asimov maintained a clear distinction between automatons and humans; but since that time other writers have shown themselves less confident that any such distinction exists. Thus Alfred Bester in 'Fondly Fahrenheit' (1954) melds an android and its master into a composite homicidal creature which speaks by turns in the voice of man, of machine, and of a collective 'we' which embraces them both. The humans who staff the army of Mars in Vonnegut's *Sirens of Titan* (1961) have radios implanted in their skulls, by means of which they may be controlled from without. They thus fulfil to perfection the ideal of mindless unanimity and precision after which merely human armies strive in vain. The title character of Michael Crichton's novel, *The Terminal Man* (1972), combines the depersonalizing metaphors of robot and computer, for his brain becomes a computer terminal, and the character himself becomes a monstrous hybrid of human desires and mechanical powers.

Cyborgs erase all distinctions between man and machine, wedding organic and mechanical parts in the same creature. As the technology of transplants and prosthetics has grown more sophisticated, cyborgs have multiplied in print and on the screen. For example, two American television series, *The Six Million Dollar Man* and *The Bionic Woman*, popular during the latter 1970s, have explored at melancholy length the exploits and dilemmas of government cyborgs. In *V.* (1963) and *Gravity's Rainbow* (1973), two mainstream novels which draw heavily upon science-fictional motifs, Thomas Pynchon uses the figure of the cyborg (together with a talking computer and radio-controlled characters) to symbolize the dehumanization which he detects in the history of our century.

Androids – robots designed to look like humans – enforce the man/machine comparison even more strongly. Subject to external control, lacking a past, immune to feeling, unable to strike or revolt, anonymous and interchangeable – androids and their mechanical kinfolk exactly suit the needs and express the fears of an industrialized and bureaucratized society. In its freedom from desire, in its perfect rationality, the android caricatures one prominent image of the scientists's personality. When Norman Mailer went to Texas and Florida to view the first moon shot, an extravaganza he describes in *Of a Fire on the Moon* (1970), he saw the engineers and astronauts as just such mechanical figures, priding themselves on their subordination to the space programme, on their functions, on their anonymity.

Androids are indistinguishable from the figures of human beings, so common in post-war SF, who have been possessed by some alien power. Instead of using electrodes and wires, these invaders take over the minds of humans by means of telepathy, or crystals embedded in brains, or by genetic duplication. Whatever the means of possession, the effect is the same: humans are turned into automatons. A classic example of this scenario is provided by Robert Heinlein's *The Puppet Masters* (1951), in which aliens establish control over their victims by attaching themselves parasitically to the base of the skull. The title creatures in Murray Leinster's *The Brain Stealers* (1954) establish their control by telepathy. In Jack Finney's *The Body Snatchers*, which Don Siegel later made into a grisly movie (*Invasion of the Body Snatchers*, 1955), aliens duplicate their human host cell-by-cell, then substitute the depersonalized replica for the original. Like androids, the transmuted creatures mimic the human originals, but they lack all emotion, obey a collective will, and devote themselves conspiratorially to spreading their control from house-to-house, town-to-town. 'It's a malignant disease spreading throughout the whole country', complains the doctor in the film version.

Exactly the same elements – invasion, possession, conspiracy – are displayed in the Cold War image of communism. The automatons resemble those monitory figures of communists portrayed by the popular media in America during the 1950s and early 1960s. In *Red Nightmare*, for example, filmed by Warner Brothers in 1962 for the Department of Defense, the central figure dreams that his town is taken over by the communists. After the transformation, everyone, including the hero's wife and children, looks exactly as before, but now each one lacks emotion, obeys party orders, and devotes himself single-mindedly to the state. A scene at the town square in which a Soviet officer lectures to the zombie-like citizens ('When the moral fiber of America weakens, you will seize control') exactly parallels scenes in *The Body Snatchers* and *The Brain Stealers*, where newly transformed automatons are sent out to spread their disease to others.

Still the grimmest literary treatment of the loss of identity through social pressures is that offered in *Nineteen Eighty-Four* by Orwell, who had contemporary Britain and America in mind as well as Stalin's Russia. In the showdown scene between Winston Smith, the rebel-against-the-system, and the inquisitor O'Brien, the dread of anonymity is described in terms parallel to those we have found in the literature of invasion and possession: 'We shall crush you down to the point from which there is no coming back', O'Brien declares.

Things will happen to you from which you could not recover, if you lived a thousand years. Never again will you be capable of ordinary human feeling. Everything will be dead inside you. Never again will you be capable of love, or friendship, or joy of living, or laughter, or curiosity, or courage, or integrity. You will be hollow. We shall squeeze you empty, and then we shall fill you with ourselves. (Part III, Ch. 2)

Here is the emotional focus of the invasion-anxiety: the self erased, hollowed-out, filled with alien spirit.

During the years in which fictional invaders, whether from Mars or Russia, were turning ordinary folk into puppets, many people were suggesting that the denizens of Unidentified Flying Objects had invaded earth for the same nefarious purpose. Arthur Clarke drew upon the flying saucer cult in his *Childhood's End* of 1953, conquering the earth in the satanic persons of alien Overlords, who were themselves puppets of an Overmind. At the novel's climax all the children of earth, their features erased and their wills extinguished, are integrated into the collective existence of the Overmind. Individuality – along with the planet – dissolves. Flying saucer lore outside of novels and movies also commonly speaks of aliens as creatures who possess the minds of their victims, paralysing their will, turning them into robots. John A. Keel's hyperbolic account of *Strange Creatures from Time and Space* (1970) may be taken as an illustration of this vast literature:

An invisible phenomenon is always stalking us and manipulating our beliefs. We see only what it chooses to let us see, and we usually react in exactly the way it might expect us to react. . . . The central phenomenon seems to have the ability to control the human mind. . . . Once you begin to understand how the many parts dovetail together you will discover that the 'invisible world' has exercised a peculiar influence over the affairs of men. . . . It is time for us bring all of the nonsense to an end. Time to smoke out the real culprits and tell them we do not much enjoy having our blood sucked and our brains boggled.

It is unlikely the culprits will ever be discovered in the thickets of prose cultivated by Keel, or by any others who postulate an 'invisible world'. The world responsible for the paranoia, for the fear of external control, for the dread of anonymity is the real one in which we live, made up of those institutions which define modern society.

Of course one could argue that all these tales of invasion and possession are merely symptoms of the Cold War anxiety about a communist takeover of America. But this anxiety itself has deeper social roots. We have projected onto the communists, onto flying saucer crews and aliens, the distaste we feel towards our own rationalized society. The regimentation enforced by these fictional creatures is only an exaggerated version of the regimentation we experience in our present world. Towns possessed by some inscrutable collective will are nightmare versions of General Motors or the US Department of Education. The stress on conformity, the discrediting of emotion, the subordination of self to collective, are all characteristics of bureaucratic organization. Techniques of brainwashing, military indoctrination, government propaganda and commercial advertising give us reason to fear that our heads *will* be hollowed out, our thoughts controlled. By blaming alien powers for our loss of identity, we are able to protest against our social condition while seeming to uphold the *status quo*. To paraphrase the comic strip character Pogo, we have met the aliens, and they are us.

VI

Monsters and supermen are the psychological twins of robots. Just as the mechanical men symbolize conformity and anonymity, so the Abominable Snowmen, King Kongs, and Creatures from the Black Lagoon, together with all the science-fictional heroes who are endowed with extraordinary powers, symbolize nonconformity and individuality. They are the eccentrics, defying laws both physical and social, insisting on their uniqueness. Dwelling on the night side of rationality, monsters are a fictional revolt against repression and regimentation. Thus an actor observes, apropos the monster from Tokyo Bay in *Godzilla* (1955), 'It seems to me there are still forces in this world that none of us can understand.' Whether wreaking havoc on Tokyo or New York or London, the monsters are enemies of order, at once the fleshly images of our own destructive impulses (the film *Forbidden Planet* of 1955 even features a 'monster from the Id') and of our mutiny against a rationalized society.

Superheroes present a more complex case than monsters. Batman and Superman, for example, cooperate with the law-enforcement agencies and identify with the middle class. Defence of property and of governmental security are their chief occupations. On his deathbed Pa Kent instructs young Clark, alias Superman, to obey the authorities. But even such establishment heroes express our yearning for individuality. Clark Kent, the mild-mannered reporter, is literally a man in a grey-flannel suit, unloved by women, invisible in the city – until he strips off his disguise to reveal himself as Superman. Disguise also enables Batman to hide himself by day in the figure of an aristocrat; by night he becomes a worker of miracles. The purest example of this wish-fulfilment is provided by the comic-strip character, Captain Marvel, who is the *alter ego* of a boy. The child, small and helpless, need only say, 'Shazam!' in order to be transformed into the muscular, famous, potent superhero. There is an obvious appeal in such figures for adolescents anxious to become adults. But there is also an appeal to the adult longing for an escape from anonymity and impotence.

It is more common for superheroes in science fiction to oppose the reigning order of things. Valentine Michael Smith, the psychic wonder who arrives from Mars in Robert Heinlein's *Stranger in a Strange Land* (1961), is typical of such subversive heroes. He challenges morals, political orders, and even physical laws. In the process he has appealed to readers because he is an exception, a unique individual in a society of drones. In *The Children of Dune* (1976), Frank Herbert presents us with the subversive hero Leto II, who employs his considerable psychic and physical powers to revolutionize the ecology of an entire planet. More humble in their rebellion, the central figures in *Player Piano* and *The City and the Stars* revolt against totalitarian computers; those in *1984*, *We*, *Fahrenheit 451* and *Brave New World*, against political tyranny; those in *The Body Snatchers* and *Childhood's End* against the regimented life imposed by aliens. Occasionally there are pockets of rebellion – the Spacers in *Caves of Steel*, the Travellers in *Earthworks*, the monks in *A Canticle for Leibowitz*, the sundry greenworlds and undergrounds – but these are marginal to the dominant society. Usually the search for identity is a lonely business, carried on against the current of history. The mutants who succeed humans in Clifford Simak's *City* (1952) epitomize this rebellion against conformity (Ch. 5):

the mutants were a different race, an offshoot that had jumped too far ahead. Men who had become true individuals with no need of society, no need of human approval, utterly lacking in the herd instinct that had held the race together, immune to social pressures.

In all these rebellious figures, struggling to become 'true individuals', fighting against 'social pressures', we find revealed the central predicament of characters in science fiction.

VII

Identity has become problematic in SF because it has become problematic in modern society. We are pushed towards anonymity by bureaucracies and technology, by the scale of life in cities, by the mass media, by the techniques of manipulation perfected in government and business. To borrow a term from Max Weber, these social phenomena are the *bearers* of the certain structures of consciousness, chief among them being the fear of *anomie*, of external control, of invisibility. Through form and theme, SF dramatizes this fear. It makes no more sense to condemn the genre for its seeming neglect of characterization than to praise the modernist novel for its cultivation of the isolated ego. Both are preoccupied with threats to identity in the modern world. Mainstream writers such as Thomas Pynchon, Anthony Burgess, and Doris Lessing, drawing upon the formal experiments of modernism and the materials of SF, have hybridized the two seemingly opposed traditions, revealing the shared social concerns which bind them together.

The forms and settings of science fiction differ from those of the nineteenth-century realist novel; but the kind of knowledge the genre provides is akin to the knowledge offered by literary realism. The SF novel, like the novels of Balzac or Dickens or Tolstoy or Mann, provides models of the essential structures, the inner processes, the typical movements of nature and history. Future-oriented fiction obviously cannot be mimetic in the Platonic sense of reproducing the sensuous appearance of things, since the future does not yet exist; but it can be mimetic in the Aristotelian sense of representing the essential features, the fundamental processes, of the experienced world. The great nineteenth-century realists, whatever their stated doctrine, worked in terms of typical characters and situations; they expressed an understanding of the world, and of history's movement, through their treatment of event, motif, plot, personality. And it is this act of modelling socio-historical patterns within fiction, not any congruence of surface details, which constitutes realism. Science fiction should therefore be viewed, not as an unprecedented event in literary history, nor as an exclusive outgrowth of the romance tradition; it is more fruitful, I think, to view SF as a dialectical extension of realism, incorporating its technical discoveries and intellectual concerns while projecting its methods of typification and modelling into the future, into other worlds, into alien lives.

Like most significant issues in literature, the problem of identity in SF is not so much formal as historical. Its solution waits upon a solution to the problem of identity in industrial society. Only when new forms of community arise, which allow for both cooperative living and richness of the self; only when technology is subjected to democratic control and humane purposes; only when cities are built on a human scale, and when the machineries of government and business are decentralized and the powers which they now exercise are returned to citizens – only then will writers find it easy to imagine complex characters who are at peace with modern society. No one expects that day to come soon; many say it will never come. In the meantime, novelists must invent their own worlds, if they are to do justice both to society and the self, if they are once again to make their characters visible.

Bibliography

Among theoretical treatments of SF as a genre, I have found the following texts useful: Darko Suvin, 'On the Poetics of the Science Fiction Genre', *College English*, **34** (Dec. 1972), 372-82; Robert Scholes, *Structural Fabulation: An Essay on Fiction of the Future* (Notre Dame, Indiana: Univ. of Notre Dame Press, 1975); David Ketterer, *New Worlds for Old: The Apocalyptic Imagination, Science Fiction, and American Literature* (Bloomington, Indiana: Indiana U.P., 1974); Joanna Russ, 'Towards an Aesthetic of Science Fiction', *Science-Fiction Studies*, **2** Part 2 (July 1975), 112-19; Fredric Jameson, 'World-Reduction in Le Guin: The Emergence of Utopian Narrative', *Science-Fiction Studies*, **2** Part 3 (Nov. 1975), 221-30.

Science-Fiction Studies, **4** Part 3 (Nov. 1977) is devoted to 'The Sociology of Science Fiction'. That issue includes 'A Select Bibliography of the Sociology of Literature' (pp. 295–308 compiled by Marc Angenot with readers and critics of SF in mind. Angenot's annotated guide is the best bibliographical introduction for anyone wishing to look further into the sociology of SF. A good introductory survey of the sociology of audience and literary production is provided by Robert Escarpit, *Sociology of Literature* (Paris, 1958; trans. London, 1965). In the same empiricist vein, see Escarpit, ed., *Le Littéraire et le social* (Paris, 1970).

To my mind the most important theorists concerning the relation between literature and society have been Marx, Engels, Georg Lukács, and Lucien Goldmann. For the basic Marxist texts, a good place to start is Lee Baxandall and Stefan Morawski, eds, *Karl Marx and Friedrich Engels on Literature and Art* (St Louis, Missouri: Telos Press, 1974). For Lukács, see *The Historical Novel* (East Berlin: 1955; trans. Boston: Humanities Press, 1963). And for Goldmann, see *Towards a Sociology of the Novel* (Paris, 1969; trans. London: Tavistock Pubns., 1975), and *Structures mentales et création culturelle* (Paris, 1970). Lukács and Goldmann are the main theorists behind Diana T. Laurenson and Alan Swingewood's useful study, *The Sociology of Literature* (London: MacGibbon and Kee, Paladin, 1972).

The finest interpreter in English of literary texts in light of shared historical experience is Raymond Williams. See in particular his *Culture and Society 1780—1950* (London: Chatto and Windus, 1958), *The Long Revolution* (London: Chatto and Windus, 1961) and *The Country and the City* (London: Chatto and Windus, 1973).

Literature on the sociology of modernization is abundant. I have found the following texts especially useful: Peter Berger, Brigitte Berger and Hansfried Kellner, *The Homeless Mind: Modernization and Consciousness* (New York: Irvington, Random House, 1973); Herbert Marcuse, *One-Dimensional Man: Studies in the Ideology of Advanced Industrial Society* (Boston: Beacon Press, 1964); H. H. Gerth and C. Wright Mills, ed, *From Max Weber: essays in sociology* (New York: Oxford U.P., 1946); and David Riesman, *The Lonely Crowd* (New York, 1953 abr. ed. New Haven: Yale U.P., 1969).

Characterization in science fiction: Two approaches
2. The alien encounter: or, Ms Brown and Mrs Le Guin

Patrick Parrinder

'But who shall dwell in these worlds if they be inhabited? . . . Are we or they Lords of the World? . . . And how are all things made for man?'
JOHANNES KEPLER
quoted by *H. G. Wells in* The War of the Worlds *(1898).*

I believe that all novels begin with an old lady in the corner opposite . . . We [must be] determined never, never to desert Mrs Brown.
VIRGINIA WOOLF
'Mr Bennett and Mrs Brown' (1924).

I

'I wonder', says a character in Roger Zelazny's *Doorways in the Sand* (1976), 'what it was really like? That first encounter – out there – with the aliens. Hard to believe that several years have passed since it happened.' Many people claim that in fact, not merely in fiction, it has already happened. Erich von Däniken's millions of readers like to be told that it has been going on since the dawn of history. NASA puts a pair of life-drawings of the human male and female into an unmanned space-probe so that, should it be intercepted by alien intelligences, they will learn some basic features of human existence. A large pavilion at the 'Man and his World' exhibition in Montreal gives to extra-terrestrials and the 'evidence' of their encounters with man the same status as the displays of Chinese, Russian, Indian and French cultures in neighbouring pavilions. Science and pseudo-science, rational speculation and neurotic cultism may be hard to distinguish at times, but it would be quite wrong to suggest that 'alien encounter' fiction makes its strongest appeal to a lunatic fringe. Stories depicting men's 'first contact' with imaginary beings touch a whole range of human concerns, from would-be realistic problems of space exploration to the historical guilts left behind by Western man's dealings with other races and cultures (e.g. the Red Indians), and our consciousness of individuality and isolation in personal relationships (can we rule out the possibility of a link between the myths of 'first contact' and 'love at first sight'?). These considerations, much too wide to go into here, suggest the many layers of response which may be activated by the alien creatures of science fiction.

By an interesting coincidence, the English word 'alien', in the special sense appropriated to it by science-fiction writers and readers, shares the same stem as one of the most fashionable twentieth-century metaphysical concepts, that of 'alienation'. The excitement and fear aroused by the prospect of encountering truly alien beings are not unlike the feelings associated with 'alienated individuals', such as the nihilists, terrorists and 'motiveless' murderers first described by Turgenev, Dostoevsky and Conrad. Nihilism involves the repudiation of common human emotions of mercy, compassion and goodwill towards others. Similarly, it seems likely that extra-terrestrial intelligences would look upon Earth, at best, in a coldly rational manner, without reverence for or even any conception of our own inbuilt prejudices in favour of humanity. At worst, like Swift's King of Brobdingnag, the extra-terrestrials might very well conclude that men were a race of 'little odious vermin' to be ruthlessly stamped out. A third possibility, that of benevolent patronage, has been much explored by SF writers, as has the idea of aliens 'inferior' to ourselves who thereby pose us with the moral dilemmas involved in 'conservation'. What is most unlikely is that we could expect to meet with aliens on unreservedly equal terms, and still less that we could experience feelings of real community with them; once an alien, always an alien may well turn out to be the law of the universe.

The satirists of the Enlightenment, such as Cyrano in *Other Worlds* (1657), Swift in *Gulliver's Travels* (1726) and Voltaire in *Micromégas* (1752), were among the first writers to exploit the advantages of seeing humanity from an alien viewpoint. (Previously, it might be argued, the concept of a god or gods had served this purpose.) Cyrano, Swift and Voltaire use encounters with aliens to show up mankind as the prisoners of an ideology, of a limited and self-interested system of thought. Ideologies habituate us to the particular conditions of the civilization we inhabit, so that we look upon these conditions as if they were normal and natural adjuncts of living. Beginning with the Russian Formalists, twentieth-century aesthetic theory has often suggested that literature is a principal means of exposing the artificial and arbitrary nature of the 'structures of feeling' (to use Raymond Williams's term) that we normally take for granted. Swift is one of the writers whom the Russian Formalist critics cited in support of their theory of poetic *ostranenie* (usually translated as 'defamiliarization'). Science fiction employs a particular kind of defamiliarization technique, since it confronts the reader with new and strange conditions of life outside his own likely or possible experience. This is the technique which Darko Suvin, who is perhaps the leading theorist of the genre, has named 'cognitive estrangement'.

Philosophically considered, the process of defamiliarization leads us to see men in their present state as the unconscious prisoners of an ideology. Nevertheless, the use of specific defamiliarizing devices in an SF novel by no means guarantees that the novel as a whole could be found subversive or even mildly critical of established norms. Most commercial SF is part of the ever-increasing quantity of 'escape' literature produced in the advanced countries in the last two centuries. Such literature encourages a vicarious escape from some aspects of the reader's social environment, but only, it would seem, in order to bind him more securely to other aspects of that environment. The 'superman' fantasy, for example, seems at first sight to embody feelings of rebellion against advanced industrial society, but it also helps to channel off such feelings, and thus to restrain them from any more political mode of expression.

Fantasies of supermen, we might say, are not really subversive because they are dictated by the rampant individualism on which bourgeois society itself is based. But, at the other extreme, any meaningful act of defamiliarization can only be relative, since it is not possible for man to imagine what is *utterly* alien to him; the utterly alien would also be the meaningless. To give meaning to something is also, inescapably, to 'humanize' it or to bring it within the bounds of our anthropomorphic world-view. This means that we can only describe something as 'alien' by contrast or analogy with what we already know. The difference between the most banal literary conceptions of the alien (supermen and bug-eyed monsters), and those which force us to reassess our own ideology-bound existence, is one of degree, not of kind, and must be decided by critical judgement. In science fiction one of the main factors influencing such a judgement is the existence of a long tradition of 'alien encounter' fictions. Among the most seminal works in this tradition is *Gulliver's Travels* by Jonathan Swift.

At the end of the fourth book of the *Travels,* Gulliver returns home after his sojourn in the land of the Houyhnhnms or rational horses. His wife tries to embrace him but, 'having not been used to the touch of that odious animal for so many years', he falls into a swoon for almost an hour. Later he sets up a stable and spends several hours each day in conversation with his horses, which, though they are not Houyhnhnms, are far preferable to brutish mankind. Gulliver has been among alien beings and comes back in a state of 'alienation' which amounts to madness. His madness has some all-too-human causes, such as gullibility, fanaticism and an overweening pride. For all this, it remains a disturbing rejection of the 'ideology' of being human, for which Gulliver has previously shown himself to be an avid spokesman.

The shock given to the reader by Gulliver's description of his wife as 'that odious animal' is caused by the reduction of a loved human being to a nauseous object. However, the tenuousness of all human self-conceit is implicit at the moment of his first meeting with a bemused Houyhnhnm:

In the midst of this distress, I observed them all to run away on a sudden as fast as they could, at which I ventured to leave the tree, and pursue the road, wondering what it was that could put them into this fright. But looking on my left hand, I saw a horse walking softly in the field; which my persecutors having sooner discovered, was the cause of their flight. The horse started a little when he came near me, but soon recovering himself, looked full in my face with manifest tokens of wonder: he viewed my hands and feet, walking round me several times. I would have pursued my journey, but he placed himself directly in the way, yet looking with a very mild aspect, never offering the least violence. We stood gazing at each other for some time; at last I took the boldness to reach my hand towards his neck, with a design to stroke it, using the common style and whistle of jockeys when they are going to handle a strange horse. But this animal seeming to receive my civilities with disdain, shook his head, and bent his brows, softly raising up his right fore-foot to remove my hand. Then he neighed three or four times, but in so different a cadence, that I almost began to think he was speaking to himself in some language of his own.

Both parties to this encounter are startled to realise that they are subject to biological investigation. The intelligence of the Houyhnhnm is denoted at first by his manifestation of the signs of mental concentration and 'tokens of wonder'; at the end of the passage it is confirmed by his possession of the *sine qua non* of intelligence, a 'language of his own'. Later it turns out that the idea of deception can only be expressed in the Houyhnhnms' language by a clumsy circumlocution, 'to say the thing which is not'. This realisation that alienness implies the possession of a language – which, necessarily, cannot be directly represented, and which in certain crucial ways also defies translation – epitomizes the literary problems of the 'alien encounter'. How does the SF writer set out to describe beings who do not share a common language with us, and who may not even have the same understanding about the purposes of language? The task is one of literary characterisation in a broad sense, and the rules involved may be compared with the rules of characterization in more conventional fiction.

II

There are two fundamentally opposing doctrines about character in the conventional novel. The first of these holds that character-creation is the fundamental purpose of the novel, while the second holds that character is subordinate to plot. In the latter case, only in those novels which take as their plot the life-history of an individual or the discovery of identity could the portrayal of the main character be said to be an end in itself. The best-known defence of Doctrine No 1 is Virginia Woolf's essay 'Mr Bennett and Mrs Brown' (1924). Recently the doctrine has been restated in a science-fiction context by Ursula K. Le Guin, under the title 'Science Fiction and Mrs Brown' (1976). Doctrine No 2 admits of many variations, one of which is Scott Sander's argument in the preceding essay that modern fiction (including SF) dramatizes the erosion of individuality in contemporary society. The 'disappearance of character' is, according to Sanders, the underlying 'plot' of such fiction.

One of the notable features of *Gulliver's Travels* is that Gulliver himself is not wholly satisfactory as a fictional character. Recent critics have often found him confused and inconsistent. It has been suggested that he is not a rounded individual so much as a variable 'point of view' to mediate Swift's satire. Gulliver's unsatisfactoriness, in fact, is not unlike that of many science-fiction characters who are simply rendered as props to help the author tell an exciting story. Ursula Le Guin argues that this near-universal failure of characterization prevents science fiction, in all but a few exceptional cases, from achieving the status of a 'true novel'. Though it may be valid as the statement of a personal aesthetic, this judgement seems to burden science fiction with a quite unnecessary stigma.

Mrs Brown, in the essay by Virginia Woolf mentioned above, was an ordinary lady sitting in a railway carriage going from Richmond to Waterloo. Her reality and her ordinariness constituted the novelist's essential subject-matter, the one thing that he or she must never desert. No doubt there are occasions when, as Ursula Le Guin puts it, the science-fiction writer would want to welcome Mrs Brown aboard his spaceship. But individual characterization is usually a secondary concern in SF, in a way that it is not likely to be in novels which take personal relationships as their principal subject-matter. This is because SF describes a world transformed by some new element. The new element – whether it is an extrapolation from present-day science or technology, or some form of intervention by extra-terrestrial sources – is bound to have a deep effect on the reactions of the human characters, so that characterization, even in the richest and most 'novelistic' of SF works, is always to a large extent functional, a means towards the most effective presentation of the *novum* which called the story into being in the first place. In science fiction it is the new element, and not the need for subtle and rounded characterization, which determines the basic rules of the genre.

Yet, if the new element is an alien life-form, the problem of characterization is reintroduced in a somewhat unfamiliar sense. It may even be that Virginia Woolf's paradigm for the novelist's situation still holds. We do not need to put Mrs Brown aboard the spaceship, kicking and screaming and laying about with her handbag as she is likely to be. Our problem is that of the alien intelligence (whom we shall call Ms Brown) encountered either on her home planet, or in some neutral part of the galaxy, or in a terrestrial railway carriage. Much depends on the nature of Ms Brown's psychology and physiology, which may vary from the comfortably near- or quasi-human to the utterly grotesque. For simplicity's sake, we may start with the most prosaic assumption: Ms Brown appears to be a perfect humanoid replica, she is clad inconspicuously in jeans and sweater (which, however, form a single garment) and is in all probability a Martian spy.

The science-fiction story which could follow from this is likely to embody one of three different narrative models, depending on the viewpoint that the author adopts. The viewpoint may be that of the human observer of Ms Brown, of the suspected Martian spy herself or of an objective narrator mediating between the two. (The author may, of course, use a 'cutting' technique to incorporate two or more of these.) The distinction holds good for any 'first contact' story, no matter what the aliens look like or where the encounter takes place.

Told by an objective narrator, the story most frequently takes the form of a puzzle. How is Ms Brown to be distinguished from a human being? What does her presence mean and what is to be done about her? The tradition of fictions of this kind might be traced back to Edgar Allan Poe's famous detective story, 'The Murders in the Rue Morgue' (1841), in which the detective deduces that the crime cannot have been committed by a human being (he manages to pin it on a stray orang-utan). 'First Contact' (1945) by Murray Leinster (which will be discussed later in this essay) tells of an encounter between two spaceships in the heart of a nebula foreign to both. How are they to get away without either destroying one another or revealing the whereabouts of their respective home bases? The solution is neatly held back to the end. Similarly, Isaac Asimov's 'Let's Get Together' (1957) deals with a Russian plot to kill top Western scientists by infiltrating humanoids carrying nuclear explosives into a robotics conference. Asimov's narrator shows us the robots through human eyes, but this is a detective story in which they are foiled by reasoning rather than by observation. No attempt is made to explain how 'mechanical men' are able to look and behave like living flesh, though the punch-line which follows the story's final shoot-out ('Not blood, but high-grade machine-oil') is one of which any pulp-magazine author would have been proud.

Both Asimov and Leinster use a narrative technique which plays down the sinister and grotesque effects liable to occur in a first-person account, when Ms Brown is scrutinized, as it were, through the eyes of the passenger sitting opposite her. Are not her ears somewhat beast-like, her nose curiously reminiscent of a muzzle – and could those small protuberances on top of 'her' head conceivably be horns? The spine-chilling characteristics so regularly associated with aliens tell us a good deal about the nature of modern mass-entertainment; they seem to be designed to relieve the tensions caused by fear of the unknown, fear of violence, fear of the basic insecurity of the modern world-system and by a pervasive xenophobia. The alien presence in the railway carriage quickly becomes evidence of an invasion, a conspiracy. Conversely, when Ms Brown is met with on another planet the intrepid human space-captain is all too likely to shoot first and ask questions afterwards.

Only in a very crude story would the reaction to the aliens be purely xenophobic. In most cases the narrator, though repelled by Ms Brown, is also curiously drawn to her. He may end up by paying her an ironic tribute ('She's almost human!'). Or he sets out to study her and her compatriots, finding in them the awesome traits of a higher civilization than our own. An 'eye-witness' story of this kind looks back to the Enlightenment and may still be written in a style modelled on eighteenth-century forms of empirical narrative such as the traveller's tale and the scientific report. Wells's *The Island of Doctor Moreau* (1896), for example, begins with a wary 'anthropological' investigation of the alien phenomenon, but ends, like *Gulliver's Travels,* by showing us the narrator's estrangement from humanity itself.

The third type of narrative viewpoint is that of the Martian visitor herself. She may be conceived either as a rational interrogator of human life, like Swift's Houyhnhnms and Brobdingnagians and Voltaire's Micromégas, or as a confused and emotional being, torn by impulses of love and hatred for humanity – the romantic model laid down by the monster in *Frankenstein.* The first tendency leads to a detached and often ironic exposure of humanity's cultural and ideological limitations. Ms Brown, in this view, may be pictured as a benign but wryly puzzled observer of terrestrial behaviour. 'Why', she asks, 'do human beings seem so startled and self-conscious in my presence? After all, the only difference between us is this tiny forked tail that I have. . . . And who would have thought that sexual differentiation, which seemed so unimportant to my inventors on Mars that they chose to ignore it, would have caused so much fuss? Do human beings really need to be sure what sex I am before they know how to react to me?'

Alternatively, the discovery that conventional human identity is a form of cultural imprisonment may be as harrowing for the alien mind as it is for those most directly concerned. Ursula Le Guin uses a mixture of human, alien and impersonal viewpoints in *The Left Hand of Darkness* (1969), which portrays the slow and difficult growth of personal love between Genly Ai (anagram of 'alien g(u)y'?), the human envoy to the planet Gethen, and the Gethenian politician Lord Estraven. Kurt Vonnegut in *The Sirens of Titan* (1959) shows both humans and aliens realising that their supposed identity is a form of conditioning, a literal 'alienation' that has been programmed into them for reasons unknown. Winston Niles Rumfoord disappears after announcing that the goal of human history has been the production of a tiny spare part for a Tralfamadorian spaceship. When Salo, the Tralfamadorian, discovers that the message his grounded spaceship is trying to deliver consists of the one word 'Greetings', he commits suicide. Samuel Delany's characters in *The Einstein Intersection* (1967) are aliens who have mysteriously come to inhabit human bodies, and to inherit human culture; this is explained as a cosmic mix-up involving Goedel's Law and the Theory of Relativity. In both Vonnegut and Delany the viewpoint of the 'alien' is hard to distinguish from that of an alienated humanity.

III

The discussion or narrative models has introduced some of the more familiar motifs and plots involving aliens in science fiction. However, the basic rules governing the characterization of aliens are common to all these narrative models. While the central feature of alien intelligence is its possession of a different language, its peripheral features consist of a multitude of different sign-systems, including such things as physical characteristics, behaviour-patterns and sexual roles, by which a Martian Ms Brown might be distinguished from her human counterpart. Science-fiction novelists very frequently ignore the special difficulties presented by the language barrier, and rely on these other sign-systems to convey the alienness of their creations. (Leinster's 'First Contact' provides a particularly clear example of this, since the aliens' mode of communication does not involve sound-waves. Once the technicians have sorted this out, instantaneous translation machines are set up in no time.) The choice of alien features is always meaningful, whether or not it carries an openly satirical, ironic or didactic reference to human life; aliens in literature must always be constructed on some principle of analogy or contrast with the human world.

It follows from this that aliens in SF invariably possess a metaphorical dimension. The two terms of the metaphor are as follows (I have used I. A. Richards's widely accepted terms 'tenor' and 'vehicle' to distinguish them). The tenor of the metaphor consists of some aspect of human behaviour or human culture which the author intends to defamiliarize, or to reveal as an artificial and, it may be, ideological construct rather than a natural necessity. The vehicle consists of a recognizable deviation from the human norm. Such a deviation will normally contain features reminiscent of:

1. the natural world; usually animals, but more rarely vegetable or mineral substances; or
2. the various types of mythological and imaginary beings, including devils, giants, dwarves and automata or intelligent machines; or
3. foreigners – especially those whose cultural distance from the writer and his audience is such as to make them familiar objects of anthropological or social-psychological speculation; or
4. some combination of the preceding types.

The metaphorical purpose of the vast majority of aliens in science fiction is immediately obvious to the careful reader. For example, such celebrated novels as Arthur C. Clarke's *Childhood's End* (1953) and James Blish's *A Case of Conscience* (1959) may easily be read as Miltonic parables in which alien tempters confront humanity with the traditional Satanic promises of knowledge and happiness. Often there is little to be said about the aliens in themselves (especially in a short story) once their metaphorical purpose has been grasped. At the same time, the metaphorical *implications* of SF stories frequently appear to go beyond their authors' conscious intentions.

A simple example is Isaac Asimov's 'Victory Unintentional' (1942), which tells of a confrontation between two types of 'alien' – Jovians and robots – each of whom differs from humanity in a single major respect. The robots are a research team designed by Earthmen to be sent as envoys to the Jovians, who are described as a proud, belligerent people contemptuous of all outsiders. The Jovians do their best to threaten and humiliate their visitors, but fail to realize that these visitors are themselves non-human. The robots only have to demonstrate a few of their 'superhuman' capacities, such as imperviousness to poison gases, ability to withstand extreme temperatures and indifference to atmospheric pressure, before their adversaries come cringing to them in submission.

Given the date of the story and the fact that the Jovians are accused of an overdeveloped 'superiority complex' and an inability to accept loss of face, there is no difficulty in recognizing them as 'foreigners', and in fact as Japanese in disguise. 'Victory Unintentional' is easily reduced to a parable suggesting that, despite their determination and overwhelming numbers, the Japanese may be defeated by their own over-confidence. ('When a superiority complex like that breaks, it breaks all the way.') The shallowness of this story is the shallowness of its basic metaphor, a mixture of war propaganda and pseudo-Freudian psychology.

However, the story has now acquired a further metaphorical significance which Asimov probably did not foresee. While the Jovian defeat is engineered by human beings, it is actually accomplished, and can only be accomplished, by robots. The robots differ from humanity not in being more psychologically acute, as far as we can tell, but in their astonishing strength. Their consciousness of their own strength allows them to speak with pity and some condescension of the dangers posed to their 'human masters' by the Jovians. Asimov has maintained that his robots are completely under human control (as in the Three Laws of Robotics), hence they are not really 'aliens'. But to the reader made uneasy by the destructive power of modern technology this is not necessarily very convincing. The story may now be read as a striking forecast of the actual process of the Japanese surrender after the dropping of the atomic bomb. If this reading is tenable, 'Victory Unintentional' may be said to defamiliarize not only the nature of Japanese aggression, but the confident American assumption that man can remain the unquestioned master of his technologies.

Murray Leinster's 'First Contact' is another political parable, which anticipates the Cold War strategies which developed after its publication in 1945. The chance meeting of two spaceships, 'ours' and 'theirs', brings about a situation which Leinster interprets as a 'balance of terror'. Each side would like to behave humanely to the other but they do not dare to. Leinster's aliens are, in fact, puzzlingly human in nearly every respect. They are professionals whose calculations simply mirror those of their terrestrial counterparts. The one substantial difference, as we have seen, is that they communicate without sound-waves. When the Earthmen present an ultimatum which exactly coincides with the ultimatum that they themselves have devised, they respond by making 'convulsive movements'. Belatedly it becomes evident that they are laughing.

The tenor of Leinster's alien metaphor is sufficiently trite: no matter what we look like, if we can laugh together we are brothers under the skin. (The story ends with the communications officers of the two ships exchanging dirty jokes.) But the ideology of this story completely undermines its optimistic message; we might be prepared for this by the fact that the supposed aliens are not really alien at all. Leinster is implying that the relationship between two great civilizations is *naturally* belligerent, so that perpetual vigilance and the maintenance of a balance of terror are the only ways of keeping the peace. Such vigilance must be entrusted to the scientific-military élite represented by the spaceship's crew. The good-fellowship stressed in the story is quite spurious, since it is inconceivable that two such Machiavellian cultures will not end up at war with one another, by proxy if not head-on. The fact that both sides think alike merely confirms the 'inevitability' of Cold War attitudes.

Both 'Victory Unintentional' and 'First Contact' are cleverly and efficiently written, but their conception of alienness is trite and shamelessly propagandistic. Stanley G. Weinbaum's 'A Martian Odyssey' and 'Valley of Dreams' (1934) are two much-praised stories which develop a more complex metaphor, although the actual level of the writing is comparatively crude. The most remarkable figure in these stories, which introduce several fantastic Martian species in quick succession, is the ostrich-like part-animal, part-vegetable called Tweel (actually his name sounds more like 'T-r-r-rwee-r-rl'!), who has the habit of zooming up into the air and then planting himself in the ea. h with his beak. Tweel speaks a genuinely alien language, but displays exemplary virtues of rationality and self-sacrificing loyalty; hence the inevitable compliment at the end of 'A Martian Odyssey' ('Thanks, Tweel. You're a man!').

The second stage of the metaphor occurs in 'Valley of Dreams', where Tweel is revealed in a von Däniken-like twist as one of the last descendants of the Egyptian god Thoth. Thoth travelled to Earth and came to be worshipped as the inventor of writing ('They must have picked up the idea from watching the Martian take notes'). Thus Tweel's race are not the Noble Savages that they at first appeared, but the inaugurators of civilization itself. (Further significance can presumably be drawn from the fact that both Tweel's race and the human explorers have a common enemy, the 'dream-beast' which snares its victims with unbridled fantasies.) Far from the rationalism of Asimov and Leinster, Weinbaum's aliens reveal a powerful, unsophisticated and largely uncontrolled use of imaginative materials. The human figures in these two stories are pathetically stereotyped.

If Weinbaum's Martians incline towards Gothic fantasy, those of H.

G. Wells, though equally grotesque, are portrayed in a much more scientific spirit. The Martians in *The War of the Worlds* (1898) are once again doubly metaphorical. At first they appear simply as terrifyingly aggressive creatures who, like Asimov's Jovians, are defeated by non-human agency; thus the outcome of the contest is both a triumph and a humiliation for humanity. By the end, guided by references in the text to Wells's article 'The Man of the Year Million' (1893), we are led to see them as possibly resembling the future descendants of man himself. To this metaphorical structure Wells adds a faculty of meticulous observation, particularly in the episode where the narrator is trapped in the ruined house and is able to subject the Martians to systematic study. The Martians are described by means of a series of highly imaginative and complex extrapolations from terrestrial zoology and physiology. Wells's invaders represent the classical portrayal in SF of hostile aliens, with a physique and intelligence explained by evolutionary biology, and with whom no intelligent contact is possible.

IV

Only at the end of the story, with their cry of 'Ulla! ulla!', do Wells's aliens break into language. Weinbaum's Martians, with their books which the narrator despairs of translating because 'they were made by minds too different from ours', are a more sophisticated creation in this one respect. Philological and anthropological awareness have played a growing part in mid-twentieth-century science fiction; C. S. Lewis's *Out of the Silent Planet* (1938), with its hero who reacts to his first alien encounter by projecting a Martian–English dictionary and a Malacandrian grammar, is an early landmark. Lewis's philologist-hero learns to speak Malacandrian easily enough, though not as quickly as the standard pulp-magazine hero would have done. It is precisely the possession of a language or other sign-system which *cannot* be easily learned, or which has radical points of difference from human language, which distinguishes the most far-reaching of recent attempts to imagine the alien.

Stanislaw Lem's *Solaris* (1961) and *The Invincible* (1963) reveal a fascination with forms of 'intelligence' which are as little anthropomorphic as it is possible to be. In *The Invincible* the planet Regis III is dominated by tiny metallic particles which have the power to gather in threatening clouds emitting electromagnetic radiation. The intelligence of *Solaris* is the planet-wide ocean, which creates a series of human simulacra, the 'Visitors', who arrive to torment the small group of scientists inhabiting a research station hovering over the planet's surface. We never learn the ocean's motives for producing the Visitors, but the shrewdest conjecture is that of the cyberneticist Snow, who muses that 'Perhaps it was sending us . . . presents.' The ceaseless self-transformations of the ocean, like the awesome cloud-formations seen by Rohan in *The Invincible,* are a form of 'language' which appears to the human observer as a fantastic dance of natural forms. Both novels combine a 'puzzle' element with the viewpoint of the human eye-witness. Rohan concludes that Regis III should be left alone in the future: 'Not everywhere has everything been intended for us, he thought.' By contrast, Kris Kelvin in *Solaris* elects to stay on the deserted planet and is last seen 'shaking hands' with the ocean, a new stage in the anthropological rituals of first contact. Kelvin's confused and quixotic renunciation of human claims may be compared to Gulliver's estrangement at the end of the *Travels*.

Lem's novels do not go beyond the limitations of the human viewpoint, and are thus the eloquent statements of an impasse. In order to bridge this impasse and adopt an alien viewpoint, it is necessary to offer some sort of verbal representation of alien language. This is normally done by subjecting the writer's own language to a controlled stylistic distortion. Such distortion is a recognised, though still relatively infrequent, method of emphasizing the alienness of setting in novels of the future or of the remote past. (It is related, of course, to such conventional devices as the representation of dialect through phonetic spelling, and the use of archaic grammatical forms in historical fiction.) Anthony Burgess invents a heavily Russianized teenage argot ('nadsat') for his first-person SF narrative in *A Clockwork Orange* (1962), and – more predictably – a kind of Shakespearian argot for his historical novel *Nothing Like the Sun* (1964). Yevgeny Zamyatin's *We* (1921) uses the methods of experimental modernist writing to convey the rationalised and mathematized experience of D-503, the inhabitant of a regimented, tyrannical state of the far future. Since the novel shows D-503's shocked rediscovery of the emotional and atavistic experiences (such as love) repressed by the State, its writing involves not only the creation of an alien style but its partial breaking-down under stress. George Orwell's *Nineteen Eighty-Four* (1949) explores a similar conflict between 'natural' and 'totalitarian' languages more simply by means of its theoretical account of Newspeak, the planned official language of Oceania. Finally, William Golding uses a narrative language in which sensations are interpreted ideographically, rather than by means of our normal conceptual apparatus, in his extraordinarily vivid evocation of the consciousness of the Neanderthal men in *The Inheritors* (1955).

These examples suggest that a discussion of alien languages in science fiction might very quickly leave behind the notion of characterization, in favour of a much more general consideration of modernist narrative techniques. Within science fiction, however, it is not necessary to break with the wider conventions of prose narrative in order to produce work that is validly experimental. The 'New Wave' writing of the 1960s, with its fragmented and surrealistic forms, has not made a lasting impact, because it cast its net too wide. To reform science fiction one must challenge the conventions of the genre on their own terms.

Brian W. Aldiss's *The Dark Light Years* (1964) – a novel which preceded the 'New Wave' – deals with humanity's discovery of the utods (upside-down utopians?), a race of intelligent, six-legged creatures with a remarkable love for their own excrement. At their first meeting on the planet Grudgrodd, the humans immediately open fire, killing six of the unarmed utods and bringing the other two back to captivity in London's Exozoo. The utods show a serene acceptance of life in captivity, with little or no desire to respond to their human keepers – even when the director of the Exozoo goes so far in comradeliness as to remove his trousers and defecate in their presence. The utods' stilted conversations with one another reveal both a healthy curiosity about alien life-forms and a strong sense of the limitations of curiosity. Speaking of mankind, one of them states that 'the thinlegs' ways of thought are too alien for us to interpret . . . any tentative explanation we may offer is bound to be utodomorphic'. The utods' language is conveyed in English distorted in the main by some Swiftian euphemisms; thus they use 'converted into the carrion stage' for 'dead', much as the Houyhnhnms accused Gulliver of 'saying the thing which was not'. The reader responds to their utodomorphic being while perceiving it, inevitably, as an inverted anthropomorphism; the utods have long ago passed through the frenzied stages of an industrial revolution, and their behaviour is constantly set off against the brutally imperialistic attitudes of human beings.

The Dark Light Years, then, offers a conception of alienness based on animals (one likely source of inspiration is the well-known popular song, 'Mud, mud, glorious mud' about the hippopotamus) and also on the difference between Western and 'native' (possibly South-East Asian) civilizations. The utods are a defamiliarization device serving to promote a reflection on human behaviour and, specifically, on the ideologies of Western industrialism and imperialism. At the same time, these dignified, sybaritic and dung-loving beings are strongly 'characterized', even if we are doomed to perceive their character through a veil of human incomprehension. Certainly the utods steal the show – as they were intended to – from the human characters of the story.

In *The Dark Light Years* and novels like it, richness of invention and exuberance of detail are combined with a clear grasp of the story's metaphorical import. Science fiction, above all when it is concerned with exploring alien modes of being, differs from other kinds of fiction in its basic premise, which is that of approaching 'man' through his contacts with the new and unknown. Yet a consideration of alien encounters involves the modification, rather than the wholesale abandonment, of the idea of rounded characterization championed by Virginia Woolf and lately by Ursula Le Guin. What is limiting about their declarations of loyalty to Mrs Brown is not the stress on characterization as such, but their belief that what is characterized most fully must always be the autonomous human beings of liberal individualism.

Is it too much of a travesty of conventional fictional theory to say that the SF novelist must never desert Ms Brown, but that *his* Ms Brown is frequently an alien, quite possibly with six legs and certainly with a language of her own?

Bibliography

'Science Fiction and Mrs Brown', by Ursula K. Le Guin, was published in *Science Fiction at Large,* ed. Peter Nicholls (London: Gollancz, 1976). (A paperback edition of this book, entitled *Explorations of the Marvellous,* was brought out by Fontana in 1978.)

For a different view of character in SF, see C. S. Lewis, *Of Other Worlds,* ed. Walter Hooper, (London: Geoffrey Bles, 1966), pp. 64–5.

Virginia Woolf's essay 'Mr Bennett and Mrs Brown' is collected in *The Captain's Death-Bed and Other Essays* (London: Hogarth Press, 1950).

For 'cognitive estrangement', see Darko Suvin, 'On the Poetics of the Science Fiction Genre', in *Science Fiction: A Collection of Critical Essays,* ed. Mark Rose (Englewood Cliffs, N. J.: Prentice-Hall, 1976). This essay and the same author's 'SF and the Novum' appear in Suvin's *Metamorphoses of Science Fiction* (New Haven: Yale U.P., 1979).

For the concept of 'defamiliarization' as developed by the Russian Formalists, see *Théorie de la Littérature,* ed. Tzvetan Todorov (Paris: Seuil, 1965), especially pp. 83-90, 290-2; and Fredric Jameson, *The Prison-House of Language,* (Princeton: Princeton U.P., 1972), pp. 56 ff. On 'structures of feeling' see Raymond Williams, *The Long Revolution* (London: Chatto & Windus, 1961), pp. 41-53.

Swift's handling of the narrator in *Gulliver's Travels* is helpfully discussed by C. J. Rawson, *Gulliver and the Gentle Reader* (London: Rouledge & Kegan Paul, 1973), Ch. 1.

American science fiction since 1960

J. A. Sutherland

I

All three elements in the title of this essay are problematic. Many of the leading practitioners of post-1960 science fiction dominated the pre-1960 field (Asimov, Heinlein, Pohl, Anderson, Blish, Van Vogt, for example, have all rumbled away more or less actively). National identity is confused by migrant American writers who have mixed with their British counterparts in a relatively new spirit of SF internationalism, as opposed to the pan-Americanism of the early post-war period (e.g. Disch, Delany, Harrison, Spinrad). Finally, science fiction has eroded as a self-evident category, to the point where either it, or allegiance to it, is routinely denied by those writers whom we associate with the genre.

A main difficulty in slicing the subject off cleanly arises from changes in the post-war literary, publishing and academic worlds which have released or expelled science fiction from its previously confined existence as a 'ghettoized' art form (the phrase is Harlan Ellison's). It has always been the case, for example, that straight novelists with moderately adventurous tendencies have dabbled in varieties of SF – Utopias, dystopias, fantasies, dream visions, etc. (e.g. *The Water Babies, The Coming Race, It Can't Happen Here, Brave New World, Nineteen Eighty-Four, The Old Men at the Zoo, The Alteration*). But in the 1960s in America, one has a generation of writers like Burroughs, Pynchon, Vonnegut, Nabokov or Barth who seem intimately and continuously involved with science fiction, or something analogous. Many of the modes of post-modernist fiction and the so-called 'literature of exhaustion' have assimilated to aspects of traditional SF. At the top of SF's literary range – in the work of a writer like Samuel Delany, for instance – there is a point where science fiction and the experimental modern novel clearly interpenetrate (though to the rage of young ambitious SF novelists the category marketing arrangements of the American book trade have maintained the artificial divisions of the shop rack). And while this fusion has occurred at the progressive tip of SF, the genre has recruited a new mass readership and audience from the cult successes of million-sellers and multi-million grossers like *Dune* (1965), *Stranger in a Strange Land* (1961), *2001: A Space Odyssey* (1968), *Star Trek, Star Wars,* the 'Perry Rhodan' series. The most successful of these (*Star Trek, Star Wars,* Rhodan) have propagated an extravagantly traditional SF. This growth in literary aspiration, together with the vast increase in the demand for 'straight' SF, has made any generalization about the genre as a whole a tricky business.

It is hard to make sense of what has happened, and what has been achieved in American SF over the last two decades unless one goes beyond the texts into the literary sociology and politics of the genre and, most importantly, into the economics of its production. The overwhelming fact which confronts one is the sheer volume increase in the field. SF is now big publishing business and the big publishers have taken over, largely pushing out the cottage industry of earlier periods. 'Grab Yourself a Piece of a 40 million dollar market' ran a 1976 advertisement in *Publishers' Weekly* (the commercial ethics implied in the imperative 'Grab' are as significant as the estimated dollar value of the market – some 10 per cent of the American book trade's annual 4 billion turnover). According to *Publishers' Weekly,* again, there were 890 titles 'at least' published in 1975, 24 per cent up on the previous year.(In the same issue, Arthur C. Clarke recalls that in his youth there were 'maybe two hardcover books a year' – he claims to feel 'sorry' for the deluged modern reader.)

The increase in production can be accounted for in a number of ways. At its simplest, SF has simply been pulled along in the train of the paperback book revolution. By the mid-1970s the paperback had overtaken the hardback in the American market (in Britain it still lags behind with about 30 per cent of total sales). SF is now primarily a paperback form, largely independent of library, book club and coffee-table book sales which preserve the hardcover book elsewhere (one says 'largely' since there is a Doubleday SF book club with 100,000 members, an estimated library sale of 1,200 for any SF hardback coming from a respectable publishing house and a minor boom in picture books on SF illustration; but none of these is formative in the overall publishing pattern for the genre). Characteristically, SF adapts to the most efficient and functional form of fiction publication available – functional and efficient, that is, in terms of cost and distribution. Hence the magazine and the pulps dominated in the 1930s, the anthology and magazine in the immediate post-war period and the paperback in the 1960s and 1970s. The reason why SF automatically accommodates to the form that will distribute it most cheaply and in the widest variety to the largest number of readers is to be found in the voracious nature of those readers. Judy-Lynn del Rey, editor of Ballantine Books' paperback SF division (generally acknowledged the best in America) describes the typical consumer from personal observation (*Publishers' Weekly,* 14 June 1976):

I travel around a lot with the sales force, and I like to go into the stores and watch people actually buying the books — that's an invaluable lesson, and one that perhaps not enough editors take. I'm convinced that if you publish good stuff it will sell — the problem is to get it to the booksellers. The younger ones are mostly interested, but the older ones are sometimes a problem. What they must realize is that science fiction readers are readers, *which is why it's mostly a paperback thing: they can buy six or seven books for the price of one hardback, and they do.*

In the beneficent conditions of the paperback boom SF's *reading* public has flourished and expanded, creating within the paperback sector a proportionate boom of its own.

Another frequently given reason for the expansion of SF in this period is cultural. We live, it is said, in a science-fiction world. The increasing penetration of technology into the fabric and consciousness of modern life has created what would seem to be doubly propitious conditions. Enchantment with technology has favoured 'hard' SF, and nostalgic essays in Space Opera; disenchantment has favoured escapist science fantasy and such ecologically concerned bestsellers as *Dune.* In a perceptive aside in *The Anatomy of Criticism* (1957) Northrop Frye commented (1966 edn, pp. 48–9) on an emerging ideological shift in this direction, which he connected with a larger return to modes of myth and romance in the modern period:

What we have said about the return of irony to myth in tragic modes thus holds equally well for comic ones. Even popular literature appears to be slowly shifting its centre of gravity from murder stories to science fiction — or at any rate a rapid growth of science fiction is certainly a fact about contemporary popular literature. Science fiction frequently tries to imagine what life would be like on a plane as far above us as we are above savagery; its setting is often of a kind that appears to us as technologically miraculous. It is thus a mode of romance with a strong inherent tendency to myth.

(Frye's observation is remarkably prescient for 1957. But his particular case seems to be better borne out by the soon subsequent craze for 'near' SF represented by Tolkien's sagas.)

At the same time that he wrote, Frye's colleagues in North American universities and colleges were beginning to take a professional interest in science fiction as something other than merely 'popular literature.' Jack Williamson and James Gunn, two academics who double as SF writers, estimate that there are now around 1,000 science fiction and fantasy courses offered in American higher education, almost all of which have been set up since 1960. If SF in the 1960s and 1970s is big business it is also respectable curriculum material. Both facts have had their effects; SF is now a genre many of whose prime products are written by humanities graduates for humanities graduates.

The invasion of SF by academics making professional careers in the criticism and teaching of the genre is regularly deplored by older writers, many of whom cherish their outlaw status or, in a number of cases, their qualifications in hard science subjects. But academic currency accounts for much of the increased literary sophistication of recent SF. It also helps explain the strong position which SF occupies in the campus bookshops that turn over some 20 per cent of the American book trade's business. And with these facts in hand one can attempt a provisional breakdown of the SF reading public into categories, or concentric groupings. In the middle are the 4,000 to 5,000 hard-core fans, those active enthusiasts who make up the attendance at such occasions as the World Science Fiction Conventions and who operate the networks of unofficial 'Fanzines.' Around them are the 80,000 to 100,000 subscribers to the above-ground magazines of the 1970s, and the main book club. These, too, may be termed fans, though of a rather more passive commitment. Around these are the occasional campus bookshop patrons, representing a shifting but fairly consistently sized selection of the 10 million young people in American higher education. Many, though by no means all, of these will carry their taste for SF into adult life. At the outer fringe are the volatile cultists, the millions of 'Trekkies' or the lemming-like crowds who have made *Star Wars,* and its tie-in paperbacks, all-time smash hits.

It would seem likely that the 'fan' component of this reading public (as I have anatomized it) is being gradually permeated by the college readers. A survey of *Fantasy and Science Fiction* (which according to 1977 figures sells up to 60,000 of each monthly issue) broke down its readership thus: 84 per cent of readers under forty-five years old, 62 per cent with college education. An Ace Books survey in 1976 found that the average initiated reader of its SF paperbacks was fifteen to thirty years in age, urban and had attended high school and college. (It also discovered that such a reader tended to buy six to twelve SF paperbacks a month, and that his favourite authors were Clarke, Heinlein, Asimov, Le Guin and Sturgeon). In all this SF would seem to have expanded with the huge higher education boom of the 1950s and 1960s, and to have been transubstantiated by it.

Whatever the reasons, and however interconnected, the fact remains that SF in the post-1960 period is produced and consumed on a larger scale than ever before. The demand of the market for an ever-increasing supply of new titles has imposed a disintegrating pressure on the writer, especially the young, intellectually ambitious writer (more so since his taskmaster is, typically, no longer the magazine editor – who might well take a pastoral interest – but the impersonal publisher). Novel for novel, SF does not sell spectacularly well. The *Dune* trilogy seems to be an all-time bestseller with a collective 2 million sales in paperback between 1965 and 1977. *Dangerous Visions* would seem to be something of a record-breaking hardback SF bestseller with some 60,000 copies sold before going out of print. One can contrast these figures with the regular 300,000 sales which Harold Robbins or Jacqueline Susann achieve in hardback, and the 10 million or more clocked up in paperback by *Jaws* or *The Exorcist.* But any kind of blockbuster, even on the relatively diminished scale of *Dune* or *Stranger in a Strange Land,* is rare in American SF. The pattern is for a large number of goodish sales, for a large number of titles, many of which must be new rather than reprint. In this SF is imprisoned in the hectic rhythm of the paperback market, in which there is a new batch of books every month, up to 50 per cent returns, where the average book has, as *Publishers' Weekly* estimates, fifteen days' shelf life before sale or return, and where there is neither backlist nor bestseller list longevity. In fact SF accommodates very well *as a genre* to this inhumanly accelerated existence. Its readers are self-motivating and require neither the blandishments of advertisement nor the instruction of reviewers; at the same time they have a steady yet massive appetite for their preferred brand of fiction. This clearly makes SF an attractive publishing investment, and encourages producers to think of their problems in merely quantitative terms: 'We're in a cycle that makes money. The trick though is to keep publishing more', as one executive candidly put it in 1976. But the pace, pressure and critical invisibility makes the science-fiction writer's life a hard one in which to operate creatively.

In present conditions the key to success in SF is Trollopian industry, rather than the long-matured single effort. Hence it is that the young luminaries of the genre have bio-bibliographies which would have made even Anthony Trollope blink with professional admiration. Barry Malzberg, for example, produced 22 novels and 250 short stories in ten years. Robert Silverberg claims to have made himself a dollar millionaire by the time he was thirty by writing 'twenty to thirty pages of publishable copy' every working day. At just over forty Harlan Ellison has 24 books and some 340 short stories and novellas credited to him (as well as a wealth of incidental writing). Even fiction as highly wrought as Samuel Delany's has appeared at a sufficient rate to give him ten novels in print by the time that he was barely thirty years old. (Compare with his coeval Thomas Pynchon who has two novels and a novella; or the college-supported John Barth, ten years older, with four full-length novels.)

With such evidence it is not myopically materialistic to assume that the SF writer, more than other kinds of ambitious novelist with a largely educated public, is in danger of writing himself out prematurely. There is no principle of conservation in the genre, no allowance for the necessary creative pause between efforts. This, of course, is not new: as Kurt Vonnegut reminds us (perhaps tongue-in-cheek), it was the furiously overworked SF writer who made the electric typewriter a commercial proposition. But it is anomalous that the modern SF novelist, who has, in general, higher artistic aspirations than his predecessor, should have to work at the same destructive pace, or even faster. The consequences were described, with only a little exaggeration, by Martin Amis in his final review of SF for *The Observer* newspaper (8 May 1977):

A promising first novel comes in; you read it with excitement, wondering vaguely what the second will be like; within what seems to be about a quarter of an hour, the second is glistening on your desk; you read it with reserved admiration, then, slap *comes the third; you read it with growing unease; then comes the fourth — and you read it if you can. The way things are, most SF authors have to write more than a book a year to go on being SF authors. They spin short stories into novellas, novellas into novels. They write faster and faster, and with less and less energy. They turn into hacks before your eyes.*

Or they are lost to the genre. Such casualties are common enough; one, particularly regrettable, is Thomas Disch (b. 1940). Disch has written two of the most striking SF novels of our period, *The Genocides* (1965) and *Camp Concentration* (1969). While at work on another, *The Pressure of Time,* he decided to pack it in:[2]

For various reasons, personal and impersonal, I never got back to work on Pressure, *and now I see I won't alas. Since* Camp Concentration *(which took 8 months to write) I realize I can't afford to spend such a lot of time on a book that earns only a standard SF advance. To earn a living writing SF I'd have to speed up my rate of production by 3 or 4 times. No.*

Science fiction of the post-1960 period has been punctuated by a series of such 'Nos' and, it seems to me, exemplary *non serviams.* The most famous is Kurt Vonnegut's, and Vonnegut is the more interesting to SF writers in that his defection has been rewarded by a brilliantly successful career outside the genre. He is now a great novelist, *tout court.* Nonetheless, Vonnegut certainly began as an SF novelist. And as an SF novelist, chained to the paperback form, he bitterly resented the critical invisibility of his work (*Wampeters, Foma and Granfalloons: Opinions,*London 1975, p. 307):

Mother Night *and* Canary in a Cathouse *and* The Sirens of Titan *were all paperback originals, and* Cat's Cradle *was written with that market in mind. Holt decided to bring out a hardcover edition of* Cat's Cradle *after the paperback rights had been sold. The thing was, I could get $3,000 immediately for a paperback original, and I always needed money right away, and no hardcover publisher would let me have it. But I was also noticing the big money and the heavy praise some of my contemporaries were getting for their books, and I would think, 'Well, shit, I'm going to have to study writing harder, because I think what I'm doing is pretty good too.' I wasn't even getting reviewed.*

Vonnegut was particularly incensed by such typical crassness as the bosomy woman with which his publisher, quite illegitimately, enhanced the cover appeal of *The Sirens of Titan* (1959). He satirizes such practices in the 'wide open beavers' with which paperback publishers invariably decorate the cosmic (and utterly unaphrodisiac) parables of his fictional *alter ego,* Kilgore Trout. (This prolific, but totally unknown master of SF, wanders in and out of several of Vonnegut's novels and has a starring part in *Breakfast of Champions,* 1973.) Trout embodies Vonnegut's mixture of admiration and exasperation with SF. He is a prodigy of invention, yet doomed to obscurity by the low esteem in which the genre is held, and holds itself. The obscurity is at least partly justified by the poor quality of writing which SF, generically, encourages: 'Jesus – if Kilgore Trout could only write', declares his one fan, Eliot Rosewater, in *Slaughterhouse-Five* (1969). The narrator adds: 'He had a point: Kilgore Trout's unpopularity was deserved. His prose was frightful. Only his ideas were good.' In his address to a convention of SF writers in *God Bless You, Mr Rosewater* (1965, Ch. 2) Rosewater is somewhat less qualified in his praise:

I love you sons of bitches. You're all I read any more. You're the only ones who'll talk about the really terrific changes going on, the only ones crazy enough to know that life is a space voyage, and not a short one, either, but one that'll last for billions of years. You're the only ones with guts to really care about the future, who really notice what machines do to us, what wars do to us, what cities do to us, what tremendous misunderstandings, mistakes, accidents and catastrophes do to us.

Yet despite this evident sympathy with its capacities, Vonnegut has disowned SF. (SF has not disowned him – Philip José Farmer has adopted Kilgore Trout as the pseudonymous narrator of some of his bawdier fiction.) It is not just the genre's insulation from objective criticism, nor the crudely functional mode of writing which it enjoins, that irks Vonnegut. He seems to have objected most to the *institution* of SF, the stifling coteries and mutually approving relationships which it sets up; its conventions (in both senses); the cosiness, which Vonnegut takes to be a refuge from creative responsibility. For those who remain, unlike himself, in the enclave Vonnegut (*Wampeters, Foma and Granfalloons,* p. 30) expresses the affectionate contempt of the adult for the permanent adolescent:

There are those who adore being classified as science fiction writers . . . who are alarmed by the possibility that they might some day be known simply as ordinary short-story writers and novelists who mention, among other things, the fruits of engineering and research. They are happy with the status quo because their colleagues love them the way members of old-fashioned big families were supposed to do. Science fiction writers meet often, comfort and praise one another, exchange single spaced letters of twenty pages and more, booze it up affectionately and one way or another have a million heart-throbs and laughs. I have run with them some, and they are generous and amusing souls, but I must now make a true statement that will put them through the roof. They are joiners. They are a lodge. If they didn't enjoy having a gang of their own so much, there would be no such category as science fiction.

Vonnegut's defection from SF, and his analysis of its stultifying intimacies, have been attended to. More so since his comments are delivered from the enviable position of a novelist with a second career in open, 'non-institutional' fiction (achieved, nonetheless, with a narrative equipment which clearly owns its origins in SF). Not surprisingly his act of repudiation has been imitated by younger writers, who would presumably like to imitate his post-*Cat's Cradle* (1963) career as well. The April 1976 issue of *Fantasy and Science Fiction* contains a remarkably concerted statement by three of the most gifted young (that is, fortyish) SF writers in America: Barry Malzberg, Robert Silverberg and Harlan Ellison. All three (Silverberg by proxy) announce their self-exile from the genre. No more SF from them. Malzberg's tone is nostalgic, but firm as he frames a valediction to his 'last' anthology of SF work, *Down Here in the Dream Quarter:*

It is true that I must leave science fiction. As the vise of the seventies comes down upon all of us in every field of the so-called arts, there is almost no room left for the kind of work which I try to do. But it is also true that this collection — which is a major effort of at least intermittent literary intention and execution — would not even exist, nor would the career it encapsules, have come to be had it not been for science fiction which gave me a market, an audience, and a receptivity for my work that I would never have found elsewhere. In this sense I owe my career and large pieces of my life as well to science fiction. (Such a career as it has been.) Where else could an unknown writer whose only virtues (other than a modicum of talent) were energy, prolificity and a gathering professionalism be able to write and sell twenty-three novels and five collections of some literary intention in a period of less than eight years? Even if I had satisfied my original ambitions I would have been dealing with a market which held me back, not only quantitatively but in terms of artistic growth. The only limits which SF imposed on me . . . were those framed by my willingness or unwillingness to turn out work of such pretension for what was, inevitably, an audience not intersecting with the academic/literary nexus.

(It may not be clear from Malzberg's delicate phraseology that he has finally got round to saying that the SF reading public is beneath him.)

Ellison is angrier and less tactful than Malzberg. He has insisted that ' "science fiction" be deleted from his books and nowhere be permitted in advertising or promotion of what he writes'.[3] Rebellious anger is, in fact, Ellison's characteristic mood. At times it has been turned to constructive use, as in the remarkable effort in authorial liberation represented by the *Dangerous Visions* anthologies. In these three hugely successful collections of the 1960s and 1970s, Ellison deliberately solicited work which was unacceptable to the censorious editors of the magazines. ('Writer after writer', Ellison affirmed, 'is finding his work precensored even before he writes it, because he knows this editor won't allow discussions of politics in his pages, and that one shies away from stories exploring sex in the future.') At other times Ellison's anger is frankly destructive, even homicidal. In a blazingly furious article in *Fantasy and Science Fiction,* July 1977, he describes, with evident relish, assaulting a fan at a convention – 'a rather large, fleshy young man festooned with buttons saying things like FIAWOL and FANSTAAFL and SF FANS EAT THEIR YOUNG.' And in his repudiation of SF Ellison is typically agressive. For him the fans are what women were for D. H. Lawrence, great lumps of inertia that stop men from reaching the stars (*Fantasy and Science Fiction,* April 1976, p. 157):

You would have all writers of surrealism, magic realism, fantasy, science fiction and a million other etcetera designations lumped together under that SF umbrella. That way all you'd have to do is go to the indicated racks in your newsstand and pick what you want. And that's fine for you. But what about those of us who want to go our own way, who want to write whatever we choose without having to be pigeonholed? Is that some terrible sin against the wonderfulness of SF? . . . Why don't *I have the right to reject a label? Do you like being labelled an uninformed fan? Why should a book like* Deathbird Stories, *clearly not SF, be reviewed with pure SF books in the* New York Times *and be found wanting on the basis of its having contained precious little SF material? And what the hell is so bloody holy about those two letters s and f? John Collier, H. G. Wells, Donald Barthelme, John Hersey, E. L. Doctorow, Vladimir Nabokov, Roald Dahl, David Lindsay and Anna Kavan managed to write sensational, immortal fiction without being bothered that what they were setting down might possibly be called SF by some, and be called other things by other people. They were* writers, *not SF* writers, *and they received universal attention because they weren't shunted off into the giant ant and space opera ghetto.*

II

Affiliation or disaffiliation, affirmation or repudiation, are critical issues in SF of the post-1960 period. Where the modern writer of science fiction is not complacent he is, typically, confused and unsure of his genre. Often the patterns of SF writers' careers show up this confusion in terms of changed directions, culs-de-sac, gestures of frustration. Robert Silverberg is a case in point. Silverberg, the Bobby Fischer of the genre, entered SF precociously young. Steeped in SF as a boy in New York, he ran his own fanzine by the time he was thirteen, sold his first sub-Heinlein novel (*Revolt in Alpha C,* 1955) as a sophomore, and was a self-supporting writer by his junior year at Columbia. At an early stage Silverberg discerned that 'if I intended to earn a livelihood writing fiction, it would be wiser to use my rapidly developing technical skills to turn out mass-produced formularized stories at high speed, rather than to lavish passion and energy on more individual works that would be difficult to sell'.[4] By the time he had left college in the early 1950s Silverberg was, as he reports, 'the complete writing machine', the perfect SF hack. At this period the magazines were riding high in an SF field that was generally unambitious in literary terms. In three months in 1956, Silverberg sold forty-nine stories. This work Silverberg now describes as 'sure-thing potboilers'. For the next five years Silverberg worked at the rate of one million written words a year, shifting the emphasis of his labours to general 'subliterature' when the bottom fell out of the SF magazine market in 1958. (This was a consequence of the asset-stripping takeover which put the American News Company out of business, and with it the main distribution chain for journals.) Silverberg continued to prosper, researching and writing a cascade of general non-fiction books through the early 1960s. In 1966 after a mysterious illness, which clearly had a transforming effect, Silverberg returned to SF in a chastened spirit – no longer as the 'mass producer of garbage' but as a self-conscious artist. SF itself had been renovated by the New Wave, and was now a congenial market for better things. It was, as a later critic put it, the sausage factory turned artist. There followed a period of high creativity in which, for the first time, quality matched quantity. The first batch of regenerate Silverberg SF appeared in 1967, with *Thorns, The Time Hoppers* and *Hawksbill Station*. The last of these, though in some ways the least regarded, fairly indicates the strengths of Silverberg's new mode of SF. It centres on a maximum security prison of the early twenty-first century, in which prisoners of a tyrannical regime are sent on a one-way time trip, back a billion years to the early Palaeozoic era. The novel is, like much of Silverberg's later work, concentrated on a situation of extreme personal isolation. The plot (which inevitably concerns the emergence of a return process, and a counter-revolution) is formulaic and has not stood up well. But the grim, monochrome, incarcerating landscape is given with an economy and power for which the years of machine-written short stories were, presumably, a perfect training (*Hawksbill Station*, Ch. 1):

He nudged the door open. Standing in the doorway of his hut, Barrett looked over his kingdom.

He saw barren rock, reaching nearly to the horizon. A shield of raw dolomite going on and on. Rain drops danced and bounced and splattered on that continental slab of glossy rock. No trees. No grass. Behind Barrett's sun lay the heavy sea, grey and vast. The sky was grey too, even when it didn't happen to be raining.

He hobbled out in the rain.

The king with a barren kingdom is a recurring figure in Silverberg's fiction.

Silverberg won a gratifying esteem with his peers. His work was put up for the two main prizes in the SF world, the Hugo and the Nebula. At the same time (1968) he was enjoying another of his phenomenal surges of energy:

I look back in wonder and awe at a year that produced To Live Again,
Masks of Time, Man in the Maze, *two 150,000 word works of history,
several short stories, and — I have as much trouble believing this as you
— no less than seven non-fiction books for young readers, each in the
60,000 word range.*

Of the SF listed here, *The Man in the Maze* (1969) is particularly
representative of Silverberg's penchant for reworking myth. Essentially it is an updating of Sophocles's *Philoctetes*; the island of Lemnos
where the bowman is stranded being converted to an electronically
booby-trapped maze, the wound which causes Philoctetes' fellow to
desert him transferred to the mind of Silverberg's hero. Silverberg has
an evident fondness for the magically endowed, but tragically isolated
figures in classical and biblical fable. (Teiresias is a favourite.)

   Silverberg continued to produce a string of highly regarded novels,
culminating in the Nebula award-winning *A Time of Changes* (1971).
As an act of contrition he went so far as to completely recast a novel
from his machine-writing days, *Recalled to Life*. 'The gulf between the
writer of 1957 and the writer of 1971', he declared in a preface to the
revised edition, 'is a great one; my fundamental approach to the art of
fiction is different today.' *Recalled to Life,* a novel about the 'Lazarus'
resuscitation process in 2033, manifests typical Silverberg thematic
obsessions, but it remains a weak performance. So, too, *A Time of
Changes* seems to me, despite its coveted prize, substandard (Silverberg's standard, that is). The narrative is, as the author puts it, 'more
emotional than most of my work and heavily pro-psychedelic'. The
drug theme, and the extravagant play with the Borthan prohibition on
personal pronouns ('I', 'me', 'myself') seems naively allegorical of the
commune idealism of the late 1960s. *A Time of Changes* was succeeded by what I take to be Silverberg's finest achievement to date,
Dying Inside (1972). This novel, which seems more deeply felt than
much of the author's previous fiction, is narrated autobiographically
by a typical hero, a Teiresian seer, sealed off by his 'gift' from human
relationships. What gives the book its novelty is that the extra-sensory
powers of David Selig are waning; he is, in fact, subsiding into normal-
ity. This twist gives the novel extraordinary piquancy, as does the
morose, neurasthenic personality of the 'superman':

*The power is deceptively strong in me today. I'm picking up plenty. This
is the strongest it's been in weeks. Surely the low humidity is a factor. But
I'm not deceived into thinking that the decline in my ability has been
checked. When I first began to lose my hair, there was a happy period
when the process of erosion seemed to halt and reverse itself, when new
patches of fine dark floss began to sprout on my denuded forehead. But
after an initial freshet of hope I took a more realistic view: this was no
miraculous reforestation but only a twitch of the hormones, a temporary
cessation of decay, not to be relied on. And in time my hairline resumed
its retreat. So too in this instance. When one knows that something is*

*dying inside one, one learns not to put too much trust in the random
vitalities of the fleeting moment.*

Like Wells's invisible man, Selig's superhuman power serves only to
alienate him. With his godlike faculty he scrapes a living writing cribs
for Columbia undergraduates. The texture of the novel is unsensation-
ally realistic. (Silverberg himself regards *Dying Inside* as principally a
'straight mainstream novel' with a science fiction theme grafted on.)
Given the actual university and contemporary New York setting, one
might characterize this as something of a campus novel. Whatever its
category, however, *Dying Inside* gives the lie to the frequently asserted
criticism that SF is incapable of dealing sensitively with character or
complex emotional situations.

After *Dying Inside* Silverberg's pace slowed down again. But quite
recently we have had *The Stochastic Man* (1975; another Teiresias,
working as a precognitive political adviser in a future New York) and
Shadrach in the Furnace (1976), a return to another favourite theme
(e.g. *The Tower of Glass* 1970), the potentate's quest for personal
immortality. Like others of Silverberg's novels this last is rich in hard
technical information (here mainly medical). The consistent solidity of
specification is, presumably, supplied by the scores of rapidly
researched non-fiction books which he has undertaken *pari passu* with
his SF.

In 1975 Silverberg declared himself a happy man, content with his
chosen literary profession and its rewards. 'I expect', he wrote, 'that
such writing as I do henceforth will be almost exclusively science
fiction.' A year later and he was reported to be withdrawing from the
writing of SF altogether. Privately he gave the reason as an irreconcilable difference of opinion with his publishers over the value of his
work, and its right to stay in print ('I find myself locked in mortal
struggle with my paperback publishers who have ceased to believe that
the kind of science fiction which I write is economically viable'). He
was, as he said, so discouraged that he could now write no SF at all.
Once more, it would seem, his career was at a drastic turning point.

I have given a disproportionate and central space to Silverberg for
two reasons. The first is that he is a considerable author, perhaps the
most considerable of the post-1960 period. The second reason is that
his career shows how the SF production system can shape, and twist
out of shape, a writer's evolution. In his first phase Silverberg went
along with the ethos of the magazines, turning himself into the machine
writer, aiming no higher than the low horizons of his paymasters and
the subscribing public of the later 1950s. When the magazines went
under he effortlessly transferred his skills to other paying varieties of
writing. After the New Wave of the early 1960s had opened a new
range of possibilities and largely liberated the writer from editorial
control, Silverberg returned to the field and produced a series of major
novels. In 1976, when the manufacturing system, dazzled by the mar-

ket revealed in the *Star Trek* cult, put a premium on 'ray gun and monster' SF, Silverberg found himself once again at a halt – forced either to conform (as he could quite easily do; he has written for *Star Trek*), or resign himself to the indignities of minority readership.

III

If some writers of this period have broken with SF, and a few may be said to have been broken by it, others have stretched and extended the genre's capacity. One useful way of conceiving the post-1960 period is in terms of a partial (and in some cases complete) decategorization by which the writer has been released to do new things. Among the more ambitious there has been a growth in literariness, itself subversive in terms of the genre's previous limitations. At the same time the permitted frame of reference has been enlarged to include a new freedom with sex and politics and a new subtlety in the treatment of religious subject matter. Generally, these innovations have been adapted to the dozen or so standard SF themes (alien contact, future dystopias, miraculous inventions, etc.). This is not, of course, to say that there has not been a new emphasis in the favoured themes of post-1960 SF. SF is a very sensitive and prompt recorder of collective neurosis or obsession. Judged by its leading products it has recently purged certain Cold War nightmares (invasion, atomic catastrophe, totalitarian tyranny) and replaced them with a new set (the electronic invasion of privacy, tyranny by the media or corporate industry, organ transplant and overpopulation nightmares). A thoroughgoing content analysis would probably turn up a very revealing shift in post-war pathology. Nonetheless what is attempted in the second half of this chapter is a general account, with specific examples, of the new freedoms of SF, and the use to which they have been put.

The inclusion of a new sexual frankness in SF can be tied in with the general literary disinhibition following the *Lady Chatterley* trials in the late 1950s. SF, however, still lags behind straight fiction in this area, though not as far behind as it used to. In many cases the freedom is uneasily handled; there will, for example, be the *de rigueur* sexual bout which the author seems to want to get over as quickly as possible. Perhaps in some cases the continuing *pudeur* is just as well. In the later work of Heinlein the more pervasive sexual additions to his fiction are often embarrassing. The coyness of the intersexual duologues in *I Will Fear No Evil* (1970), for instance, is beyond bearing. The following, where the amalgamated Johann Sebastian Bach Smith and Eunice Smith (his former secretary) converse in their shared mentality is typical; the occasion is one of mutual inspection, after the transplant which has lodged the man's consciousness in the woman's mind and body (Ch. 10):

(Beautiful. Utterly gorgeous. Eunice beloved, I always wanted to see you stark naked. And now I do.)

(So you do. I wish I had had time to get looking nice before you saw me. Hair a mess. And — yes, I thought so. We stink.) (Hey!) (Sorry, hit the panic button by mistake. Boss, we're going to have a hot, soapy bath before we get back into that bed. That's straight from Washington. We can't do much about flab in one day — but we can get clean.) She turned and inspected her buttocks. (Oh, dear! A broad should be broad — but not that broad.) (Eunice, that's the prettiest fanny in the state. In the whole country.) (Used to be, maybe. And it's going to be again and that's a promise, Boss. Tomorrow morning we start systematic exercise. Tighten up everything.) (Okay, if you say so — though I still say you're the most gorgeously beautiful thing I ever saw in my life. Uh, Eunice? That mermaid getup you wore once — You were wearing a trick bra with it . . . weren't you?)

She giggled. (Heavens, no. Just me, Boss. And paint. But my breasts were firm as rocks then.)

This leering prurience, reminiscent of Vonnegut's 'I see England, I see France, I see a little girl's underpants', is enough to make one long for the old days of titanium brassieres. One feels a similar discomfort about the sexual passages in Frederik Pohl's 1976 novel *Man Plus* (though there is one fine moment when the surgically enhanced eyes of the hero perceive a subliminal blush on the cheeks of his cuckolder – otherwise a barefaced liar).

The most flamboyant celebration of the new licence is to be found in the late 1960s with Philip José Farmer's Herald Childe (i.e. Childe Harold) romances. What follows is the overture to the first of the hero's many sexual encounters in *Blown* (1969 Ch. 2):

Childe anticipated what would happen next. He felt sick, and he knew he should halt the monstrous rape, but he was also gripped with the desire to witness what, as far as he knew, no man alive had seen. Emphasis on the alive. Vivienne waited and then the lips of her slit bulged open. The thick mat of rich red hair was pushed aside . . .

There is a brutal shock achieved by these novels which violently juxtapose the clichés of the Los Angeles private detective novel (Childe is a private dick, appropriately enough), SF and hard core pornography. In mitigation it should be noted that Farmer has been battering away at SF's sexual reticence ever since the novella *The Lovers*, in 1952. His calculated offensiveness does, however, seem an immature response to a resented discipline. In *A Feast Unknown* (1969), for example, he quite calculatedly does dirt on two of SF's icons from the age of Edgar Rice Burroughs innocence. Tarzan and Doc Savage are presented as warring sexual athletes in a mish-mash of sado-masochistic fantasy. What Farmer achieves, as with the Childe sequence (which preposterously turns out to be a quest for the Holy Grail) is travesty. In a field as morally conformist as SF, travesty has some diagnostic interest. The intrinsic literary merits of the exercise are harder to perceive.

A more constructive employment of the new freedom with sexual reference is found in the work of younger writers, to whom it comes naturally as a permission which has always, rather than just recently, been a fact of their writing environment. Ursula Le Guin has never, presumably, felt any prohibition on writing a fiction as sexually imaginative as *The Left Hand of Darkness* (1969) in which the setting is a planet populated by intricately versatile and erotically hyperactive hermaphrodites. On the other hand, Heinlein could never have got *I Will Fear No Evil* into print in the early 1950s, even though he was the leading SF writer in the world and otherwise possessed of immense authority. (The novel even raised eyebrows when it was serialized in part in *Galaxy*, twenty years later; though this is probably a reflection of the anachronistically conservative ethos of the remaining magazines.) Not surprisingly there is a certain 'look at me, I'm talking dirty' feel to the work of older writers when they handle sexually charged material.

It is the ability to introduce sexual explicitness with emotional neutrality which marks off the younger American SF writers, especially those involved in the transatlantic exchanges of the New Wave. A novel which is singularly successful in its unselfconsciousness in this regard is Norman Spinrad's *Bug Jack Barron* (1969). (This is also, as far as I know, the only SF novel ever to have attracted official disapprobation for its 'obscenity'). *Bug Jack Barron* is set in future America, and centred on a hero (Barron) who is a television personality whose nationwide phone-in ('vidphone in') programme deals with the gripes of his 100 million audience. The advertisement breaks promote such commodities as Acapulco Gold Marijuana. Barron is a casual, but virtuosic lover *à la mode* 1990 (Ch. 3):

'*Ah,*' *he said,* '*gotcha! You caught the show tonight. (Sharp chick, but not* that *sharp.) Don't tell me, you're an old and loyal fan of mine.*'
Tiny flicker of annoyance told him (would never admit it) that she was, as she said, taking another drag, '*I'm no fan of yours. I just dig . . .*'
'*The smell of blood?*' *he suggested. She favoured him with a wee bit feral smile as the grass began to hit, began to loosen thighs, loosen centres of hunger reality hunger make it hunger drag a piece of the action hunger ersatz power hunger fuck me into mystic circle power where it's all at hunger make me real with your living-colour prick hunger.*
'*Yeah, we all dig the smell of blood,*' *Barron said, glancing around the carefully musk-dusky room.*

Bug Jack Barron is a moment worth marking in a recent history of SF. It has an easy trans-generic quality which makes it at once SF, social criticism, experimental novel. It is very long – around 300 pages. Such space is rarely allowed the SF novelist, except in 'epics' which impose limitations of another kind. The cool, consistently inventive narrative in this novel would have made one optimistic for the form, were one writing in 1970, the year after it was written. From today's viewpoint the breakthrough Spinrad achieved seems not to have been followed up, least of all by Spinrad himself (though I confess I have some difficulty in piecing his subsequent career together.)

A final aspect of disinhibited sexual reference in SF may be cited as a definite gain for the form. It has often been the case that SF writers have wanted their novels to terrify. Where sexual matters came into it, the writer was usually constrained to muffle his shock effects by euphemism or vagueness. This constraint has been largely lifted. As a result the impact of much recent dystopian fiction is genuinely shocking. The following is a description of a post-revolutionary slave state America, in which childbirth has been mechanized (the influence of Huxley's *Brave New World* is evident enough, though the earlier novel is milk and water in comparison). It comes from Charles W. Runyon's *Pigworld* (1971) Ch. 2:

They rode an endless belt through a vast amphitheatre where women lay strapped in long rows, their legs hoisted up. 'This is our main birth centre,' said Quampa, 'capable of processing a thousand women per day. We hope to have one for every fifty thousand people in the New Democracy. So far twelve hundred have been built.'

A woman screamed. The belt stopped, and Ross watched the babies emerge like turtle eggs, one-two-three-four-five-six-seven, each one a tiny human being. A technician cleaned them and placed them on an endless belt with a hundred others. A line of assistants poked, prodded and stethoscoped the little bodies and took samples of their blood. About one in ten was lifted off the main belt and shunted through a cabinet which resembled a restaurant dishwashing machine. The rejected babies went under the flap kicking and screaming and emerged silently from the other end, to drop off the belt and roll down a chute into an incinerator.

IV

Taking the universe as its province, science fiction has rarely been afraid of religion or much constrained in its reference to religious matters. Wells, Stapledon and C. S. Lewis are only three pioneers who used SF as a vehicle for theological speculation or assertion. A number of classic stories from SF's 'golden age' have also dealt successfully with religious themes. The work of Arthur C. Clarke, the best known of all SF writers, is saturated with a religiosity which probably derives from Stapledon's cosmic humanism. Other writers, such as Asimov, offer a technological-utilitarian philosophy founded on an articulate atheism.

Around the 1960s two writers in particular dealt with familiar religious subject-matter in a way that was quite novel in its subtlety. These were James Blish, best known for *A Case of Conscience* (1958), and Walter M. Miller, author of *A Canticle for Leibowitz* (1959). Of the two, Miller has had an immense influence on the post-1960 SF field (most of Blish's career is contained in the earlier period). In many ways *A Canticle for Leibowitz* suggests comparison with William Golding's *Lord of the Flies* (1954). Like the earlier novel it circulated for many years as an 'underground' classic. Like *Lord of the Flies*, *A Canticle for Leibowitz* juxtaposes the theological concept of Manichaean struggle with modern man's atomic destructiveness. Beelzebub haunts the one novel, Lucifer the other. (It would, in fact, have made a nice symmetry if Miller had entitled his novel *Lord of Light*; in view of Lucifer's final victory over the planet it would not have been inappropriate.)

A Canticle for Leibowitz takes a huge time span for its narrative, imagining a completed cycle from atomic destruction in the near future to atomic destruction in the far future, two millennia hence. In scale it bears comparison with Asimov's *Foundation* trilogy (although, as the bare synopsis above witnesses, Leibowitz's novel does not share Asimov's Manhattan-Project-inspired optimism in science's powers of redemption). It is SF's privilege to deal in these vast segments of time; the price which is exacted is in depth of characterization and scene development. *A Canticle for Leibowitz* pays the price. The identifications which the reader makes with certain characters (notably Francis and Zerchi) are broken off uncomfortably abruptly. (One may suspect that Miller may not have been entirely sure of his motives when he started writing; the first section seems to promise a less synoptic narrative than we are finally given.) The connection of the three original novelettes into a tripartite novel may also be thought schematic and arbitrary.

But more than most genres, SF can survive faults in construction, and *A Canticle for Leibowitz* remains an extraordinary achievement. And however disjointed in structure, Miller's novel is unified in its sequence and variety of moods. The predominant mood is, largely speaking, pessimistic; the novel is heavily steeped in the gloom of the immediate post-Hiroshima age, expressing a confidence in catastrophic conclusions which is typical of later 1950s SF. Yet the surface of *A Canticle for Leibowitz* is enlightened by a delicately comic handling of certain scenes (notably in Francis's ordeal in the Utah desert, but also in such incidental byplay as Zerchi's running battle with the 'Abominable Autoscribe'); and the original *donnée* of the work – a Jewish electrical engineer's relics sanctified – is rich in ironic possibilities. The middle and later section of the novel tend towards the sombre and symbolic; but even in the most horrific depictions of dark age barbarism Miller's narrative style is leavened with a sardonic wit (Ch. 15):

Hongan Os was essentially a just and kindly man. When he saw a party of his warriors making sport of the Laredan captives, he paused to watch; but when they tied three Laredans by their ankles between horses and whipped the horses into frenzied flight, Hongan Os decided to intervene. He ordered that the warriors be flogged on the spot, for

Hongan Os — Mad Bear — was known to be a merciful chieftain. He had never mistreated a horse.

The main theme of *A Canticle for Leibowitz* concerns the historic dualism of science and religion, as Catholicism contests with rationalism (and both combine against barbarism) in the embryonic civilization of the post-atomic era. Superficially science is progressive and open-minded, the Church conservative and superstitious. Other works of literature have been made out a clear-cut notion of this clash of ideologies and institutions: Brecht's *Leben des Galilei*, for instance, or at a lower level Pierre Boulle's *Planet of the Apes* and (as low as one can get), its tie-in movies. But Miller's evident sympathy for Catholicism and his inwardness with it precludes any such clear-cut treatment. In *A Canticle for Leibowitz* the Church plays a profoundly equivocal part in the advance of civilization. It is instinctively conservative – yet among other things it conserves the foundations of scientific progress. The blueprint which Francis spends fifteen years illuminating is one of the Leibowitzian 'memorabilia' – relics; yet these relics are also the enshrinement of the future technological aspirations of mankind and, in some cases, the key by which scientific rediscoveries are made (not, as the scholar Thon finds to his chagrin, discoveries). The cumulative irony is that the painful dialectical advance of the two ideologies will result in the second atomic devastation. In preparation for this, each of the three sections charts a step forward for mankind, and finishes on a plunge back into darkness and suffering, which, we are led to believe, may or may not be purgatorial.

The action of *A Canticle for Leibowitz* is organized on a number of oppositional scenes. In the last and most poignant of these Abbott Zerchi and a rationalist physician argue the legitimacy of euthanasia for hopelessly irradiated refugees. As usual the Church appears pigheaded and cruelly dogmatic in its resistance to the well-intentioned 'Mercy Cadres,' refusing to shelter their operations on Church land. But the uncompromising dedication to religious principle is vindicated in the climatic scene of the novel when a mortally wounded Zerchi, trapped in the debris of the second holocaust, is vouchsafed a divine vision in the form of a mutant second head ('Rachel') of Mrs Grales, an itinerant peddler. In a scene of great power this child of radiation declines baptism, offers Zerchi the host and in her primal innocence commands, 'Live.' It is Zerchi's promise of resurrection: 'One glimpse had been a bounty, and he wept in gratitude. Afterwards he lay with his face in the wet dirt and waited' (Ch. 29).

And yet the novel does not end on this scene. Equivocally, the epilogue, in a much less intense style of narration, presents a party of monks taking off in a starship for a new life in a new Order of Leibowitz across the galaxy (Ch. 30):

The last monk, upon entering, paused in the lock. He stood in the open hatchway and took off his sandals. 'Sic transit mundus', *he murmured, looking back at the glow. He slapped the soles of his sandals together, beating the dirt out of them. The glow was engulfing a third of the heavens. He scratched his beard, took one last look at the ocean, then stepped back and closed the hatch.*

There came a blur, a glare of light, a high thin whining sound, and the starship thrust itself heavenward.

The final juxtaposition of the starship with its cargo of medievally clad monks and their Leibowitzian relics is ambiguous in the extreme. To the end Miller sustains the tensions of the novel's central dualism. Is it religion, science or some complex relationship of the two that embodies whatever hope (and the novel is not optimistic about the colonial prospects for the pilgrims) that remains for mankind?[5]

V

It is a feature of SF of the post-1960 period that it has attempted a more direct political intervention than hitherto, and that it has taken its various stands on a political base which is diverse and frequently adversary. In view of the conformist patriotism of much earlier SF (exemplified, say, in the fiction of Heinlein and Poul Anderson and the editorial policies of John W. Campbell), this has been a controversial development. Dark allegations are made against the 'decadence' and 'nihilism' of modern SF by those who cleave to traditional values. There are those who assert that SF, *sui generis,* is optimistic and simple in its ideology: that it embodies the idealism of the free human mind making its destiny manifest throughout the created universe (an idealism which, coincidentally, happens to be exactly consonant with the American Dream). Thus the veteran Donald A. Wollheim finishes his 1971 survey of SF, *The Universe Makers,* with the rousing paraphrase:

> We are not going to end with a bang.
> We are not going to end with a whimper.
> We are not going to end.
> That's all.

There is, however, no longer any consensus. Nor is it just a domestic SF matter. In SF of the 1960s, particularly, one can see the stress lines which shattered the solidarity of the Cold War period. A central event, and one which reverberates in much writing of the decade, is the assassination of President Kennedy. The assassin was not, as innumerable SF novels had predicted, an 'alien,' but an American. The emotional confusion produced by this national disaster is given literary expression in one of the most ambitious political fables the genre has produced, Barry Malzberg's *The Destruction of the Temple* (1974). In the complex narrative of this novel the traumatic events in Dallas are rehearsed time and again, in the search for 'final' meaning. Another traumatic experience was the Vietnamese involvement which created in SF, as in other areas of American life, a division largely along generation lines. A measure of the rift which emerged can be taken by comparing, in rather more detail, representatively antagonistic novels by an old guard and a New Wave writer. The novels are *Farnham's Freehold* (1964) by Robert Heinlein (b. 1907) and *Camp Concentration* (1968) by Thomas M. Disch (b. 1940).

The inspiration of *Farnham's Freehold* seems to have been a complex mixture of apprehension, panic and rage at such events as the Cuban missile crisis, the race riots in American cities in the early 1960s and the fallout shelter neurosis of the late 1950s. In the earlier decade Heinlein's political views, always reactionary, underwent an intensification, putting him in a position 'slightly to the right of Joseph McCarthy'. The setting of *Farnham's Freehold* is contemporary, indicating Heinlein's conviction that in 1964 the future had at long last arrived. The dramatis personae are the Farnham family, plus a nubile young houseguest and a docile black servant; the daughter is somewhat insipid, the son, a lawyer, is a sophisticate but essentially spineless; the wife, of more patrician origins than her self-made husband, an advanced alcoholic. The 'hero' (literally and unremittingly heroic throughout the action) is a middle-aged Second World War veteran, Hugh Farnham. In the early sections of the novel Farnham is never without a radio to his ear, listening for the four minutes' warning of the inevitable sneak attack by Khruschev's barbarians. He has constructed a sturdy fallout shelter, though his intentions are far from being merely passive. As he explains to his son (Ch. 1):

'If those lying, cheating bastards ever throw their murder weapons at the United States, I want to live long enough to go to hell in style — with eight Russian sideboys!'

Farnham twisted in his chair. 'I mean it Duke. America is the best thing in history, I think, and if those scoundrels kill our country, I want to kill a few of them. Eight sideboys. Not less. I felt relieved when Grace refused to consider moving.'

'Why, dad?'

'Because I don't want that pig-faced peasant with the manners of a pig to run me out of my home! I'm a free man. I intend to stay free.'

The pig-faced peasant does his worst and, with the addition of the first SF element in the action, the Farnham fallout shelter is blasted into the future and a parallel universe. There follows a pioneer interlude in the natural world where Farnham, now completely in charge, inspires the young Barbara to fall in love with him (is he not a 'real man' unlike his effete son?), and his daughter dies in childbirth. This episode is shattered when the party is captured by the hitherto unsuspected rulers of the planet ('The Protectorate') who turn out to be black Muslims ('The Chosen'). In their dynastic households whites are kept either as gelded slaves or, as it eventually transpires, as battery-reared food supply for the cannibalistic ruling élite. Farnham's wife is taken as a concubine by the head of the household, Ponse (an interestingly revealing choice of name), his son is castrated and settles down happily as a neutered courtier. The black servant becomes a senior member of Ponse's entourage and, in the spirit of 'I've got my sergeant working under me now', proceeds to lord it over his former masters ('I thought you were a gentleman', Farnham tells him accusingly). Farnham is now the father of twins by Barbara. In an increasingly improbable sequence of events he contrives to be transported back in time, and across universes, to the period just before the bombs drops. The Farnhams (new wife and new children) survive and set to restoring civilization. In the epilogue we are shown 'Farnham's Freehold', a model of emergent free-enterprise trading which offers, among other commodities, 'Jerked Quisling, by the neck'.

Farnham's Freehold is a remarkably efficiently told tale, its techniques honed by twenty years of high-quality SF writing. Heinlein understands the dynamics of his chosen fiction intimately. Surprise (such as the revelation of the Chosen's diet) is withheld to the perfect moment. The authenticating descriptions of the Protectorate's caste system and its rigidly deferential modes of language are expertly done. Like the best 'classic' SF, *Farnham's Freehold* cannot be put down once one has started reading it. It bears out Heinlein's expressed conviction that SF must grip on an elemental level, satisfying appetite rather than critical sensibility (*Analog,* January 1974, p. 167):

My purpose is to make what I write entertaining enough to compete with beer. Not to be as great as Shakespeare or as immortal as Homer but simply to write well enough to persuade the cash consumer to spend money on one of my paperback reprints when he could spend it on beer.

And yet, for all its efficient appeal, *Farnham's Freehold* is painfully extreme in its motivating ideas and energies. An unprovoked attack by the 'reds' is succeeded by a vile tyranny under the 'blacks'. The younger generation of males is manifestly degenerate, having lost the pioneer resourcefulness of its parents. The castration of the only son (in which Farnham has a hand, albeit by default) displays an oddly reversed Oedipal obsession. For all its narrative control, *Farnham's Freehold* is, apparently, driven by the uncontrolled emotional responses of the nightmare. There is clearly no deliberate allegory, but one is reminded of Norman Spinrad's brilliant fantasia, *The Iron Dream* (1972), in which an Adolf Hitler emigrates from Munich in 1919 after dabbling in radical politics. 'Hitler' becomes an illustrator for early SF magazines and writes his *chef d'œuvre, Lord of The Swastika,* which wins a posthumous Hugo in 1955. (Exactly the period, incidentally, when Heinlein was pulling Hugos with annual regularity.) *Farnham's Freehold* is not the work of a diverted Hitler; but it is fair to say that in a parallel universe Barry Goldwater could have written it.

Disch's *Camp Concentration* also has much of the nightmare about it
– though it is a younger man's nightmare, and a younger man whose
work Heinlein would disdain as tainted with 'custard-headed pacifism'. It is also, by contrast, a self-consciously literary work aiming at
something more than equality with a can of beer. In the dedication
Disch genuflects to Thomas Mann ('a good writer'), the epigraph is
from the verse prologue to *The Pilgrim's Progress* and on the first page
we are directed to note the work's similarity to Dostoevsky's *House of
the Dead*. Thereafter literary allusions come thick and fast. The form of
the novel, the personal journal of an academic poet (who has a Ph.D.
thesis on the recusant Winstanley in his background), encourages a
mandarin, elegant play with cultural reference.

Camp Concentration, as the title implies, derives in part from the
Second World War, seen not as a victory but as a demonstration of
ultimate inhumanity. (Disch's other main novel, *The Genocides,* is
similarly derivative.) At the same time the basic idea of *Camp Concentration* is almost witty and elegant. Many of the great men of history
have suffered from syphilis – could there not be a link between greatness and the disease, between 'syphilization' and 'civilization'? (There
is, the novel reveals.) In Camp Archimedes, therefore, subjects are
deliberately infected with spirochetae. The allusion to obscene Nazi
experiments is clear enough, but in this case the main experimental
subject is a thirty-five-year-old draft resister to what we understand to
be the Vietnam War (at the beginning of the novel 'President
McNamara' – a joke that may not have lasted too well – has just
decided to use tactical nuclear weapons). *Camp Concentration* thus
makes the same equation as the omnipresent slogan of the 1960s,
US=SS. For Disch America is not, needless to say, 'the best thing in
history'.

It is likely that Disch had some inspiration for his novel from Daniel
Keyes's *Flowers for Algernon* which won the Nebula two years before
in 1966. In this novel (also in the form of a journal) a moron is
chemically operated on to bring him, temporarily, to genius mentality.
As in Keyes's novel, the syphilis-inducing drug gives only nine months
of enhanced powers of mind before death supervenes. But Keyes's
novel, powerful and pathetic as it is, has none of the horror of *Camp
Concentration,* where the 'criminals', subjected involuntarily, are draft
dodgers, deserters, military insubordinates. Nor does Keyes make
Disch's allegations against the military–industrial complex which
funds Camp Archimedes. Most of all, Keyes does not rise to the
challenge of actually displaying the intellectual powers of Charly as
they wax (it is easy enough to do it, of course, as they wane). Disch
does; the inmates of Camp Archimedes are made to discourse and
display their horribly induced genius, as their senses and bodies decay
under the influence of the drug.

The journal monologues, and the reported dialogues are brilliantly
impressive. But if there is a fault in the novel, it resides in that area where

Heinlein's mastery is most sure, the movement of the plot. *Camp Concentration* is a situation novel, which resolves itself with a last-minute *deus ex machina* device; a clandestine prisoners' rebellion is revealed, in which a metempsychosis process has been evolved by the super-intelligent prisoners, who proceed to occupy their custodians' bodies. Disch can write well-plotted fiction (*vide The Genocides* or the rather slighter *Echo round his Bones*); it seems that in this novel he had more important aims in mind, and that he achieved them most impressively.

Disch's novel has not had the general recognition it deserves, I feel. On the other hand, another novel patently allusive to the Vietnamese experience, Joe Haldeman's *The Forever War,* won both the Hugo and Nebula prizes in 1976. This acclaim is probably accounted for by the conciliatory nature of the book. *The Forever War* is a fascinating exercise in the combination of Heinleinian virtues (direct narrative, plenty of action, economical 'unliterary' style) with Disch's anti-war stance. The warriors of *The Forever War* are a specially trained *corps d'élite,* Green Berets of the future, set loose against a subhuman alien enemy (post-hypnotic suggestion reinforces their dedication to slaughter). In the technology race, time jumps are developed. These gain a military advantage but they separate the soldiers from the world they knew and to which, by the laws of relativity, they can never return. Similarly, the chances of individual postings and tours of duty separate them from friends and lovers they may have found in the service. This alienation, and the ultimate futility of the 1,143-year war, is patently allegorical of the experience of soldiers returning from South-East Asia. In mood, Haldeman's book is reminiscent of another anti-war novel of the period, Robert Stone's *Dog Soldiers*. At the same time *The Forever War* communicates an evident fascination with military hardware, with battle and with the machismo of the fighting soldier. (In the climax of the action 42 earthmen overcome 600 aliens in an epic battle; one is reminded of Farnham's determination to outfight his Russians eight to one.)

It may be that *The Forever War* announces a new compromise by which old and recent trends will find some mode of coexistence in the genre. Nonetheless, in the field generally there seems to have been a definitive shift towards a more liberal, and sometimes radical position. This can be shown, almost clinically, by examination of the novels which have won both the Nebula and Hugo prizes. Since the one is awarded on the vote of the Science Fiction Writers of America and the other on the vote of fans at the main annual convention, any joint winner represents the choice of a broad constituency of those active in the field. *Dune* (the first joint winner) confirmed the existence of an axis between SF and alternative culture when it was recommended as an ecological primer in *The Last Whole Earth Catalog.* Herbert's book returns the compliment by being dedicated 'to the people whose labours go beyond ideas into the realm of "real materials" – to the dry land ecologists'. Ursula Le Guin's *The Left Hand of Darkness* (Nebula 1969, Hugo 1970) tells the story of a non-interventionary black ambassador from a kind of galactic United Nations, Ekumen, assigned to planet Gethen. As the names suggest, oecumenicalism and anthropological respect is endorsed in Le Guin's novel. 'Ekumen', we are told 'doesn't rule, it co-ordinates. Its power is precisely the power of its member states and worlds' (Ch. 1). *The Left Hand of Darkness* opposes the standard 'earthman (white earthman) normal: extraterrestrial alien' formula, offering instead something along the lines of 'everything is normal from its own standpoint'. This 'oecumenical' view is embodied in the narrative which imaginatively shifts from human to Gethenian viewpoints. And the comradely love which develops between Estraven and Genly Ai is as innovatory, in its way, as the inter-racial relationships in, say, the fiction of James Baldwin. Finally, although he has only a Hugo for *The Man in the High Castle* (1962), the large following which Philip K. Dick has attracted indicates a new sympathy with SF which takes its start from frankly heterodox attitudes. (Philip K. Dick describes his development thus: 'In my early novels and stories I often used sociological and political themes; later I branched into drug trips and also theological trips – which angered many readers, both those who used drugs as well as those who used God.'[6] The influence of psychotropic drugs on SF of the post-1960s is profound; though for obvious reasons any investigation of the subject is difficult.) Dick's evolution as a writer has been anything but steady. But in his best work he makes a brilliant and quite idiosyncratic play with alternative realities. And the characteristically West Coast flavour to his fiction should remind us that within American science fiction there are important regional variations to be taken account of. (It will be interesting in this respect to see if Silverberg's SF – assuming he writes any – changes under the influence of his removal from New York to California.)

Having made the point, one should also acknowledge that there is a temptation to concentrate on 'excellence' and 'innovation', and to overlook the bulk of merely good fiction of a traditional kind which has been produced since 1960. Among many others one could cite Keith Laumer with his consistently inventive time-game novels, or Harry Harrison whose 'Deathworld' and 'Stainless Steel Rat' reveal an ability to refresh and rework formulae which in less deft hands would be threadbare half-way through the second instalment. (Harrison, incidentally, has also written the more ambitious overpopulation novel *Make Room! Make Room!* (1966). But he seems a writer consistently forced to work below his best by financial stringencies, a common enough affliction in SF.) At a somewhat higher level the theorist and novelist Alexei Panshin has argued and demonstrated (in the exquisite *Rite of Passage*) that the traditional and original values of SF need not be broken with by the creative writer.

Much depends in the future on how SF writers are *allowed* to write.

It used to be that they were oppressed by commercial pressure, editorial discipline and widespread deprecation of their form. Now the combination of oppressions would seem to be different. There is a discrepancy between what is given the ambitious writer in terms of time and money, and what is held out to him as the potential literary achievement of the genre. How this problem will be resolved, if indeed it ever is resolved, remains to be seen.

Notes

1. Ace figures from the *New York Times Book Review*, 'Paperback Talk', 1 Feb. 1976, p.39.
2. *Again Dangerous Visions*, II. Ed. H. Ellison (1972, repr, New York: 1973), p. 246. Disch informs me that he has, in fact, done SF work since this declaration. But his main creative effort has shifted away from the field into 'straight' fiction.
3. *Fantasy and Science Fiction*, July 1977, p. 54.
4. *Hell's Cartographers*, Ed. Brian Aldiss and Harry Harrison. London: 1975, p. 19. The subsequent account is largely taken from Silverberg's chapter in this volume, pp. 7-45.
5. See Tom Woodman's essay in this volume for a somewhat different interpretation of the novel's ending.
6. *Contemporary Novelists*. Ed. J. Vinson. London: 1976, p. 363.

Bibliography

The booktrade material in this essay is taken largely from *Publishers' Weekly*, particularly that journal's issue devoted to SF, 14 June 1976. I have also made use of the booktrade columns which appear at the end of the Sunday *New York Times Book Review*.

The most informative single study on the publishing of SF, and its commercial market, is provided by Frederik Pohl in his contribution to the critical anthology *Science Fiction, Today and Tomorrow*, ed. R. Bretnor (New York: Harper and Row, 1974). Pohl has the unique distinction of having been over the last thirty years an SF magazine editor, literary editor, and a leading SF novelist. The figure for the number of SF courses is taken from Jack Williamson's essay 'Science Fiction, Teaching, and Criticism' in the same volume.

The magazine which I have used most extensively in this essay is *Fantasy and Science Fiction*. This seems to me to have been the journal which has, more than any other, fostered informed critical debate on the genre.

In the discussion of Robert Silverberg at the centre of my essay, extensive use is made of Brian Aldiss and Harry Harrison's *Hell's Cartographers* (London: Weidenfeld & Nicolson, 1975). The editors' invitation to leading SF writers to provide professional autobiographies elicited a remarkably frank and illuminating response from Silverberg. The garrulous introductions, prefaces and afterwords to Harlan Ellison's *Dangerous Visions* anthologies provide an outsider with a unique insight into the social world of SF and its practitioners. The somewhat cross-grained reflections of Kurt Vonnegut on SF are taken from his collected journalism, interviews, etc. *Wampeters, Foma and Granfalloons: Opinions* (London: Jonathan Cape, 1975).

British science fiction

Christopher Priest

Modern science fiction is a primarily American phenomenon, and much of the genre is written either by Americans or by authors who adopt the American idiom.

This dominance has nothing whatsoever to do with unassailable literary excellence, except in individual cases, but is the product of various related factors. In the first place, English is a world language of literature, and American publishers, with modern promotion and distribution techniques, have access to the world market with books of all kinds. Secondly, the process of dynamic social change – whose own product is an awakening of public curiosity about the prospect of more change, and an arousing of interest in the future, within which social environment science fiction thrives – moved through American society earlier and more dramatically than it did elsewhere. Thirdly, there was and is a geographical concentration of writers, publishers and readers in America, living in a society which welcomes new technology, which enjoys novelty, which embraces change and expansion.

Science fiction, in the modern sense, has no actual existence except as a publishers' category. The only completely reliable definition of science fiction is that anything *labelled* as science fiction *is* science fiction, and although at first sight this appears to be a cynical viewpoint, it is essential to an understanding of the SF phenomenon.

Science fiction did not exist as a discrete literature until Hugo Gernsback created *Amazing Stories* in 1926. His idea was to abstract a 'type' of fiction (epitomized in those days by the work of H. G. Wells, Edgar Allan Poe and Jules Verne) from general literature. All science fiction has grown from there, because the existence of the early pulp-magazines attracted writers who wrote specially for them, imitating each other and influencing each other. This process of imitation continues until the present day, accounting for the unwritten 'rules' of science fiction, the high proportion of mediocre work that appears, the recurrent use of shorthand and jargon . . . and perhaps most noticeable of all, the hostility to the outside world that is subliminally manifest in many utterances of science fiction writers. (One American author recently defined general fiction as being 'gossip about people you don't know'; David Gerrold, Introduction, *Science Fiction Emphasis,* 1.)

Many of the prominent authors in the field declare themselves to be 'science-fiction writers', with the same apparent desire to be categorized as the specialist journalist who wants to be known as a 'football writer' or 'political commentator'. The field has been dominated by doctrinaire editors like Hugo Gernsback and John W. Campbell Jr, who were unreceptive, to say the least, to the unorthodox, and many authors acknowledge a debt they see as due to them.

All this happens because the trappings of the genre are seen to be a good rather than a bad thing. After all, the argument goes, science fiction is hugely popular, it makes a lot of money for its authors, and, best of all, it is even being taken seriously by educators and literary academics. One hears of the acquisition of respectability, and of the maturity of the field now that it has outgrown its pulp-magazine origins; science-fiction writers are eagerly sought as lecturers and television pundits; the first coffee-table books of science-fiction 'art' are already going into second editions.

A few authors – remarkably few, when all is considered – do not subscribe to this notion of science fiction, and although a few of this minority are Americans, a large number of them are British writers.

Science-fiction writers in Britain have an uneasy relationship with the genre. Because Britain and America share a language it has always been relatively easy for a British writer to sell his work in the States; unlike foreign-language authors, to whom the science-fiction markets have long been virtually closed.

With a few exceptions, though, British writers have not 'written for market' by pitching their work at the imagined demands of American magazines or publishers, choosing instead to go their own way and find their own voice. This article is concerned with those writers who have been doing this, but before considering them, it is worth describing how the American idiom has crossed the Atlantic in other ways.

British publishers market science fiction in the same way as their American colleagues, which is by having a separate category for the genre; every major commercial paperback house in Britain now has a science-fiction list. There is nothing particularly unusual or undesirable in this, except to point out that the modern paperback book is a descendant of the American mass-market pulp-magazines, and that most of the categories – thrillers, westerns, science fiction, etc. – have survived intact.

British science-fiction magazines, when there have been any at all, have usually been copies of the American original. Up to the Second World War there were a few titles published, and these were in the large-page format. After the war, *New Worlds* was created by the joint efforts and capital of various British fans and writers, and was edited for more than seventeen years by E. J. Carnell. In its early years, *New Worlds* looked rather like the American *Astounding Stories,* but latterly looked rather more like *Galaxy.* Although most of its contributors were British or Australian, the stories apparently favoured were the puzzle-on-an-alien-planet sort of thing, commonly found in

Astounding Stories of the time. Unsurprisingly, there was an unsatis-factory quality to many of the stories – although there were, of course, notable exceptions – because the idiom was a received one. Some years later, in 1964, *New Worlds* underwent a radical change for the better when Michael Moorcock took over the editorship.

British science fiction, however, existed long before such temporary phenomena as SF magazines came into being. Fantasy has been an element of European literature from the time the first words of fiction were written or uttered. But so far as the modern fantastic novel is concerned, British science fiction, and science fiction itself, began simultaneously.

The first literary work which was indisputably a science-fiction novel, in the modern sense, was Mary Shelley's *Frankenstein* (1818). The circumstances in which the novel was conceived are well known, and described by Mary Shelley in the Preface to the 1831 edition: she, Byron, Shelley and a Doctor Polidori were staying on the banks of Lake Geneva during the summer of 1816. After reading a volume of ghost stories, the four set themselves the task of writing a ghost story. Of the four attempts, only one was finished, and that was *Frankenstein*.

Many and long were the conversations between Lord Byron and Shel-ley, to which I was a devout but nearly silent listener. During one of these various philosophical doctrines were discussed, and among others the nature of the principle of life, and whether there was any probability of its ever being discovered and communicated. They talked of the experi-ments of Dr (Erasmus) Darwin . . . who preserved a piece of vermicelli in a glass cage till by some extraordinary means it began to move with voluntary motion. . . . Perhaps a corpse would be re-animated; galvan-ism had given token of such things; perhaps the component parts of a creature might be manufactured, brought together, and endued with vital warmth.

During the night following this conversation, Mary Shelley had a nightmare, the content of which she describes in her Preface, and which soon became the substance of the first words of *Frankenstein* that she put down: these are now the first few paragraphs of Chapter V.

Mary Shelley set out to write a ghost story (today we would call it a Gothic novel), but inadvertently she created a piece of science fiction. *Frankenstein* is in almost every respect a Gothic novel, for most of the elements of the genre – which was already popular in Mary Shelley's day – are there: the brooding atmosphere, the craggy scenery, the terrifying visitations, the brutal murders, the quest for revenge. The Gothic idiom, however, is one rooted in the natural or supernatural. The drama is one of madness, or suicide, or incest, or infanticide . . . the visitations are explicable to deliria, or to ghosts.

Mary Shelley, sharing the company of two of the most brilliant and witty poets of the day, growing up (she was yet only nineteen) in a society that was increasingly interested in technology and its potential, unconsciously changed the idiom. The madness she described was the madness of scientific ambition; the phantasm she created was the product of scientific method. *Frankenstein* has a quality new to the Gothic idiom: it is a fable of moral responsibility and conscience. Because a scientist, Victor Frankenstein, dares to play God, he has to pay the price for his hubris; his monster, a lamenting Nemesis, his head furnished with *Paradise Lost* and Plutarch's *Lives,* exacts an entirely moral revenge.

Frankenstein is in the literature of the fantastic, but unlike its predecessors it is *about* something. Its thrills and *frissons* (which manage to survive the author's sometimes turgid prose) come not from the playing on the primaeval fears and superstitions of the reader, but from the presentation of a plausible improbability.

The Frankenstein theme, providentially discovered by Mary Shelley, informs a huge amount of the writing in modern science fiction. It is found in any story about robots, androids and computers, including such disparate works as *The Island of Doctor Moreau, Player Piano, The Caves of Steel* and *2001: A Space Odyssey*; it is present, in effect, in any fiction where man or woman aspires to a higher state of being or knowledge by creating a machine or human-substitute which improves on the five natural senses. It is no longer a uniquely British theme. In the nineteenth century it was Britain that led the world in scientific research; today it is West Germany, Japan and the United States, and the Frankenstein theme has been taken to the bosom of the American imagination as if it was born there.

If Mary Shelley's discovery of a major speculative theme was accidental, then H. G. Wells's role in the creation of the genre was no less so.

By the middle of the 1920s, Wells was a world figure. He had written two major histories, a number of books on warfare, politics, democracy, Russia and the United States, and a huge number of novels, many of which like *Ann Veronica* (1909), expressed his personal ideas or ideology. He was probably the most famous living author in Britain, and one of the most controversial. His early scientific romances were still immensely popular with the public, but as John Huntington has pointed out elsewhere in this book they were ignored by most critics, and even Wells and his publishers seemed anxious to underplay them; opposite the title-page of *Meanwhile* (1927), for example, there is a list of Wells's previous novels, and underneath, in much smaller type, attention is drawn to 'the following fantastic and imaginative romances'.

That Wells himself, at this time, saw his early science fiction as being less important than his 'real' novels probably goes without saying, even though for the rest of his life he thought of himself as soothsayer and prophet. At the actual time of composition, though, when he was at the beginning of his career, there is nothing in his letters to suggest that he saw his books as hackwork, and in fact there is evidence that he treated them with the greatest seriousness.[1]

The magazines where Wells's early work was published – *Pearson's, the Strand,* the *New Review,* the *Pall Mall Budget* and others – were not science-fiction magazines in the way we would understand them today. They were general magazines, read by a wide audience. This new young author would have been read and enjoyed without preconceptions, and he made quite a mark.

Although several of the early short stories are anecdotal and undeveloped, by today's standards, they are remarkable firstly for the innovative nature of their notions, and secondly for their scientific imagination. In later years, Wells himself sometimes failed to distinguish between actual prophecy and an ability to conceive imaginatively of a possible scientific development. Take, for instance, this description of an aeroplane, from 'The argonauts of the Air' (1895):

The thing . . . was driven by a huge screw behind in place of the tail; and so hovering . . . was rendered impossible. The body of the machine was small, almost cylindrical, and pointed. Forward and aft on the pointed ends were two small petroleum engines for the screw, and the navigators sat deep in a canoe-like recess, the foremost one steering, and being protected by a low screen, with two plateglass windows, from the blinding rush of air. On either side a monstrous flat framework with a curved front border could be adjusted so as either to lie horizontally, or to be tilted upward or down. These wings worked rigidly together, or, by releasing a pin, one could be tilted through a small angle independently of its fellow. The front edge of either wing could also be shifted back so as to diminish the wing-area about one-sixth.

This description, written at least eight years before the Wright brothers' first flight, and at a time when heavier-than-air flight was assumed to be possible only by mechanically imitating the movements of a bird (the 'ornithopter'), is a clear description of a modern monoplane. Wells anticipates the propeller (he uses the word 'screw', probably literally, but even today propellers are still called 'airscrews'), petrol engines, fuselage, aerofoil wings, windscreen, ailerons and elevators . . . even retractable flaps. But is Wells *prophesying* a machine, or is he simply using contemporary ideas in an imaginative way, and assembling them into a logical whole? (In *The War in the Air* (1908), Wells anticipated, by imaginative extension, the use of aeroplanes in war. In 1921, when the book was reprinted, Wells wrote a Preface, pointing out the warning prophecy he had made; in 1941 the book was again reprinted, and Wells, then aged seventy-five, asked that his epitaph should be: 'I told you so. You *damned* fools.')

When Hugo Gernsback published the first issue of *Amazing Stories,* H. G. Wells was sixty. One can only guess at the feelings of this historian, novelist, social thinker and statesman's confidant, to see a brightly packaged commercial magazine dedicated to the scientific romance, and one which was busily reprinting nearly all his early works. Wells was regularly included in the first issues of *Amazing Stories* (together with Poe and Verne), his work apparently exemplifying, in Gernsback's mind, the sort of fiction which would awaken and excite the interest of the general public in crystal sets and atomic bombs. Gernsback's dependence on Wells was almost total: in the first three years he published no less than seventeen of Wells's short stories, and serialized six of his novels!

So it was that Wells inadvertently helped create the modern science-fiction idiom. It is not that his early work would now be forgotten but for Gernsback – a ludicrous claim that is sometimes made in the science-fiction world; the romances were popular with an audience far wider than that sought by Gernsback – but that all writing within a commercial genre is inherently imitative, and it was Wells's stories, some of which were more than thirty years old, that provided the original.

For the two decades following the introduction of *Amazing Stories,* and the magazines created by other companies to rival it, there was no such thing as 'British' science fiction. True, there were British writers who were selling to the American magazines – including John Beynon Harris (later known as John Wyndham), William F. Temple and John Russell Fearn, who used a number of pseudonyms – but their work, in differing respects, was written with the magazines in mind, and for all useful purposes is indistinguishable from the work of contemporary American writers.

This article is primarily concerned with science-fiction writers (that is, authors who either call themselves science-fiction writers, or whose work is in general closely identified with the field), but it would be a gross omission not to mention Aldous Huxley, Olaf Stapledon or George Orwell.

Of the three it is possible that only Orwell had knowledge of the existence of the American pulps, and even then his interest in them would have been of the same order as, say, his social-history interest in seaside postcards or boys' comics. None of his work was ever printed or reprinted in American pulps, and the notion that he would ever think of writing specifically for them can be discounted entirely. In the case of Olaf Stapledon, he was once shown some science-fiction magazines and told that his work had certain affinities with their contents; this information left him puzzled and hurt. Even so, all three writers produced novels which we can identify as being science-fictional, or fantastic, in nature.

Of the three, Olaf Stapledon is probably the most isolated: he has never been fully embraced by the science-fiction world, in spite of much critical advocacy from within, and nor has he been recognized by the larger world of letters (for example, the *Oxford Companion to English Literature* has entries for Orwell and Huxley, but not for

Stapledon). His novels are of visionary intensity, his scope universal; millennia pass within a paragraph. But Stapledon does not have a character protagonist (in the usual sense) in his masterworks – *Last and First Men* and *Star Maker* – and nor does he have a plot as such. To the science fiction reader, brought up on the muscular storytelling of the Americal style, these are serious failings.

The title alone of Aldous Huxley's *Brave New World* (1932) has acquired a catchphrase, shorthand meaning; one sees constant reference to it whenever utopian or satirical writing is discussed, and yet one suspects it is not often read these days by science-fiction fans or critics. It is not at all the prophetic nightmare of received wisdom, but a witty if elbow-nudging satire on the hedonism of the 1920s. The novel takes on a different momentum with the appearance of the Shakespeare-quoting Savage, but the author's feelings about his imagined world, from a modern reading at least, seem ambiguous.

George Orwell is known in the science-fiction world for his novel *Nineteen Eighty-Four* (1949), and to a lesser extent for *Animal Farm* (1945), but to claim him as a science-fiction writer would be to ignore the major part of his work. His novels, including the non-fantastic early books, must be looked at in the context of Orwell's career as a political journalist (perhaps the most brilliant of the century). *Animal Farm* (which Orwell started writing in 1943, but which was not published until 1945, after many setbacks), is a satire on post-revolutionary socialist states; quite apart from the unambiguous statement which is made in the book, Orwell was writing during the latter years of the Second World War, and his journalism and diaries contain many observations of the political double-thinking that was going on in Britain and the States about the expedient alliance with Stalin's Russia. The actual setting of *Nineteen Eighty-Four* is 1948 – the year in which it was written – not 1984, and as such is an entirely lucid symbolic description of Britain in the immediate post-war years. The fact that it can be read as a hortatory vision, in the extrapolative mould of the science-fiction idiom, is partly propitious, and partly the probable result of Orwell's admiration of E. I. Zamyatin's *We* (1920), a novel he had first encountered in 1945, and for which he had been trying to find an English publisher for some time. As with Huxley's novel, the title has become synonymous with oppressive dictatorships, both in fact and in fiction. It can still be read today without any sort of allowance for its age or period; it is one of the most important novels of the twentieth century.

In the early 1950s, British science fiction took a new turn, although this was attributable, initially, to the fact that American science fiction was itself moving forward.

In the first place, there was a considerable boom in the sales of magazines. Secondly, new publications, like *Galaxy* and *The Magazine of Fantasy & Science Fiction,* came into being, and the editorial policies were less conservative and more concerned with good writing than those of the pulp-magazines: a number of excellent American writers came into prominence, including Sheckley, Pohl, Dick, Tenn, Bester, Kornbluth, Bradbury and Matheson. Thirdly, Britain at last had regular science-fiction magazines of its own: primarily *New Worlds,* which started publication soon after the war, and to a lesser extent *Authentic Science Fiction* and the Scottish magazine *Nebula.*

John Wyndham (whose real name was John Wyndham Parkes Lucas Beynon Harris) was one of several fans and writers who put up the capital to create Nova Publications Ltd, publishers of *New Worlds.* As already mentioned, Wyndham had sold a number of stories to American magazines before the war, and additionally had published two novels in 1935, *The Secret People* and *Stowaway to Mars* (both serialized in *The Passing Show,* the latter under the title *Planet Plane*). Both of these novels, although written in the racy, extravagant mode of the American idiom, are unmistakably British in origin, with the hero calling the heroine a 'brick' at one point, and Mars being claimed for the British Commonwealth and Empire, which if nothing else certainly made for a change.

Wyndham is best remembered for several novels he published in the 1950s, namely *The Day of the Triffids* (1951), *The Kraken Wakes* (1953), *The Chrysalids* (1955) and *The Midwich Cuckoos* (1957).[2] What is important about these novels is not the huge success each has enjoyed (success which continues to the present), but the fact that while being unmistakably science-fictional in kind, and in many cases actually borrowing some of the standard notions from the pulp-magazines – perambulating plants, telepathic children, etc. – they are firmly British in manner, style and locale. (The exception is *The Chrysalids,* which is set in post-holocaust Canada; even in this book, however, the writing is 'British' in cadence and vocabulary.)

Wyndham is the master of the middle-class catastrophe; his characters are of the bourgeoisie, and his books lament the collapse of law and order, the failure of communications, the looting of shopping precincts and the absence of the daily newspaper. One step up the social scale from Wells, Wyndham's debt to the old master is different in kind from Gernsback's, but no less in degree. Many of Wells's best literary devices – especially the almost surreal juxtaposition of the familiar and reassuring against the exotic and menacing – are strongly evident in Wyndham's books.

However, Wyndham's major contribution to British science fiction lies in his approach to the subject-matter. He was the first science-fiction writer in Britain to turn away from the American idiom; he knew the genre, had read (and written for) the pulps, was involved with other SF writers in London . . . but he went his own way. His books are comedies of English manners, examples of that peculiarly British type of novel, and yet he was wildly successful, both in Britain and in the States. The lesson, if not taken directly from the books, was not lost on other British writers.

John Wyndham's novels are archetypes of a sub-category within science fiction, known by a number of names, but perhaps best described as 'the British disaster novel'. Almost every British writer seems at some time in his career to turn his hand to the theme – reflecting, it might be argued, an unconscious response to the loss of the Empire – but with one or two renowned exceptions it has never been as popular with writers in the States.

The theme is attractively (and perhaps deceptively) simple: the *status quo* is overturned by some hitherto unanticipated development – which might be natural catastrophe, scientific advance, social revolution or alien intervention – and the story follows a small group of ordinary people as they confront the upheaval.

H. G. Wells's *The War of the Worlds* is one such novel. A partial listing of other titles would be: *The Tide Went Out* by Charles Eric Maine (1958), *The Giant Stumbles* by John Lymington (1960), *The Fittest* by J. T. McIntosh (1955), *The Wind from Nowhere* by J. G. Ballard (1962), *The Hopkins Manuscript* by R. C. Sherriff (1939), *Fugue For a Darkening Island* by Christopher Priest (1972), *White August* by John Boland (1955), *The Twilight of Briareus* by Richard Cowper (1974), *The Scent of New-Mown Hay* by John Blackburn (1958), *The Iron Rain* by Donald Malcolm (1976), and *The Primal Urge* and *Greybeard* by Brian W. Aldiss (1961,1964).

John Wyndham's closest rival for pre-eminence in this sub-category was John Christopher (C. S. Youd). Christopher is best known as an author of children's novels (many of which have a fantasy background), but his early work included a number of remarkable adult novels. Of these perhaps the best, and the best known, is *The Death of Grass* (1956; U.S. title *No Blade of Grass*).

In absolute terms, *The Death of Grass* is probably a better novel than anything Wyndham wrote; it is certainly more atmospheric and 'realistic', and has the added benefit of concentrating much of its attention on the personality development and regression, respectively, of the two leading characters. Unlike Wyndham, Christopher sensed that when the thin protective veneer of civilization is stripped away from otherwise normal people, the bestial soon emerges. *The Death of Grass* is a fine essay on the brutalization of man by the reduction of his circumstances.

These novels aside, the centre of science fiction in Britain during the 1950s and the early 1960s was the group of magazines edited by John Carnell. The three titles were: *New Worlds, Science Fantasy* and *Science Fiction Adventures* (this last one was an oddity: it was originally a reprint of an American magazine of the same title, but when the American publication went out of business, Carnell continued publishing with original material).

Carnell expended much time and energy on these magazines, but the period was one of transition, creatively. Although writers like Wyndham were showing the way towards finding a singular voice, there were a great many writers in Britain who could not find either the nerve or the inspiration to take a chance on individual merit. The propaganda coming across the Atlantic from energetic editors like Anthony Boucher (of *Fantasy and Science Fiction*) and H. L. Gold (of *Galaxy*) was very persuasive, and the revolution in the States, although of a different sort, was showing results. Consequently, many British writers felt compelled to write in an alien idiom, one they imagined was nearer to 'pure' SF. Like all imitations the work was inferior to the real thing, although a few writers made repeated sales to American publishers. Among these were Eric Frank Russell, Kenneth Bulmer and, most prolific of all, John Brunner. Those whose work did not survive the Atlantic passage, and saw it return on the next boat, sold to the British magazines. *New Worlds* and the other Carnell-edited magazines were therefore somewhat overweighted with ersatz material, an undue percentage of which dealt with the adventures of Anglo-Saxons on puzzling alien planets.

There were exceptions, though, and Arthur C. Clarke is one of them.

Although Clarke is an over-rated writer – his work is redolent of a naive romanticism, made palatable by homely similes, and simple, logical plotting – he has achieved a worldwide popularity, and this is no doubt due to the fact that his voice is undoubtedly his own; much of this is in turn due to a wholehearted, if facile, Englishness. Clarke's Bill-and-Jimmy heroes are a likeable lot, pursuing their adventures through a wonderland universe (apparently inspired by Arthur Mee's encyclopaedia), displaying both niceness and the sort of grit they drill into you at boarding-school. Clarke's admirers will point to a lyrical turn of phrase, and an ability to describe the most complex concept with evocative similes, and these are indeed his best qualities as a writer. Of his novels, two of the earliest, *The City and the Stars* (1956) and *Childhood's End* (1953), are typical of his more successful writing; two of his latest, *Rendezvous with Rama* (1973) and *Imperial Earth* (1975), while seeming to have much the same sort of visionary force behind them, actually reveal a gaucherie about character motivations and a pedestrianism of plotting that were better concealed before.

During Carnell's editorship of *New Worlds,* two British writers emerged who have become, each in his own way, major authors. Both have gone on to greater things than their early published work, but from the outset it was clear that each had an individual voice. They are Brian W. Aldiss and J. G. Ballard.

Aldiss's history of science fiction, *Billion Year Spree* (1973), is probably the best and most controversial of all surveys so far published of the field, and although it is complete in many ways, there is one major omission. Aldiss neglects to mention his own contribution as a writer.

In some respects Aldiss is the complete British science-fiction writer: he has a comprehensive knowledge and understanding of the genre, and a great liking for it, he is and has been involved with a number of behind-the-scenes activities (it was he, for instance, who initiated the Arts Council grant for *New Worlds* in 1967), but at the same time he has never lost a sense of perspective.

With the advantage of hindsight we can see that his first book, *The Brightfount Diaries* (1955), was typically untypical: it is an utterly English novel, based on a series of fictionalized articles, first published in *The Bookseller,* about an Oxford bookshop assistant. This was not his first published work: short stories had been appearing in SF magazines since 1954, and most of the early ones were collected in *Space, Time and Nathaniel* (1957). His first science-fiction novel, *Non-Stop* (1958; US title *Starship*), which many people still consider to be one of his best, is a useful one to consider when examining the virtues of British science fiction.

Unlike Wyndham, who had apparently turned his back on the established SF idiom, Aldiss confronted it head-on. He took one of the standard science-fiction plot-situations – a long-journey starship, populated by descendants of the original crew – and approached it with such vigour that it was as if he had originated the idea. *Non-Stop* acts as a kind of bridge between American science fiction and British: it has a strong storyline, played out against a background of lost races, telepathic mutants, advanced machinery and stellar exploration, and yet there is a closeness of focus on the characters that one would not find in many American novels of similar background, and a joy of using language, an exhilaration, in fact, at the discovery of science fiction.

Aldiss has been a prolific writer, having authored something like eighteen novels, several story-collections, and three works of non-fiction, as well as editing a large number of books of different kinds. It is not possible to do justice to his work in this space. His best early novels are *Non-Stop* and *Greybeard*; of his later works, *Frankenstein Unbound* (1973) and *The Malacia Tapestry* (1976) are outstanding. Some of his best work is not science fiction at all, notably the Horatio Stubbs novels, *The Hand-Reared Boy* (1970) and *A Soldier Erect* (1971), and a large body of critical work.

If Wyndham made a point with his books about the British approach to science-fiction content, Aldiss makes one of similar strength about the actual writing of SF. He is a writer endowed with a felicity of expression; there is nothing of his in print that is not crafted with precision, wit and style. Like any other good writer he is inimitable, but many writers who followed have drawn inspiration from his example.

After Aldiss first made his presence felt, it was no longer good enough merely to imitate the Americans.

J. G. Ballard's first short story, 'Prima Belladonna', was published in John Carnell's *Science Fantasy* in 1956, and it was immediately clear that he was a writer unique in both subject-matter and prose-style. His development as a writer – which for some time was through short stories – appears to have proceeded without any obvious influence from the genre, although nearly all his early stories were published in science-fiction magazines.

Ballard, born in Shanghai of British parents, was interned by the Japanese throughout the war, and came to Britain when he was sixteen. Virtually every other science-fiction author will confess to having read SF at an impressionable age, but Ballard was effectively insulated from this. Instead, he experienced at first hand one of the great examples of human misbehaviour, and probably as a direct consequence his writing has a vision of peculiarly twentieth-century intensity.

His haunting short stories – like Wells's work, like Wyndham's, though here the similarity ends – are a disconcerting blend of the naggingly familiar and the bizarrely surreal, full of powerful visual images and a vague but quite tangible sense of doom and wreckage. These early stories – most of which are still in print – were the basis for his increasing reputation within the SF world, but it was his novels, especially *The Drowned World* (1962), which brought him the first critical acclaim from outside.

When Michael Moorcock took over the editorship of *New Worlds* in 1964, Ballard had started publishing his stories in the States, but with Moorcock's encouragement he returned to his former fold and began a series of experimental 'condensed novels'. These stories – eventually collected as *The Atrocity Exhibition* (1970) – are almost impossible to analyse except in the context of Ballard's own work, being a nightmarish juxtaposition of seminal images: advertising hoardings, crashed automobiles, film-stars, cityscapes, cosmetic surgery, abandoned hotels. It was as if Ballard was distilling his previous work into a potent metaphor of the times.

Later, he returned to more conventional work, notably what is probably his best novel so far, *Crash* (1973). Set in a landscape of elevated motorways, airport approaches and high-rise suburbs, and peopled by screenwriters and plastic surgeons and air-hostesses, *Crash* deals with the extraordinary link between technology and eroticism. Written with an obsessive attention to detail, and an equally obsessive repetition of the theme, the book eventually draws the reader into an understanding of its surreal world. *Crash* is one of the best novels of any kind of the 1970s, and probably not by intent – though this is true of all Ballard's work – it is also an example of high science fiction.

Both Aldiss and Ballard were regular contributors to *New Worlds* while it was edited by Michael Moorcock, and to a large measure helped shape the 'New Wave' that came as a result.

Moorcock's work on *New Worlds* was from 1964 to 1971, and throughout the period he encouraged both new and established writers to seek an individual voice. I have written elsewhere of Moorcock's influence,³ and what follows is a mere précis of one of the major revolutions within the genre.

By a combination of polemical editorials and the enlightened choice of material (some of which tended toward the experimental), Moorcock showed that the traditional idiom of science fiction – as represented by the work of popular authors like Heinlein, Asimov and Van Vogt – need not be an exclusive one. He argued that the speculative notion need not be applied just to alien cultures, space travel, etc. but might also be used to explore internal concerns, such as madness or loneliness, or to describe transitory experiences, such as drug-taking or listening to music.

This was during the 1960s, when an awareness of social change was sweeping through Western culture, and a new generation of writers joined Moorcock's crusade. The New Wave was always an essentially British phenomenon, because there was a genuine spirit of revolt within it, and the revolution was against the axioms of the American school. However, a number of independently minded American writers – notably Thomas M. Disch and Samuel R. Delany – visited London and became regular contributors to *New Worlds*, and in due course the New Wave crossed the Atlantic.

Outside Britain, the New Wave was treated differently. It was seen to be a new 'type' of writing: eclectic in source, often explicit in sexual content, frequently experimental in form. Any fiction that was the least bit obscure, or daring in subject-matter, or innovative in its typography – however traditional it might be in other respects – was dubbed 'New Wave'. The result was that a sub-category came into being, and without the revolutionary instinct behind it the New Wave became identified with anything that made perfunctory gestures towards the avant-garde.

The New Wave's least contribution to science fiction was therefore the introduction of a new mannerism: self-conscious obscurity hiding an emptiness of meaning.

Its greatest contribution was the public proclamation of the individual writer's voice, and New Wave sub-category or no, it is only by individual talent that a writer can make his way.

This, then, is the essence of the British contribution to the science-fiction category. For a number of reasons, some of them evolutionary, some of them cultural, some geographical, Britain has produced a large number of writers who have found acceptance within the genre as it is generally recognized; they are established, though, not because they have met the category on its own terms, but because the category itself – although severely restricted in some respects – is broad enough to include them.

The authors mentioned here are only a handful of the whole; they have been mentioned, because, to one degree or another, their work has signalled some kind of turning-point in British science-fiction activity. An incomplete listing of other writers who are presently working in fertile ground would be: Angela Carter, D. G. Compton, Michael G. Coney, Richard Cowper, Robert P. Holdstock, Keith Roberts and Ian Watson. This has to be incomplete, because at a recent estimate it was found that there are something like sixty people living in Britain today who are writing or who have written science fiction professionally; twenty-five of those are full-time authors, most of whose output is science fiction or closely similar work. Expressed as a percentage of overall population, this figure must compare favourably with almost any other Western nation.

This is partly due to economics: the way science fiction is published has changed considerably in recent years, and America is no longer the most important market. Science fiction is published throughout Europe, in Japan, in South America; translation-fees, although individually small, are increasingly important to authors. British writers, with their European sensibilities, translate well. Probably more significant, though, is the British sense of individuality.

To return to an earlier point, much of the writing within the genre is inherently imitative; although this seems to be a dismissive observation, it has not been a completely bad thing. The idiom has its strengths, one of which is its naturalism. Science fiction achieves many of its effects by the description of real-seeming people experiencing real-seeming events in a bizarre or unlikely set of circumstances. Put another way, the idiom is one of verisimilitude within a fantastic metaphor.

British writers have always seemed more at ease with an instinctive grasp of the fantastic metaphor. Theirs is a more 'literary' approach; the form is of equal importance to the content.

An interesting comparison can be made between two novels, one American and one British, which deal with the same sort of central notion.

Larry Niven's *Ringworld* (1970) describes a huge, artificially constructed ring, which circles a distant star; Bob Shaw's *Orbitsville* (1975) describes a huge, artificially constructed hollow sphere, also circling a distant star. Both books deal with the discovery and exploration of these artefacts.

In Niven's book the protagonist is the artefact itself. Although a group of explorers spend much of their time travelling around the ringworld, and making various discoveries, by the end of the book nothing of any real interest or importance has been discovered about either the characters or the artefact. The book ends as it has begun, with a mystery. *Ringworld* has enjoyed a large and admiring audience, and it is a novel often quoted as being central to science fiction. In fact it is no such thing. *Ringworld* consists simply of a notion, one that is described through fictional prose.

In Shaw's book the protagonist is a man, Garamond, who is motivated by a need to escape from an industrialist who has hitherto controlled his life. Far from this escape being simply a plot-motivation, as the novel proceeds it becomes clear that Garamond's journey, while being described in a matter-of-fact narrative, with spaceships galore, is also a journey through the subconscious. His discovery of the artificial sphere is one that ensures his freedom from the industrialist; when the industrialist follows, it is the sphere that eventually liberates him again. At the conclusion of the book, we discover that the sphere has a larger purpose.

Both books are firmly in the traditional mode of science fiction, and both are superficially entertaining because of the various contrivances that the authors produce. *Orbitsville,* however, entertains on a more subtle level. Because the reader can sense that there is in the story a deeper movement of events than just plot-happenings – in effect it is *about* something more than invented incident – it is ultimately a more satisfactory book than *Ringworld*.

To treat either of these books as being examples of the conscious use of metaphor would be wrong. In Niven's case, it is self-evident from the writing that the book simply does not operate on that level; in the case of Shaw, it is probable that the book was conceived and written on a straightforward basis. And yet one can find, and respond to, a metaphorical content in *Orbitsville*.

Niven's book is one that can only be judged in the context of science fiction as a whole; it would be largely incomprehensible to anyone who has not read SF. Shaw's novel is more personal, the product of an individual imagination. It can be read as a novel on its own terms, with no pre-knowledge of jargon or idiom required of the reader.

This is not to praise Shaw at the expense of burying Niven, but merely to point up possible differences between a British and an American approach. Nor is it to make a larger case, that British science fiction is *per se* 'better' than American. Many of the most influential and remarkable examples of modern SF have come from the States.

However, if a general case can be made, it would be to say that a mediocre American science-fiction novel is usually poor in an uninteresting way, and a mediocre British science-fiction novel is poor in an interesting way.

British science fiction does not often surround itself with razzmatazz; its virtues are modest ones. British books do not often figure in the competition for the annual SF awards. With the possible exceptions of Wells and Tolkien, Britain does not have authors of the same legendary stature as, say, Asimov or Heinlein.

Instead, Britain has a number of excellent writers, each of whom goes his or her own way. The work is in general literate and fresh, displaying qualities of landscape, irony, language and subtlety that any other nation, English-speaking or otherwise, would find hard to match.

Notes

1. George Orwell, writing in Tribune, 7 Feb. 1947, offers this insight into Wells's attitude to his own work: 'When H. G. Wells's *The Island of Doctor Moreau* was reprinted in the Penguin Library, I looked to see whether the slips and misprints which I remembered in earlier editions had been repeated in it. Sure enough, they were still there. One of them is a particularly stupid misprint, of a kind to make most writers squirm. In 1941 I pointed this out to H. G. Wells, and asked him why he did not remove it. It had persisted through edition after edition ever since 1896. Rather to my surprise, he said that he remembered the misprint, but could not be bothered to do anything about it. He no longer took the faintest interest in his early books: they had been written so long ago that he no longer felt them to be part of himself. I have never been quite sure whether to admire this attitude or not.'

2. The last three of these appeared in the US under the titles *Out of the Deep, Re-Birth* and *Village of the Damned,* respectively.

3. See Christopher Priest, 'New Wave Science Fiction', in *The Encyclopaedia of Science Fiction* (London: Octopus Books, 1978).

European science fiction

Franz Rottensteiner

Science fiction from the continent of Europe is still relatively unknown in the English-speaking countries, despite the efforts of publishers such as Seabury Press, Daw Books and Macmillan; translations are few and far between, and they are often of a poor quality. Condescending remarks have rarely been tempered by any knowledge. One thing seems certain about SF, anywhere in the world: there is far too much of the stuff, and there is more bad science fiction than Sturgeon's Law of the '90 per cent crud' in any field would allow for. It must be admitted right at the beginning that this is especially true of many European countries, where science fiction as a specialist branch of writing and a mass phenomenon is of fairly recent origin, although there have always been writers attracted by the unusual, the outré, and the fantastic. This isolation from world SF has resulted in a certain clumsiness and technical backwardness, as science fiction in those countries had slowly to catch up with the general level achieved by American and British science fiction. But such generalizations are only true of the average science fiction, and definitely not for the very best efforts.

It is my belief that science fiction is a minor branch of fiction, minor at least in artistic terms, that the current commercial popularity of SF has not changed anything about this, and that any writer who would write *only* science fiction can only be a minor writer. The greatest works of SF have always been written by people who were good writers anyway, choosing the form of science fiction only when it was the best expression for the things they had to say; that is true for H. G. Wells, Karel Čapek and to a lesser extent even for Jules Verne, and it is also true for the novels of George Orwell, Aldous Huxley and others that might be called SF. Of course, any writer has a right to be judged as an individual on his own merits, and it would be ridiculous to evaluate a writer on the average level of the literature of his environment. Indeed, I do believe that a large SF field, while it may raise the general standard of SF to a higher degree of mediocrity, is absolutely detrimental to the production of really first-rate works (as opposed to the Nebula and Hugo-winning popular trash that succeeds in the US paperback market). American SF may serve as an example: it has produced a dense accumulation of writers capable of producing good commerical fiction, but not any really outstanding figures comparable in stature to an

H. G. Wells, a Karel Čapek or a Jules Verne. Why some people are writers of great capability, and others are not, is never a matter of the environment, but remains a secret of the creative personality, a 'lucky throw of the genetic dice' as a philosopher once put it; and more important than any SF environment is always the wider field of literature, to which anybody can have access if he but wants to have it.

Science-fiction readers, naturally, often feel that only familiarity with SF produces good SF, and that something that doesn't conform to their expectations is therefore *a priori* somewhat unsophisticated. This is a criticism that has been levelled often by ghetto critics at writers like Stanislaw Lem, whom I personally consider the most important SF writer anywhere in the world.[1] The simple truth is that Lem's reputation extends far beyond the usual SF audience, and that in fact he is much more popular among the general literary public than among habitual SF readers. Literary critics, after all, do not care for SF fandom's criteria of writing excellence. Often cited has been Lem's impressive record of sales and translations, now approaching 9 million copies in more than 30 languages, with 4 million in the Soviet Union alone: all the more remarkable for a writer writing in so inaccessible a language as Polish. In fact, with close to 200 translations now, Lem is the most often translated author in modern Polish literature. This success has sometimes been attributed to a lack of competition; this is undoubtedly true for the early years, but it is not true any more, for Lem is just as successful in West Germany, Sweden or the United States, where there are very competitive SF markets; and he also appears in countries like Israel, Greece, Turkey or Finland, where little SF of any kind is being published.

Poland

In SF terms, Lem may be an isolated figure; in terms of literature, he is not. He is creating in a science-fiction desert, although it is by no means true that he is the only SF writer producing in Poland. There are about two dozen regular SF writers, among whom Czeslaw Chruszczewski, Konrad Fialkowski and Krzysztof Borún may be the best known. Other names in Polish science fiction are Stefan Weinfeld, Ryszard Sawwa, Janusz A. Zajdel, Witold Zegalski and Andrzej Czechowski. They are mostly scientists for whom writing is a hobby, and they publish their work in popular science magazines for a very young audience; some others are journalists. Some Polish SF has been translated into Russian and German, and Konrad Fialkowski and Czeslaw Chruszczewski have had volumes of short stories published in Germany. The general level of writing is low; by Western standards it resembles the kind of fiction published in *Wonder Stories,* naively enthusiastic about technical hardware. (Much the same is true for the mass of Soviet SF.) Of quite a good quality is the yearly almanac of science fiction, *Krokie w nieznane,* edited by Lech Jeczmyk, who is a translator himself. These almanacs present a spectrum of international science fiction, including the leading American and English authors, and also provide a forum for original Polish SF stories.

More interesting than the modern efforts are some older novels. Antoni Slonimski was one of the grand old men of Polish literature; in his youth he made an excursion into speculative terrain, namely into alternative history, that branch of speculative fiction well represented in the USA by Ward Moore's Civil War story *Bring the Jubilee* (1953). Slonimski's subject-matter is the Napoleonic Wars, and the misery entailed by them. His heroes set out to change history with their time torpedo (*Torpeda czasu*, 1921) to prevent all this suffering, but while they do indeed manage to change history, all that they bring about is a different kind of misery. It is the book of a young man, as evidenced by the exuberance of its mannered style, and although the writing now appears dated, the whole idea is very clever and was original to the author. A still earlier writer, Jerzy Zulawski, was a celebrated playwright and man of letters, who wrote around the turn of the century a remarkable lunar trilogy. The first and best-known of these novels is *Na srebnym globie* (*The Silver Globe*, 1903), which was translated into Russian and German. It deals with the first journey to the moon, and the efforts of the survivors to create a new society under most unfavourable circumstances. The second book, *Zwyciezca* (*The Victor*, 1910), introduces religion as subject-matter when another visitor from Earth, more than a century later, finds himself cast into the role of a saviour supposed to deliver the lunar colony from their bondage to a race of alien monsters. The trilogy is concluded in *Stara Ziemia* (*The Old Earth*, 1911).

So much for the SF background. In such an environment, a writer like Lem must appear as a mutant. What distinguishes him from other writers of science fiction is, apart from his erudition and depth of knowledge, his infallible ear for the slightest nuances of language, and his overabundance of imagination and ideas. His works are the products of a personality exerting the whole range of his intellectual faculties to the utmost; not, as all too often in science fiction, merely playing with stock devices that have been used and recombined so often that all that remains for the writer to do is to invent some minor twist or to improve the level of the writing a little. Lem's imagination never seems to tire, and he gets better, and his ideas become more daring, the older he gets. Most writers in the field of SF are soon burnt-out cases, bound to repeat themselves for ever. This was true of the greatest of them all, H. G. Wells, whose later SF novels never achieved the poetic freshness and vigour of his earliest masterpieces; this is true of an American SF writer like Ray Bradbury, who, after two or three remarkable books, lives on as the empty hull of his own fame; and this is also true of many lesser writers, including Heinlein, Asimov or Clarke. Many young SF writers manage to write in their twenties as if they were already very old men, so empty their work appears to be.

Lem, on the other hand, gets better the older he gets, and although he, like many a great writer, treats only a few great themes – chance and necessity, cybernetics, and most prominently the role of consciousness in the universe, whatever its material substratum, human, alien or robotic – he extracts infinite variety from them.

Lem's beginnings were fairly humble. Finding that a novel about the German occupation of Poland couldn't get published for political reasons, he turned to writing science fiction. *Astronauci* (*The Astronauts*, 1951) and *Oblok Magellana* (*The Magellan Nebula*, 1955) are conventional SF novels; the first is about an expedition to Venus, a planet found devastated by atomic war; the second about a utopian society aboard a gigantic space ship on its way to the stars. Both books still abound in lecturing, some of it of an improving kind, although they also contain the graphically vivid descriptions of alien worlds which distinguish later books like *The Invincible, Eden* and above all *Solaris*. Their social ruminations secured these books a ready acceptance in the socialist countries, and they make up a large proportion of Lem's Soviet editions.

Dissatisfied with these early efforts, Lem soon moved into new literary territory: Ijon Tichy is a cosmic Baron Münchhausen, a teller of tall stories that parody both Lem's own apprentice SF and other common SF motifs, such as various forms of time and space travel, or the acceptance of Earth into a Galactic Federation as in the 8th Journey of Ijon Tichy. These stories, to which Lem has been constantly adding in the last decades, emulate and parody an astonishing range of styles, from political speeches to scientific treatises and philosophical essays, poking fun at human failings and at a variety of philosophical ideas.

Pirx the pilot presents another aspect of Lem's literary universe; he is a more serious pendant to Ijon Tichy, embodying a different viewpoint: he is a courageous and sympathetic, yet bungling, hero who achieves his greatest victories by indecision, by failing to act; compared to the perfect electronic machines he represents man's inefficiency and slowness. A man-machine confrontation occurs frequently in the ten Pirx stories so far, and it is always Pirx's self-doubts, his indecision, that enable him to grasp a situation better than the machines can.

Pirx is a good illustration of the essence of Lem's fiction. His is a work that does not provide any ready-made answers, and offers no simple solutions; it poses rather a complex set of questions, establishing a 'field' of meaning rather than any fixed single meaning. His work is a balancing-act, a careful manoeuvring between various theories and hypotheses, all of them qualified by many conditions, and made more complex by Lem's oscillation between jest and earnest, so that it is often difficult to decide when he is serious about something and when he is just playing the devil's advocate. Take science, for instance: Lem loves science, but that doesn't make it sacrosanct for him, and he extends his method of critical doubt to science itself, which can give the wrong impression that he is anti-science (an impression belied by the considerable body of scientific knowledge displayed in his books). What some reviewers consider a weakness, is in fact one of Lem's greatest strengths: that problems usually are not resolved, but left open; or if resolved, they are likely to open another, greater mystery. The greatest weakness of SF writers is that they feel obliged to provide 'solutions'; this they do either in a trivial way, by asking the wrong questions in the first place; or they offer incredibly pat 'solutions' to what are really very complex problems that admit of no easy answers. Lem distrusts any final and easy answers; he prefers to let the problems dangle – though at a higher level of understanding at the end of the story – constructing in most cases only a net of various, usually contradictory hypotheses; in analogy to the situation in many fields of science, where there is as yet no generally accepted explanation. Although Lem's writing eschews physical action (except for his comic writing, where it is apt to be exaggerated) it is nevertheless exciting and highly dynamic, deriving its dynamics either from a battle of wits, a veritable verbal fireworks in his humorous writings, or from the dialectical interaction of the theories themselves in his serious novels.

More so than Wells's novels, Lem's are genuine scientific works. Wells's primary concern was with evolution, with the various stages of man's development, and the pitfalls and challenges encountered by mankind at selected points on his journey into the unknown future, translated into timeless poetic symbols or frozen moments of time – especially in *The Time Machine, The First Men in the Moon, The War of the Worlds* and *The Island of Doctor Moreau* – and not with evolution as an abstract concept. Lem, however, is interested in the process of cognition itself, in the way in which theories and hypotheses are formulated, tested, and revised – the process of the system of science: ever changeable, ever in flux, always prepared to revise its own position when new facts make it mandatory. The central position of Lem's philosophy is perhaps best characterized by a quotation from Lessing:

If God had enclosed in this hand the whole truth and in his left only the ceaseless striving, the ever active impulse toward truth although with the condition that I must always and eternally err, and he said to me: 'Choose!' I would turn in humility to his left hand, and say: 'Father, give me this; pure truth is for Thee alone.' . . . [For] the worth of man lies not in the truth which he possesses or believes himself to possess, but in the sincere effort he has made to get at the truth. Not by the possession of truth but by the search after truth are man's powers enlarged. And man's ever increasing perfection consists in such enlargement, while possession fosters but contentment, indolence, and pride.

This strikes me as a good description of Lem, and it can serve as an explanation why his work is likely to appeal to sophisticated readers, and not to those who are willing to accept the most silly explanations, if only they get an explanation at all. Lem is a man hungering for absolute truths, and yet only too painfully aware that there are none; that all our knowledge is conditional and temporary, and is ever likely to be superseded. But although there are many things to which no conclusive scientific answers are yet available, and perhaps never will be, man is nevertheless forced to act on incomplete, perhaps even erroneous information, and to act in a moral way in shifting situations. Lem doesn't advocate any form of passivism; on the contrary, he urges responsible action, and the need to create ethical systems in a world devoid of higher meaning, lacking absolute values, a world that just *is*. That is the existential situation of Lem's heroes: yearning for the haven of absolutes, they are faced with the recognition that they don't exist, that man is alone, and confronted with the task of creating his own, necessarily relative standards of moral action. Lem is a moralist who doesn't believe in unchangeable moral laws, but who urges intelligent action in the most testing situations.

Much of the intellectual tension of Lem's novels is derived from the contrast between the essence of things, and their outward appearance, and never more so than in his masterpiece *Solaris* (1961). The appearance of the planet Solaris, covered by a mysterious ocean, is described in every particular, and the more the reader learns about it, the clearer it becomes that the question of the nature of the ocean remains insoluble. In *Solaris* the riddle of the living ocean is inextricably connected with a poignant personal problem, the duplication by the ocean of the deepest guilts of man's subconscious. For the hero Kris Kelvin this is his dead lover, a woman he had once betrayed. This brilliant connection of abstract theory (the nature of the ocean which produces assorted strange phenomena) with a deeply felt human problem of guilt and rekindled love, gives this novel its particular emotional and symbolic power, while in some others – *The Invincible* (1964), *The Investigation* (1959) or *His Master's Voice* (1968) – the theories themselves are more prominent, though coupled always with very human dilemmas. In the ironically named novel *The Invincible* Lem emphatically stresses the right of existence of other life-forms, even if they are clouds of cybernetic flies, and in the impressive ending of the book, where the humans keep their humanity in acknowledging their defeat, Rohan, the hero, experiences a brief moment of communication with his adversaries. In Lem's theoretically most accomplished novel *His Master's Voice* (1968) it is a message from space, partly decoded by the scientists of an American project resembling the set-up of the Manhattan Project, that leads only further into a labyrinthine net of theories, while the responsibility of the scientist for the results of his work, the social implications of science, contribute to the ethical theme of the novel.

Lem's work can be classed into several groups. First there are his serious novels and short stories, books such as *Solaris, The Invincible, Return from the Stars* (1961), *The Tales of Pirx the Pilot* (first collected in one volume in 1968). Another group are his humorous writings such as the Ijon Tichy cycle, partially translated in the English volumes *The Star Diaries* (1976) and the short novel *The Futurological Congress* (1971, translated 1974), *The Fables for Robots* (1964, translated as *Mortal Engines,* 1977) and *The Cyberiad* (1965, translated 1974), my personal favourite. The latter two are books of fables as they might be invented by robots for robots, extolling their own kind, and vilifying the humans, who appear as 'palefaces', as foul protein-slime, the utmost horror in the robot world. The robots here are not naturalistic beings but fairy-tale characters with the properties of traditional fairy-tale characters, though aggrandized by the arsenal of scientific terms; and the final joke of these stories is that after all there is not much difference between the robots and the humans. The robots are just as villainous as human beings, and they are tyrannized and tortured by their own kings and princes, who are exaggerated versions of human kings and princes. These often involved stories, with Oriental-like stories-within-stories, are impossible to synopsize; they are a whirlwind of wordplay, punning and verbal inventiveness, in which things are created by naming them. And yet, behind all the joking and often childlike fun there are levels of more serious meaning. For instance, some stories illustrate real problems of physics: 'The Dragons of Probability' for instance, deals with the genuine properties of atomic particles, and 'How Trurl and Klapaucius Created a Demon of the Second Kind to Defeat the Pirate Pugg' uses an idea taken from the cyberneticist W. R. Ashby. On still another level, these stories probe into philosophical problems of consciousness, justice and happiness, and in no frivolous spirit, despite their jocular manner. There is a tendency in SF to equate a tone of pontifical exclamation with seriousness, and to think comic writing *a priori* minor. This strikes me as nonsense, and I feel that Lem's comic marriage of fable with the latest scientific vocabulary is not only one of the most hilarious achievements of SF, but also one of the profoundest.

A third group is formed by Lem's philosophical writings on cybernetics, the future and literary theory. In them he vents in serious form the thoughts that appear also in his science fiction. These books are *Dialogi* (1957), *Summa technologiae* (1964), *The Philosopy of Chance* (1968) and *Science Fiction and Futurology* (1971). During the last few years Lem has created a form halfway between his purely discursive work and his fiction: reviews of non-existent books (*A Perfect Vacuum,* 1971), and introductions to non-existent books (*Imaginary Magnitude,* 1973), respectively. Much more could be said about Lem, whose literary universe is more varied than the SF field of many a country and who is undoubtedly one of the most interesting writers in Europe today. There is already a large body of criticism on his writings in Poland and Germany, and he is receiving increasing attention in the English-speaking world.

The Soviet Union

It is only after Lem that one should turn to the most important SF field in Europe, that of the Soviet Union. There is a natural curiosity about that enigmatic colossus, and the fears and hopes as well as the current situation of the Russian peoples are reflected in its science fiction. It is characteristic that the best-known Russian SF book, one mentioned in almost any history of anti-utopias or SF, could never appear in the Soviet Union, and indeed is often denounced as a mere piece of anti-Soviet writing: Evgeni Zamyatin's *We* (1920); a fate it shares with some later major satirical works, such as *The Makepeace Experiment* (1965) by Abram Tertz (pseudonym for Andrei Sinyavski) or *The Ugly Swans* (1972) by Arkadi and Boris Strugatsky, published only by the anti-Soviet publishing house Possev in Frankfurt. Anti-Soviet *We* hardly is, but certainly uncomfortable, for it is not easily reconcilable with a communist ideology that has long since degenerated into a narrow Russian nationalism and a smug self-satisfaction hardly different from that of Russia under the late Czars. But above all, *We* is a work of art, a dynamic, living masterpiece, not one of those unreadable dusty old works that usually pass for classics in science fiction. *We* is a tightly reasoned fusion between the cold mathematical calculation (after all, Zamyatin was an engineer by profession), the poetic vision, and a passionate outcry for freedom against the regulation of life, whether in the name of science or of an ideology claiming to possess final answers. Just as there is no final number, for the mathematically trained Zamyatin there can be no final revolution, and no end to the changes that make up life itself. In this view he is remarkably modern, and even optimistic, despite the gloomy ending in which the brain-washed hero, D-503, builder of the rocket-ship *Integral,* calmly watches as I-330, the girl who had led him on his path to rebellion, and whom he has betrayed, is being tortured. Quite contrary to the pseudo-realism usually affected by science fiction, Zamyatin chose a highly subjective method of presentation, the diary of a man who is often in doubt how to interpret his observations. As Patrick Parrinder has shown, it is rather in aspects like these that Zamyatin's modernity and importance lies, than in innovations like the dictatorial United State ruled by a Well-Doer (a predecessor of Aldous Huxley's World Controller and Orwell's Big Brother), the Taylorian tables which regulate even such intimate matters as sex, the antiseptic city within the Green Wall, or the pattern of temptation and revolt in a world of rigid regimentation – though all these are dwelt upon in any study of anti-utopias. *We* undoubtedly influenced Orwell's *Nineteen Eighty-Four* and may have been an influence on Huxley's *Brave New World;* it is itself partly a reaction to some of Wells's ideas, though Zamyatin admired Wells as a literary innovator.

We has become a part of world literature, as the officially acceptable Soviet science fiction has not. Abroad, Soviet SF is usually thought of as a kind of awkwardly written fiction, similar to the American SF of four decades ago, optimistic about hardware, and fettered by an ideology that assumes the future will get better and better, producing a new kind of happy human beings populating a Socialist paradise on Earth. Such a paradise might be good for human beings if it could be achieved, but makes for dull fiction, for fiction lives from conflict, especially the conflict in human souls, and where the only problems are the minor errors of almost perfect individuals, there is no chance of fiction coming alive dramatically. Most of Soviet SF is really very dull, and not only the novels of a writer like Nemtsov, in which uncommonly good Soviet engineers battle with the forces of nature, conquering Siberia for Soviet man, while the plans of evil capitalists and their lackeys are thwarted. The sterile qualities that seem to be an inevitable side-effect of the best of all worlds are evident even in Ivan Efremov's *Andromeda* (1957-8), by far the most influential and successful of all Soviet SF novels. It describes in great detail an ideal Communist society of the future, combined with the adventure of the exploration of outer space, where a communication network of civilizations exists, the Iron Ring. Efremov's views of the ideal Communist future elicited an enormous mass of comment in the Soviet Union, but the artistic level of his work is not very high.

Much superior are the best books of the Strugatsky brothers, dynamic, ironic, mature and complex statements on the human condition. Russian SF has always been strongest in satire, and this seems to be the case in any society where there is little freedom of expression. One involuntarily thinks of Karl Kraus's statement that those who get to jail for their satires are rightly imprisoned, for it means that even the censor understood their work. Censorship seems to sharpen the wits: where everything can be said, it can also be said crudely; but where it is dangerous to say certain things, it is necessary to disguise them, and that makes for literary subtlety. Thus, some works of the Strugatskys may appear unfocused and unclear to the Western reader, but I think that this ambiguity is not a disadvantage, and may even form part of their attraction. Any successful satire should contain, aside from its purely local and temporary components, some universal meaning; and this the books of the Strugatskys amply have. In a certain sense they are very much the pupils of Lem: in their unwillingness to provide final answers, and in the way in which they pose complex ethical problems, establishing an element of doubt, an area where ethical disagreement is possible. But they do not have Lem's detachment, his Voltairean attitude of looking down upon human foibles and weakness from a superior philosophical position. Their writing is more activistic than contemplative, more political than philosophical, and is firmly anchored in history. The Strugatskys are genuinely angry about the injustices of the world, and what they want is action, not just cognition: in this respect they may be genuine Marxists. Their engagement makes their books more immediately acceptable than Lem's novels, which often appear cold. The colourful and varied characters of the Strugatskys are usually close to Russian life, both high and low, and they draw upon the richness of Russian folk-tales and the Russian literary tradition, especially Gogol. Like Gogol, the Strugatskys are skilled in drawing grotesque characters, and like him they direct their fury against fumbling, self-seeking and self-aggrandizing bureaucrats who are allowed to condemn themselves out of their own mouths by the sheer ingenuousness with which they distort truth and logic into the most outrageous falsehoods.

The satirical works of the Strugatskys employ a traditional fairy-tale and folk-tale frame, cross-bred with the jargon of science to satirize the inefficiency and corruption of the Russian bureaucracy. *Monday Begins on Saturday* (1965) is located in an Institute for Magics and Wizardry somewhere in Russia; it is both a delightful take-off of pseudo-scientific research (an attempt to build a perfectly happy consumer) and its bureaucratic management, and a spoof on several dominant kinds of (Western and Soviet) SF. The wildly grotesque *Tale of the Troika* (1968), recently published in an excellent translation by Macmillan in their series of Soviet SF, is more complex and more profound, and its many allusions to Soviet conditions are wholly understandable only to those familiar with life in the Soviet Union; still, the story has its universal applications, and its pure inventiveness can be enjoyed even if its final purpose remains hidden from the reader. In this story V. Nestruev, the charlatan of *Monday Begins on Saturday,* is at it again, acting as a scientific adviser for a bureaucratic triumvirate in a fairy-tale land located on the seventy-sixth floor of an artificial world of the far future. It is a country haunted by assorted strange phenomena, including an alien with seventy-seven parents of seven different sexes, whose existence is quite beyond the mental horizons of those petty-minded Russian servants of Red Tape who do their utmost to explain him away. This hilarious farce deserves to stand beside the work of Gogol and Mikhail Bulgakov.

Even more complex and surrealist, perhaps even a bit obscure, is *The Snail on the Slope* (*Ulitka na sklone*), published in the Soviet Union only in two independent parts in an anthology and a little magazine, but designed by the authors in the form of alternate, inter-locked chapters. In one series of chapters the swamp forest peopled by the monsters of modern science – a forest which serves as a metaphor for the world – is seen from inside, while the other series portrays the hesitations of a member of the uncomprehending bureaucracy that, paradoxically, is responsible both for preserving and destroying the forest.

Some other books by the Strugatskys deal with the problem of interference or non-interference with another civilization, even one appearing primitive and gruesome by our standards, a theme treated earlier by Lem in his novel *Eden* (1959). In Lem's novel, a spaceship crew, crash-landed on the ironically named planet Eden, is faced with the dual task of repairing their ship and understanding the strange civilization they encounter. What little they manage to find out about Eden suggests that the curious inhabitants of the planet, the 'doubles', are victims of a genetic experiment gone wrong; and that there are mass-slaughters going on to dispose of the unhappy failures of the experiment. It seems that the government is distorting and manipulating information in order to deny not only the failure of the experiment, but even that it ever took place, or indeed that there is a government. All the evidence seems to point towards the fact that Eden is under the thumb of a cruel tyranny, a mindless social mechanism grinding its victims to dust. Lem's spacemen are enraged, but they finally do nothing, for they cannot be sure that their interpretation of the goings-on on Eden is correct; the happenings in an alien society may be quite different from what we imagine them to be.

Suffering and tyranny are less an abstract cognitive problem for the Strugatskys than an urgent and concrete historical issue, though one that appears displaced in time and space. This is so in their early short novel *Attempted Escape* (1962), where the feudal tyranny and its concentration camps on another planet are definitely linked with the Russian trauma of the struggle against the fascist invaders in the Second World War, and it is even more true of their masterpiece *Hard To Be a God* (1964). Rumata, the novel's hero, is an emissary of the Terran Institute for Experimental History to the feudal empire of Arkanar on another planet. He has strict directives to observe but not to interfere. Perfectly disguised as a native prince, he watches angrily as things turn from bad to worse, oppression is increased, and pogroms and 'nights of the long knives' take place. Although he knows that any intervention by force would be hazardous and would bring about only superficial changes in the consciousness of the people – who have to find their own path to historical progress, however slow and painful – his humanity rebels against his orders, and when he loses his beloved mistress, his personal grief and anger win over his instructions. Where angels fear to tread, the heroes of most SF written in English boldly step in with their full armoury, 'solving' any social problems; the Strugatskys, on the other hand, construct a convincing personal drama, an intense psychological conflict over the choice of the right way of action. It is this responsible maturity, together with its clearly and inventively visualized scenes and characters – its fullness of life – that makes *Hard To Be a God* the most important book of modern Soviet SF.

The pseudo-medieval society of Arkanar embodies some of the features of fascism and Stalinism, and this is even more pronounced in their later novel *Prisoners of Power* (1971, originally titled *The Inhabited Island*) whose hero, Maxim, stranded on another world ruled by All-Powerful Creators, fights against the tyrants and their mind-control for a more humane society. In this novel, Maxim is something of a superman, the issues appear less complex, the background is more that of an ordinary SF novel, and the adventurous elements dominate. Nevertheless, this is a good book, with some impressive descriptive passages, for example those concerning the forest of mechanisms. The

Strugatskys have returned to the same issues yet one more time, in *The Guy from Hell* (1974), a more trivialized account.

One of their latest novels, *Roadside Picnic* (1972), which like *Prisoners of Power* is also in Macmillan's Soviet SF series, poses another puzzle: various deadly zones have come to exist on Earth, where alien tourists are presumed to have carelessly left their litter. At great personal danger, human prospectors manage to retrieve certain valuable objects whose original purposes remain unknown. Unlike Lem's *His Master's Voice,* where the author presents intricate theories about the signals from outer space, the Strugatskys confine themselves to making a few suggestions about what the zones may be, concentrating with great resourcefulness on the picaresque human types, prospectors, bureaucrats and scientists, who become involved. The novel ends on a mystical note, with the zones appearing to be an experimental set-up which brings out in each human being what is in him: greed, ambition, hate, but also loyalty, comradeship and love.

Compared to the versatility and literary achievement of the Strugatsky brothers, most other Soviet SF pales, although there are a number of authors who have produced some interesting short stories, especially Sever Gansovsky, Anatoli Dneprov, Genrikh Altov, Vadim Shefner, Ilya Varshavsky, and even Alexei Beliaev, that old pioneer of Soviet SF who has at least written some passable adventure novels. But none of these writers has produced work of consistently high quality, and their output is rather erratic. Ilya Varshavsky has some good humorous vignettes, and Sever Gansovsky, among many weaker stories, has produced some well-executed tales exploring the social consequences of various scientific inventions. Gansovsky's 'Day of Wrath' raises the old problem of scientific responsibility, juxtaposing an intellectually superior, but totally unemotional race of intelligent bears with the suffering of common peasants in a dramatically perfect tale; 'Proving Ground' is a chilling shocker of a story, while 'Vincent van Gogh' is both one of the better time-travel stories and a very credible portrait of the artist.

But it must be admitted that the bulk of Soviet science fiction is no less banal than its Western counterpart, exploring the same trite old SF problems (with some limitations imposed by ideology – time-travel stories can only confirm the Socialist future; a story wherein time-travel led to an alternative, non-Communist future would have no chance of appearing), perhaps more technology-oriented than American SF, and certainly far worse written. And what is sometimes said (at least by some European critics) to be the advantage of Soviet SF, its utopian orientation, its brighter outlook on the future, is often hardly more than a cliché, a thinly applied coating to make it more acceptable to the officials in charge of publishing.

Czechoslovakia

The third Slavic country to be considered here, Czechoslovakia, produced one of the prime influences in modern science fiction, Karel Čapek (1890-1938), the man who gave the word 'robot' (actually coined by his brother Josef) to the world in his play *R.U.R.* (1921). The title stands for Rossum's Universal Robots. Čapek's robots, or rather androids, artificially created organical beings, are a stripped-down, depersonalized version of humankind; human beings reduced to the working process, without any of the higher faculties that are detrimental to industrial efficiency, such as love; mass production become manifest, equally usable for the production of goods or for obedient, unquestioning destruction of their masters. Designed by the engineer Rossum, the son of the old inventor, to meet the requirements of industrial production, these tools intended to free mankind from the toils of labour, turn first into instruments for the collapse of the economy, then into the means to suppress the discontented, and finally into tools for the destruction of mankind. Once equipped with feelings by another scientist, the robots acquire the ability to procreate, and the cycle of civilization can go on anew.

Čapek's other plays and novels display the same uneasiness about science and the dangers of industrial production methods, with their dehumanizing and dispossessing effects, for the common man. In *Krakatit* (1924) the threat is atomic power and its destructive potential in the hands of the ruling classes, against which the idealistic inventor Prokop, half-crazed by feverish dreams, and lured by promises of money, power and sex, holds out alone. This hectic novel has a surrealist tone, and while the general situation and psychic conflicts of the hero appear to be typical of the 1920s, and so somewhat old-fashioned today, the problem itself remains as poignant as ever. The oppressive social forces of capitalism and industrialization and the erosion of peaceful life in the countryside are again the butt of *The Absolute at Large* (1922); God or the absolute is being set free as a by-product of cheap atomic generators or 'Karburators', and it turns out that human society cannot bear the absolute, which tends to destroy the state, the press, the individual, and even the church. The result is a hilarious chaos that soon turns most bitter as a giant war ravages the Earth and exhausts itself only when all the atomic generators have been destroyed.

The robotization of life is more clearly linked with fascism in Čapek's masterpiece *War with the Newts* (1936). The coldly intelligent newts turn from exploited working armies used for cheap labour into real armies, making war upon mankind, and sinking the continents. Partly this is a political parable, paralleling the march of the Nazi newts in neighbouring Germany, and Čapek was to become increasingly political in his later plays 'The White Sickness' (1937) and 'The Mother' (1938). But there's more than that. As a spokesman for and sympathizer with the common people, Čapek saw human individualism threatened, on the one hand, by the dehumanizing processes of industry and the political and economical forces behind it; and on the other hand, by the masses of part-slaves, part-potential supermen reaching for power, that modern industry was creating. His robots and newts are symbols for very real forces in human society; efficient, anonymous, mechanical forces, crushing human individuality and human feeling.

Not quite in a class with Čapek was Jan Weiss, whose *House with a Thousand Storeys* (1929) is the expressionist fever-dream of a soldier lying in a typhoid barracks; a dream about a power-hungry industrial magnate aspiring to mastery of the world, as symbolized by the thousand-storey house he had built. The ideas in the novel include interstellar space travel (but only as a metaphor) and artificial stimulation of the brain, opening up for man new senses and new pleasures. Weiss certainly had a considerable imagination, but he was unable to sustain his vision.

A worthy successor to Čapek is Josef Nesvadba, who has written several volumes with satirical SF pieces, and who has been widely anthologized and translated, appearing in several anthologies of the year's best SF stories. A book in English translation is *In the Footsteps of the Abominable Snowman* (1970, American title *The Lost Face*). In his novella 'The Absolute Machine', a complex tale of humans and robots, Nesvadba had paid his tribute to Čapek, after whom one of his characters is named. Nesvadba's stories nearly always have a satirical bent, treating familiar themes of science fiction and adventure (Tarzan, the Abominable Snowman, time travel, robots) in a tongue-in-cheek way, and twisting them into quite startling ironies. A psychiatrist, he achieves his effects not by probing into the minds of his characters, but rather by externalizing psychic conditions in surprising plot situations. The connection of science with political machinations is one of his characteristic concerns.

Other Slavic Countries: Albania, Bulgaria, Hungary

Nothing is known about Albanian SF (if it exists), and little Bulgarian SF has found its way abroad, although there exist some German and Russian translations, and one story by A. Donev was included in Darko Suvin's *Other Worlds, Other Seas* (1970). Translations, however, appear to be quite numerous, Ray Bradbury, Isaac Asimov and Stanislaw Lem have all had Bulgarian books, and even some SF clubs exist there. An article by Elka Konstantinova, a well-known Bulgarian SF personality, 'Modern Times and the Fantastic' in *Obzor* (Autumn 1975) discusses works by Alexander Gerov, Lyuben Dilov, Pavel Vezhinov and Atanas Nakovski, amongst others.

The Hungarians have a well-developed SF field, including many books, one of the most beautiful and most determinedly international SF magazines in the world, *Galaktika,* and a theoretical magazine on SF, *SF Tájékoztato,* published by the SF section of the Hungarian

Writers' Union. The prime mover of SF in Hungary is Péter Kuczka, a well-known poet and scriptwriter who edits a beautiful, also very international SF series for Kozmosz. Among the forerunners of SF in Hungary was Mór Jokai (1825-1904), a prolific writer of historical romances, who published, besides a story of Atlantis, a huge *Novel of the Coming Century* (*A jövö század regenye*) in 1872, which contained many inventions (such as the electrical airship), and even more adventures. Frigyes Karinthy (1887-1938) wrote a couple of SF short stories on topics such as suspended animation, but his major SF works are two sequels to *Gulliver's Travels,* a 'Voyage to Faremido' (1916), and a 'Voyage to Capillaria' in which the narrator encounters intelligent machines and other wonders. Current names in Hungarian SF include György Botond-Bolics, József Cserna, Zoltán Csernai, Gyula Fekete, Gyula Hernádi, Péter Lengyel, Péter Zsoldos and Maria Szepes. Hungarian literature has particular difficulties in getting translated; but what has so far appeared of Hungarian SF in German translation suggests only a space-opera level.

Yugoslavia

Yugoslavia's most prominent contribution to international SF is of course in the field of criticism: Professor Darko Suvin, currently of McGill University in Montreal, has established himself as one of the foremost historians and especially theoreticians of SF, whose writings have appeared in many languages. He is one of the few SF critics able to read the most important European SF in the original languages. In his anthology *Other Worlds, Other Seas* (1970) he has mentioned some Yugoslav SF stories, but even he couldn't produce an example, for the authors of his own country modestly refused him permission to translate a story. But although no Yugoslav SF stories seem to have crossed the border, they certainly do exist. For instance, some are included in *Andromeda 1—3,* beautiful, huge and quite international anthologies of SF stories, poems and criticism, which have appeared since 1976 in Belgrade as special yearbooks of the popular science magazine *Galaksija*. The major authors like Asimov, Clarke or Lem get regularly published in Yugoslavia, and the Yugoslavs were also very quick to pick up *Star Wars,* in several of their languages. The enthusiastic force behind much of Yugoslav SF, at least that published in Serbo-Croat, appears to be Zoran Zivković, who has also edited an anthology of international SF criticism, *Naucna fantastika* (1976).

France

Now that there is very little SF being published in the Soviet Union, France undoubtedly has the strongest native SF field in Europe, quite aside from the many translations. Albin Michel, Calmann-Levy,

Robert Laffont, Editions Denoël, J'ai lui and Jean-Claude Lattès all have their own series (although some publish only translations), and there is the magazine *Fiction,* principally a French edition of the American parent *The Magazine of Fantasy and Science Fiction* but which has published hundreds of original French short stories. *Galaxie,* however, folded in 1977. Gérard Klein, editor of 'Ailleurs et Demain' with Robert Laffont, and himself one of the most important French SF writers, has especially propagated SF in France, while Denoël has Jean-Pierre Andrevon, one of the most talented of the newer writers. Fleuve Noir relies almost exclusively on French authors for its series of space operas. The novels of Pierre Barbet published by Daw Books in the USA (*The Napoleons of Eridanus, The Enchanted Planet, Baphomet's Meteor, The Games Psyborgs Play*) are typical examples of the low-grade space opera that is Fleuve Noir's speciality. Gérard Klein publishes both new French works (by André Ruellan – who is better known under his pseudonym Kurt Steiner, and is a prolific author for Fleuve Noir – Jacques Sternberg, Philippe Curval, Pierre-Jean Brouillard, Christian Léourier, Michel Jeury and Gérard Klein himself), and a series of 'classics': Kurt Steiner, Gilles d'Argyre (i.e. Klein), B. R. Bruss, Stefan Wul, Jacques Spitz and others.

If we are to believe what the French say about themselves (e.g. Klein's forewords to the 'classics' edited by him, or Jacques Sadoul's *Histoire de la Science Fiction moderne,* 1973), their SF is leading in Europe, and as good as English and American science fiction. An opinion almost as exaggerated is voiced by the English-born but French-educated Maxim Jakubowski, in the introduction to his anthology of French SF, *Travelling towards Epsilon* (London, 1976). Like Damon Knight's earlier *13 French SF Stories* (1965), this anthology serves mostly to demonstrate not so much the technical backwardness as the slightness and shallowness of French SF; most stories are only a pale imitation of Anglo-Saxon kinds of SF that were not very good in the first place, with the same trite old plots of robots and time travel, alien invasion and so on, reworked one more time. Some of these stories are certainly quite smoothly written, in fact too smoothly, but they signify nothing.

Michel Jeury, author of *Le Temps Incertain* (*Uncertain Time,* 1973) and *Les Singes du Temps* (*The Apes of Time,* 1974) is a star in France, considered to be the equivalent of Philip K. Dick, by whom he professes to have been influenced. Like Dick, he plays with different levels of reality, different time-tracks, and consciousness-expanding and -distorting drugs. But all he does with these elements is to play around with them, juggling with time and space, but never achieving a consistent whole or the sharpness of vision that distinguishes Dick's best novels like *Ubik.* The central question that decides the value of any fiction must be: What does it mean? Without a positive answer to that question, all mere stylistic excellence, all technical accomplishment that a piece of writing may possess, comes to nothing and all that remains is an empty bag of tricks of the trade that result only in final disappointment.

Gérard Klein, a similar case in point, began in his short stories as a disciple of Ray Bradbury, i.e. as a writer with a good lyrical style, trying to generate a melancholy mood in a fiction of slight content; this he did reasonably well, but strictly as an imitator, without any originality of his own. His later short stories, especially those collected in *Un Chant de Pierre* (1966) are more independent in spirit, and contain some fascinating ideas, especially his space tales like 'The Valley of Echoes', 'Jonah' (in Jakubowski's anthology) or 'Le cavalier au centipede'. The latter are vaguely reminiscent of some writings of Alfred Bester and Cordwainer Smith, show the stylistic influence of Saint-Exupéry, and at their best succeed in evoking a feeling of awe for the cosmos. These stories are more striking for their pathos than for their intellectual impact, and this is what characterizes French SF in general. Its defenders claim that French SF was always more concerned with psychology, and that this is good: but what sort of psychology it is! It is a kind of sticky syrup indiscriminately applied to everything, and smothering any genuine problem in sentimental verbiage. What the readers usually encounter is strange beings acting in strange ways in strange surroundings, and this is just too much strangeness, resulting in an arbitrariness that lacks any firm anchoring in the real world, and allows the reader no possibility of understanding, only blind acceptance. The result is a pseudo-profundity based on mind-boggling concepts or mere name-calling. More than in the short stories this is evident in French SF novels, such as those of Klein, which show the pernicious influences of A. E. van Vogt and of French pseudo-scientific theoreticians like Jacques Bergier, a predecessor of von Däniken, and an indefatigable collector of crank theories of ancient civilizations, visitors from space, UFOs and ESP. Just like van Vogt, French SF authors have a love for time travel, complicating the threads of their narratives so much that the readers are lost rather than persuaded, although as a result of the confusion, some become convinced that the author must have said something terribly profound. In two of Gérard Klein's translated novels, *The Day Before Tomorrow* (*Le Temps n'a pas d'odeur*, 1967) and *The Overlords of War* (*Les seigneurs de la guerre*, 1971) there are plots and counter-plots in time, anomalies of time, monsters, meetings of the characters with their own duplicates, and galactic warfare, in the manner of van Vogt, including van Vogt's tendency to obfuscate all happenings by obscure explanation: in short, typical SF talk about the mysteries of time and space, but really quite meaningless.

It is, however, not all due to the influence of van Vogt. The Belgian Jean Ray (1887–1964) for instance, primarily a writer of horror stories, was also attracted by time; he has streets or houses leading into other times, telephone conversations with the future, doorways into other dimensions, and similar effects. There is also René Barjavel's novel *Le Voyageur Imprudent* (1944, translated as *Future Times Three*). The imprudent time traveller of the title sets out to assassinate Napoleon Bonaparte before he can do any historical harm, but only succeeds in blotting out his own existence by killing an ancestor, landing instead in some horrible future society dominated by an entomological hive-creature. This novel, considered a classic in France, makes for extremely dull reading; the beginning is most clumsy, and the time paradoxes are of a simplistic kind. Barjavel's other SF classic *Ravage* (*Ashes, Ashes,* 1943) is just as bad, describing very quaint scientific phenomena.

Jules Verne is, of course, rightly considered to be one of the founding fathers of the SF genre, and his synthesis of the popularization of scientific facts with the adventurous spirit and the voyage of discovery is still viable, but most other writers presented as classics of French SF are very dated, and sometimes quite unreadable. This applies also to J. H. Rosny Aîné (pseudonym of Joseph Henri Böex, 1856-1940), an author of mostly forgotten social-historical novels; only his prehistoric adventure novels still enjoy some reputation. His SF work often aims at presenting true alienness and human encounters with alien life, sometimes in a prehistoric setting, as in 'Les Xipehuz' ('The Xipehuz', 1887) or in the two Martian novels *Les Navigateurs de l'infini* (*The Navigators of the Infinite,* 1925) and its sequel *Les Astronautes* (*The Astronauts,* 1960), in which he also describes puzzling sentient life-forms. Rosny is, however, only a moderately gifted author, and since his concept of alien beings lacks any underlying philosophical principle, his stories just make for some more curiosities in the big garden of science fiction. *La Mort de la Terre* (1910) presents the familiar end of the human species, which is being replaced by ferro-magnetic life-forms. In *La Force Mystérieuse* (*The Mysterious Force,* 1913) there is a weakening of the light spectrum when Earth comes under the temporary influence of an extraterrestrial energy storm; one of the effects is a revolution in human relationships, since mankind can bear only to live in small groups, and any separation of an individual from his particular group results in nausea and death. Men revert to barbarism and even to cannibalism, but finally the old order is restored.

Quite ridiculous are some other 'classics', such as Gustave Le Rouge's *Le Prisonnier de la Planète Mars* (*The Prisoner of Mars,* 1909) and *La Guerre des Vampires* (*War of the Vampires,* 1909), and Régis Messac's *La Cité des Asphyxiés* (*City of the Asphyxiated,* 1937) and *Quinzinzinzili* (1935), which have all been reissued in recent years. Of Jacques Spitz's writings the best-known is probably the novel *La Guerre des Mouches* (*The War Against the Flies,* 1938), yet another thriller.

These writers continue to exert an influence on the lower forms of the genre in France, but the more highly regarded French SF has taken a different track: that of the New Wave: characteristically not so much J. G. Ballard (who is very successful in France, especially his recent novels) as Harlan Ellison and Roger Zelazny and the more self-indulgent aspects of the British New Wave; the result is a further step towards baroque, vaguely symbolic writing, imprecise language and a 'psychology' that is a cloud of murky sentiments. The prime offender in this regard is Daniel Walther, whose stories try to achieve psychological depth, but happen to be awfully over-written, painful examples of purple prose. The one of his stories available in English, 'The Gunboat Dread' in the Jakubowski anthology reads almost like its own parody. One thing that the French do is to remind the reader that human beings have sexual organs, but the sexual explicitness of some stories serves rather to make them the more unpalatable, and the new sexual relationships described appear strained (e.g. 'Delta' by Christine Renard and Claude F. Cheinisse), while others are mere pot-boilers, rehashes of themes that have been treated many times in Anglo-American SF.

It is characteristic that what is perhaps the best novel in modern French science fiction, Edward de Capoulet-Junac's *Pallas ou la Tribulation* (1967) is usually treated with scorn in French accounts of SF, or ignored altogether, yet this is the purest example of French *esprit,* undiluted by any aspirations to grandeur and significance. In style and form quite simple, it is at first glance a space opera, a monster story, in which extraterrestrial monsters invade the Earth, capturing a number of human beings and taking them to a place that has nothing in common with the asteroid Pallas. These humans are not used as slaves, not subjected to inhuman experiments, nor are they forced to betray the secrets of human science. They are not treated as intellectual partners but simply as pet animals who are sometimes allowed to indulge in their whims, and sometimes punished when they misbehave. Attempts at revolt are rather pitiful, and there are no glorious revolutions to restore human dignity and the supremacy of mankind over the cosmos; instead there are petty feuds among the humans themselves, and a passive acceptance, an adaptation to the new role, and even an erotic submissiveness: love for the new masters. This ironical, debunking attitude, which is presented with great psychological skill by quite simple narrative means, is probably what made the novel obnoxious to SF fans, who prefer a huge apparatus producing virtually nothing to the psychological complexity of an apparently quite simple tale. The Kleins, Andrevons, Walthers, Jeurys, and the other 'masters' of French SF cannot hold a candle to this novel, and it also compares favourably to the excursions of writers like Pierre Bouille and Robert Merle into the SF field.

Other Romance countries

If French SF has found any disciples in Europe, it is in Rumania, where the ties with French culture are still strong, and where some French SF has been translated. However, what shows most in Rumanian SF is its isolation from the literature of other countries. Most SF there is very naive, exhibiting a dearth of ideas and literary values. Even the best Rumanian SF, such as that written by Vladimir Colin and Adrian Rogoz, is usually better only in regard to style, while the stories themselves are old-fashioned, resembling more fairy-tales translated into the SF idiom than SF proper. Nevertheless, Vladimir Colin is a fine writer, and he has had a volume of his short SF translated by Robert Laffont in France, and a volume of fantasy stories from Marabout in Belgium (the same publisher also produced an anthology of Rumanian SF, edited by Vladimir Colin). Adrian Rogoz was editor of the now defunct SF magazine *Povestiri Stiintifico Fantastice* which was for many years the mainstay of Rumanian SF. As a writer he produced the long novel *Omul si naluca* (*The Man and the Phantom*, 1965), the story of a journey to Venus and a romantic love encountered there. Rogoz is a cultured writer, a surrealist at heart, and parts of his book are written in a synthetic pseudo-Joycean language, a mixture of various existing tongues. Thanks to the efforts of Ion Hobana, the leading Rumanian SF historian, the history of Rumanian SF is readily accessible, and may be read up in two articles of his (see Bibliography).

Among the many works cited by Hobana is Felix Aderca's *The Undersea Cities* (1935), a journalistic effort whose brevity of expression is quite engaging. Two ways of saving the inhabitants of a doomed world are realized: a migration towards the still warm core of the planet, and space travel to another world, undertaken by a young couple. This period piece has a a certain nostalgic charm.

The other Romance countries, Italy and Spain, now have large SF markets, but they consist mostly of translated material, while SF in Portuguese appears to be published mostly in Brazil. The Spanish *Nueva Dimension,* a periodical founded by fans, is one of the most attractively produced SF magazines in the world, and there are a handful of writers like Carlos Buiza and Domingo Santos, but Spain has yet to make an original contribution to SF. Much the same is true for Italy, where there are only a few more than occasional writers of science fiction; Sandro Sandrelli and Lino Aldani are among the older writers, while Ugo Malaguti, Piero Prosperi, Gianfranco de Turris and Gianni Montanari represent the younger generation, sometimes with New Wave ambitions. Some of Aldani's short stories are quite good, and they have been translated into several languages, but they are only on the level of the stories found in any of the better SF anthologies anywhere.

Germany

Germany is a somewhat paradoxical case; it boasts one of the largest SF markets in the world, and it generated what must certainly be the most successful SF series of all time (seen purely in commercial terms), the interminable *Perry Rhodan* series, with nearly 900 dime novels by now, some 200 full-sized paperback novels and a companion series *Atlan* which now consists of several hundred novels; altogether, world sales of about 300 million copies. Written by a team of authors, these novels are the ultimate compendium of SF, with all the SF ideas that ever were rolled into one gigantic package. The originators of the series are the prolific SF writers K. H. Scheer and Clark Darlton (i.e. Walter Ernsting).

In Germany, there is a marked gulf between the cheap dime novels such as *Perry Rhodan,* saddle-stitched publications of sixty-four pages each, and the large paperback field which consists almost exclusively of translations; expensive SF hardcover editions have all failed in Germany.

There are almost no better SF authors in West Germany today, although Germany produced a genuine classic, *On Two Planets* (1897) by Kurd Lasswitz (1848–1910), translated into English as late as 1972. Despite being enthusiastically received in its day, translated into several European languages and constantly reprinted, it never exerted an influence comparable to that of H. G. Wells's or Jules Verne's books. Lasswitz was, of course, not the literary peer of these men; he was very much a schoolteacher, and his work shows it. He tends to expound German idealism and to lecture his readers. Still, his work, especially *On Two Planets,* is a respectable attempt to infuse philosophical ideas into SF, and to combine them with technological forecasts, such as the space station and space travel. The subject-matter of *On Two Planets* is a conflict between Earth and a superior Martian civilization, and unlike many invasion novels, *On Two Planets* gives serious attention to the ethical aspects of the problem, as the victorious Martians are corrupted by their own power.

Much more successful in Germany than Lasswitz was Hans Dominik (1872-1946), an engineer whose books sold in hundreds of thousands, and still sell best of all SF published in Germany. His novels concentrate on a single invention, and the background is always a slightly changed present, only with different political groupings. His plots revolve around the villains' attempts to get hold of the amazing new invention – a space drive, atomic power, a source of energy from the atmosphere, a new kind of rubber, an incredibly dense steel – and out of this he spins a tale of intrigue and espionage, culminating in open warfare between the great power blocs. In these intensely nationalistic novels the 'good' side is either the German one (with various foreign nations as adversaries) or, frequently, the white races – in which case the opponents belong to the species of the 'yellow peril'. Dominik's first novel, *Die Macht der drei* (1922) may also be his best.

Modern German SF of any quality consists, aside from some short stories by Wolfgang Jeschke and others, of little more than one man, the Viennese physicist Herbert W. Franke. Franke's stories are not what one would call beautiful; he deliberately fails to write anything that one is taught makes worthwhile fiction. His work is almost totally bare of similes, metaphors, poetic images, beautiful expressions. He cultivates an unadorned, unaffected, simple style, metallic, precise, describing the mere necessities, trying to give an impression of scientific and technical processes. Reading Franke, one sees the cogs and wheels turn, as it were. Interestingly enough, he is not so much concerned with scientific thought itself as with the social consequences of scientific processes, the political uses and misuses of science. His stories, and especially his novels, belong to the species of anti-utopia, and he singlemindedly creates one technological hell after another in which the individual is manipulated by sinister social groups distorting information with the most up-to-date technical means. This is so in his first novel *Das Gedankennetz* (1961), translated as *The Mind Net,* and it is the same in his latest novel *Ypsilon minus* (1976). Franke is guilty of the occasional over-simplification; his characters are mere strands in a larger design, of no interest in themselves, and his plots tend to be more involved than is advantageous for them; and yet, although his novels structurally resemble ugly concrete blocks, he has managed to create out of this poetic desert a prose that is equal to the task of expressing scientific and ethical ideas in an adventurous form, without any great pretensions to literature.

East Germany

In the other part of Germany, the German Democratic Republic, there also exists a considerable SF field, although both the number of titles published and the print-runs are totally insufficient to satisfy the demand, so that SF books are usually out of print within a few days. Most translations are from the other Communist countries, especially the Soviet Union. What East German SF authors there are write mostly in the juvenile field, such as Carlos Rasch, Günter Krupkat, Curt Letsche, Eberhardt dell'Antonio and Gerhard Branstner, but it is an indication of the growing acceptance of science fiction there that even literary writers such as Anna Seghers, Rolf Schneider and Günter Kunert now and then produce an SF story. But only the husband-and-wife team of Johanna and Günter Braun have moved further into SF. They have developed a highly mannered individual style and an absurdist outlook, beginning with *Der Irrtum des Grossen Zauberers* (1972), through their best novel *Unheimliche Erscheinungsformen auf Omega XI* (1974) to a collection of short stories called *Der Fehlfaktor* (1975). These books provide an entirely fresh viewpoint that seems to be genuinely Socialist, though not uncritically so.

Northern Europe

The remaining European countries can be presented briefly. The Netherlands resemble Germany is so far as there is a booming SF market, but very little original work. Norway is the domain of the two young writers Ion Bing and Tor Age Bringsvaerd, who practically control the field, both as writers and editors; though some other Norwegian SF gets published, such as the anthology *Malstrøm* (1972). The works of Bing and Bringsvaerd range from fairly conventional SF (see Ion Bing's story 'A Whiter Shade of Pale' in Donald A. Wollheim's anthology *The Best from the Rest of the World*, 1976) to experimental, often wildly comical and sometimes obscure writings, for example, Ion Bing's *Det Myke Landskapet* (1970) or Bringsvaerd's *Blotkakemannen & Apache-pikene* (1972) and *Sesam 71* (1971). Only a few of their stories have been translated into English, but Bing and Bringsvaerd have had a number of translations into other languages. Danish SF might be said to be Jannick Storm, who has done much for it as an editor; as writers, Niels E. Nielsen and Anders Bodelsen are more important.

Sweden's SF showpiece is Sam J. Lundwall, truly an international SF personality who writes in English as well as in his native Swedish; his first two novels were written first in English (*Alice's World* and *No Time for Heroes*, 1971). His later *2018 A.D. or King Kong Blues* (1975) was a bestseller in Sweden. It is not a very good book, though, but rather a rambling, unfocused satire on everything that happens to occur to the author, from contemporary Swedish conditions via conventional features of anti-utopias to SF ideas. His earlier books were outrageous space operas, treating well-worn SF themes with a touch of ridicule just sufficient to make them readable again, and crossing their original appeal with a little satire; fun to read, but rather rough going. Lundwall is one of those people who have made SF a way of life. He engages in every sort of SF activity, from fandom to bibliography, translating, writing, editing and publishing. He has founded his own publishing house (Delta Forlags), has written a lively little book on SF (*Science Fiction: What It's All About*, 1971), as well as an illustrated history, and is working on a huge SF Encyclopaedia subsidized by the Swedish government.

After this high-speed tour through so disparate a field as European science fiction, it would be very difficult to arrive at some sort of conclusion. I do not think that there is any quality common to European SF; by and large, it is not very significant either in numbers or quality. But since in literature only the best counts, it is valuable above all for the works of Stanislaw Lem and Arkadi and Boris Strugatsky, which alone are more important than the writings of several dozens of lesser authors. And not because they would exemplify the virtues of European SF, whatever they may be, to the highest degree; but rather because they – Lem certainly, and to some degree also the Strugatskys – have nothing in common with it. They are simply talented writers, working in a rich literary tradition, who happen to have a preference for science and the fantastic; that is all.

Notes

1. Dr Rottensteiner is well known as Stanislaw Lem's literary agent, and he wishes me to point out that he does not and cannot write about Lem disinterestedly. The claims that he makes for Lem's stature in this essay are widely shared among SF writers and critics (Editor's Note).

Bibliography

In addition to anthologies of the SF of individual countries such as France and the USSR, there are three anthologies of European SF in English translation: Darko Suvin's *Other Worlds, Other Seas: Science-Fiction Stories from Socialist Countries* (New York: Random House 1970); Franz Rottensteiner's *View from Another Shore* (New York: Seabury Press, 1973); and Donald A. Wollheim's *The Best from the Rest of the World* (New York: Doubleday, 1976). All of these contain lengthy introductions.

For a more detailed discussion of Stanislaw Lem, see especially Jerzy Jarzębski's essay 'Stanislaw Lem, Rationalist and Visionary', *Science-Fiction Studies*, **4**, Part 2 (July 1977), 110-26, and Michael Kandel's introduction to *Mortal Engines* (New York: Seabury Press, 1977).

On Zamyatin, see Alex M. Shane, *The Life and Works of Evgenij Zamyatin* (Berkeley and Los Angeles: California U.P., 1968), and Patrick Parrinder, 'Imagining the Future: Zamyatin and Wells' *Science-Fiction Studies*, **1**, Part 1 (Spring 1973), 17–26.

On the Strugatskys and Soviet SF, the reader is referred to the many writings of Darko Suvin: e.g. the foreword to *Other Worlds, Other Seas* (cited above); *Russian Science Fiction 1956-74: A Bibliography* (Elizabethtown, N.Y.: 1976); 'The Utopian Tradition of Russian Science Fiction', in *Modern Language Review*, **66** (Jan. 1971), 139-58; 'Criticism of the Strugatskii Brothers' Work', *Canadian-American Slavic Studies*, **6** (1972), 286–307; and 'The Literary Opus of the Strugatskii Brothers', *Canadian-American Slavic Studies*, **8** (1974).

On Karel Čapek, see Darko Suvin's introduction to *War with the Newts* (Boston: Gregg Press, 1975).

A number of essays and reviews on Hungarian SF are to be found in the two English-language issues of the journal of the SF Working Committee of the Hungarian Writers' Union, *SF Tájékoztato*: No. 6 (1972) and No. 18 (1976).

On French SF see Maxim Jakubowski's anthology *Travelling Towards Epsilon,* (London: New English Library, 1976), with a useful introduction; also Peter Fitting, 'SF Criticism in France', *Science-Fiction Studies* 1, Part 3 (Spring 1974), 173-81, and J.-P. Vernier, 'The SF of J. H. Rosny the Elder', *Science-Fiction Studies*, 2 Part 2 (July 1975), 156–63.

Ion Hobana's 'A Survey of Romanian Science-Fiction' appears together with some other pieces on Rumanian SF in *Romanian Review*, **22**, No. 1 (1968). See also Hobana's 'Futurism and Fantasy in Romanian Science-Fiction', *Cahiers roumains d'études littéraires*, 1974, No. 2 72-84.

Franz Rottensteiner's 'Kurd Lasswitz: A German Pioneer of Science Fiction' appears in *SF: The Other Side of Realism,* ed. Thomas D. Clareson (Bowling Green, Ohio: Popular Press, 1971), pp. 289-306.

Notes on the editor and contributors

Patrick Parrinder teaches English at the University of Reading and is the author of *H. G. Wells* (1970), *Authors and Authority* (1977) and of numerous articles and reviews. He is an editorial consultant for *Science-Fiction Studies* and has lectured on science fiction in the UK and at universities in Canada, the United States and West Germany.

Mark R. Hillegas, of Southern Illinois University at Carbondale, taught his first science fiction course at Colgate in 1962. He is the author of *The Future as Nightmare: H. G. Wells and the Anti-Utopians* (1967) and *Shadows of Imagination: The Fantasies of C. S. Lewis, J. R. R. Tolkien and Charles Williams* (1969).

Marc Angenot is of Belgian origin and teaches French and Comparative Literature at McGill University. He is the author of *Le Roman populaire: Recherches en paralittérature* (1975) and of *Les Champions des femmes* (1977), and is an editor of *Science-Fiction Studies*.

John Huntington, of the University of Illinois at Chicago Circle, is author of a number of essays on science fiction and on Renaissance poetry.

Raymond Williams is Professor of Drama at the University of Cambridge. His most recent books include *The Country and the City* (1973) and *Marxism and Literature* (1977).

T. A. Shippey lectures in English at St John's College, Oxford. He is the author of *Old English Verse* (1972) and has reviewed science fiction for *Foundation, The Times Literary Supplement* and *The Guardian*.

Tom Woodman took his Ph.D. in eighteenth-century studies at Yale. He has taught at St David's College, Lampeter and is now a Lecturer in English at the University of Reading.

Scott Sanders, Associate Professor of English at Indiana University, is author of *D. H. Lawrence: The World of the Major Novels* (1973) and of several novels and short stories.

J. A. Sutherland is author of *Victorian Novelists and Publishers* (1976) and *Fiction and the Fiction Industry* (1978). He teaches in the English Department at University College, London

Christopher Priest is a well-known science fiction writer and former Associate Editor of *Foundation*. His novels include *Inverted World* (1974), *The Space Machine* (1976) and *A Dream of Wessex* (1977).

Franz Rottensteiner is author of *The Science Fiction Book: An Illustrated History* (1975) and editor of the SF magazine *Quarber Merkur*. He lives in Vienna.

Index

(of names, authors, and works cited in the text, excluding bibliographies)